Be to Me a Father and a Priest

Be to Me
a Father and a Priest

REV. PETER M. J. STRAVINSKAS

NEWMAN HOUSE PRESS

FIRST EDITION
Copyright © 2009
by Rev. Peter M. J. Stravinskas
All rights reserved

Published in 2009 by
Newman House Press
601 Buhler Court
Pine Beach, New Jersey 08741

ISBN 978-0-9778846-3-6

Printed in the United States of America

CONTENTS

Preface   7

ESSAYS AND REVIEWS
The Priest, Youth, and Religious Education   15
Religion, Relevancy, and Youth   18
Solving the Vocation Crisis   21
The Parish: Crucible of Priestly Formation   24
The Prophetic Priest Today   30
The Priest as Consoler   39
Christmas Thoughts of a Celibate Lover   41
The Thorn Birds—Worth Watching, with Reservations   42
The Priesthood   46
Holy Orders   49
Why Can't Our Women Be Ordained?   53
Christus Dominus   56
Optatam Totius   60
Review: *Theology of the Priesthood* (Galot)   63
Presbyterorum Ordinis   65
A Cry for Help   68
"Father, Did You Lose Something?"   71
The Priests We Deserve   72
The Role of the Deacon   75
The Priesthood and Celibacy   78
Reviews: Four Books on Church Ministry   80
Review: *Old Testament Priests . . .* (Vanhoye)   84
Pastors and Money   86
Ministry and Priesthood   88
Smearing Future Priests   90
Review: Two Books on Parish Ministry   92
Questions of Identity   94
Personally Responding to God's Call   96
Helping Priests Be Celibate   98
Review: *Last Priests in America* (Unsworth)   100
A Few Good Men   102
Another Modest Proposal   105
Vocations and Visibility   107
Leader of the Parochial School   111

Scholars and Intellectual Explorers	115
Service as Visible Public Witnesses	119
The Priest and Prayer	122
The Priest as Preacher	126
Bring Back the Black	129
The Greek Orthodox Church and Celibacy	131
Priest—A Year Later	133
Catholic Higher Education as a Source of Priestly and Religious Vocations	136
Can Anyone Say "Forever"?	140
Review: *Clerical Celibacy* (Phipps)	145

HOMILIES

Mass of Thanksgiving (1977)	151
Fifth Anniversary of Ordination (1982)	153
Mass of Christian Burial of My Father (1983)	155
Silver Jubilee of the Reverend Perry W. Dodds	158
First Solemn Mass of the Reverend J. H. Scott Newman	163
First Solemn Mass of the Reverend Joel M. Kovanis	170
First Solemn Mass of the Reverend Nicholas L. Gregoris	179
First Solemn Mass of the Reverend Thomas Kocik	190
Tenth Anniversary of the Priestly Ordination of the Reverend Michael Lankford	199
On the Occasion of My Mother's Death (2004)	207

LECTURES AND PAPERS

Recruiting Candidates for What?	215
Holy Orders	221
The Holy Spirit in the Sacraments and His Gifts	225
The Understanding of Holy Orders in the Roman Catholic Church Since Vatican II	239
Gentlemen and Scholars: Priests for the Third Millennium	260
Celibacy and the Meaning of the Priesthood	273
An Open Letter to My Brother Priests	287

Preface

People love vocation stories, so let me begin with mine. It wasn't a profound event; it might even be considered silly, but God works in strange ways. As an only child, I truly looked forward to school, because I would have the company of other children. On my first day of kindergarten at St. Rose of Lima School in Newark, New Jersey, Monsignor John Gormley, the pastor, came into class to welcome us. When I got home that afternoon, my mother asked how everything had gone at school: How did I find Sister? The other kids? Did I learn anything? Enthusiastically, I replied: "Everything was great. And I learned what I want to be when I grow up—a monsignor! I really like his outfit." I hope my appreciation for the priesthood has grown since that first spark of interest, but that's how it all started.

From that rather fragile beginning, the priestly vocation of the grandson of immigrants was nurtured by excellent priests and women religious of three different congregations in three different schools in two different dioceses. An interesting side-effect of it all was that my non-practicing parents were brought back to a fervent living of the Catholic Faith and were nothing but supportive of their son's youthful but unshakeable resolve.

Having received a stellar education—human, spiritual, and academic—I walked into Seton Hall University ready for any challenge, and actually completed my bachelor's degree in three years, with a double major in Classical Languages and French. The greatest achievement of my elementary and secondary schooling, however, was not the academics (as impressive as they were) but that I had come to know and love Christ and His Church and was totally prepared to give my life to them both in the holy priesthood at the age of seventeen. I had learned not simply isolated theological facts or catechism questions; I had been introduced to a Catholic culture, a way of life, which gave me the desire for more and the capacity to make a decision with firmness and conviction.

The assuredness of my first seventeen years was quickly shattered as ecclesiastical life began to unravel, for I had entered the seminary less than a month after *Humanae Vitae,* with all the confusion and dissent conjured up by the mention of that watershed event in the life of the Church—an iconic conversation-stopper in 1968 and ever since, as Pope Benedict XVI has observed on many occasions. Not a few people over the years have opined: "You couldn't have picked a worse time to enter the seminary." How right they were. While the college seminary experience was not all that bad, the theology years were horrific, as I met truly bad priests for the first time in my life (along with some very saintly ones). The stock-in-trade, though, was heresy in the classroom, liturgical abuses on a grand scale, degradation of traditional notions of priesthood, sexual immorality, and active persecution of seminarians who adhered to orthodox views of the Church and the ordained ministry. Add to that, the approximately hundred thousand priests around the world who left the active ministry during the last ten years of the pontificate of Pope Paul VI; it's a miracle the suction didn't take us all with them.

When such a laundry list is recited, a common response is: "Then why did you stay?" For one simple reason: I knew that I had to be a priest to be truly happy and fulfilled as a human being and as a Christian. Of course, as one might suppose, it was a rather rocky road to the altar, with massive doses of psycho-babble attempting to convince me (and others of my stripe) that we were "unsuited for ministry in the post-conciliar Church." We knew those "formators" were wrong, but it was hard to counteract their pontifications. To be sure, the Tradition of the Church was clear, but that was scoffed at, and contemporary authoritative documentation was scarce.

Ordination did finally come (in 1977), and eventually some clarity began to emerge with the accession of Pope John Paul II to the Chair of Peter. Between the steady stream of documents flowing from the papal pen and his non-stop comments on the nature of the priesthood, especially during his globe-trotting pastoral visits, an arsenal of material was available to build up a case for the priesthood as the Church had always known it.

My priestly ministry has been far more challenging, interesting, and multi-faceted than I ever imagined on that August evening in 1968 as I crossed the threshold of the college seminary. Although teaching in, administering, and establishing Catholic schools (elementary, secondary, university, and seminary) have been a constant from my first days as a seminarian, I have also worn many other "hats"—from serving as a pastor, vocations director, and bishop's secretary, to public relations work for the Church, to writing and lecturing on timely topics throughout the country and abroad, to founding a community of secular clergy devoted to the new evangelization, liturgical renewal, and Catholic education.

This book is a product of the many ways in which I have been a priest, as each assignment has contributed insights into the identity and mission of priests. It is an anthology of all my reflections on that vocation, without which the Church cannot exist, as John Paul II pointed out in a most persuasive manner in the final encyclical of his life, *Ecclesia de Eucharistia.*

Julius Caesar tells us in *De Bello Gallico* that *"Gallia omnis divisa est in partes tres"* (All Gaul is divided into three parts). And so is this volume. The first part is a collection of my essays on the priesthood, which have appeared in popular Catholic periodicals over a thirty-five-year span; the second part offers homilies on the same topic, mostly preached at First Masses or anniversaries; the third part presents more scholarly reflections for more select audiences.

The idea for the anthology came from readers and friends who noticed what I seemed not to notice, namely, that much of my writing has been concerned with the priesthood. As I took their suggestion more seriously, I discovered that they were right and that there was a lot of material. As I arranged it in chronological order, I likewise saw an amazing consistency in positions I have espoused over the years. In fact, I cannot detect any significant change on any substantive issue throughout. Now, some might be quick to quote Ralph Waldo Emerson to the effect that "a foolish consistency is the hobgoblin of little minds," causing me swiftly to call their attention to the adjective "foolish." I hope no one finds my consistency foolish. Instead, I would like to claim as my own (with appropriate and necessary modifications) the comment of John Henry Cardinal Newman in his *Apologia pro Vita Sua*:

> From the time that I became a Catholic, of course I have no further history of my religious opinions to narrate. In saying this, I do not mean to say that my mind has been idle, or that I have given up thinking on theological subjects; but that I have had no variations to record, and have had no anxiety of heart whatever. I have been in perfect peace and contentment; I never have had one doubt. I was not conscious to myself, on my conversion, of any change, intellectual or moral, wrought in my mind. I was not conscious of firmer faith in the fundamental truths of Revelation, or of more self-command; I had not more fervour; but it was like coming into port after a rough sea; and my happiness on that score remains to this day without interruption.

Because most of my writing is "occasional," in the sense that the topics are "occasioned" or dictated by life's exigencies, the second observation I made was that there was also an amazing consistency as to the same problems surfacing. That consistency is disturbing: after nearly forty years, we priests continue to suffer the same ills that have been responsible for low morale, which, in turn, results in minimal efforts at vocational recruitment. Simply put, if priests do not taste satisfaction from their pastoral efforts, they become bad advertisements for their vocation.

One of the basic difficulties has been a certain ecclesial amnesia in regard to the priesthood and even a taking of it for granted. In many parochial situations today, the priest finds himself caught most unpleasantly in a "vise" between the many hyperactive laity who really want to *be* priests (without the attendant burdens) and the more-than-few intrusive diocesan bureaucrats who constantly second-guess the parish priest. Some wags have commented that while Vatican Council I solidified the place of the Pope in the Church and Vatican Council II promoted the dignity of both bishops and laity, a Vatican Council III might be needed to highlight the essential and irreplaceable role of the priest. Without going so far as to convoke a council to deal with the matter, Pope Benedict has surely acknowledged the problem by declaring June 2009 the beginning of "The Year for Priests," during which he hopes priests will have their identities strengthened, their value affirmed, their vocation promoted and appreciated by the whole Church.

As the Prefect of the Congregation for the Clergy, Claudio Cardinal Hummes, has put it: ". . . the Pope wants to give priests a special importance and to say how much he loves them, how much he wants them to live their vocation and mission with joy and fervor."

This "Year for Priests" takes place within the context of the celebration of the one hundred-fiftieth anniversary of the death of St. John Mary Vianney, commonly known as the "Curé of Ars" and revered as the patron of parish priests. I am pleased that the Holy Father has now expanded the Saint's patronage to all priests, especially because a large portion of my priestly life has found me outside the realm of parochial ministry. This initiative of the Pope provides all priests—in any apostolate—with both a heavenly example and a heavenly intercessor. It also reminds us that the essence of priesthood does not reside in what a priest does, but in who he is—whether he be teaching, doing research, studying, administering institutions, or doing parish work. St. John Vianney is also an apt patron for yet another reason: The age in which the Lord called him to minister as a priest was not unlike our own—a time of profound and troubling change, rapid secularization, relativistic thinking, and hostility to religion. In placing the Curé of Ars before the minds' eye of priests, Benedict XVI is saying: "If he could make the Gospel the center of people's lives then, you can do it now."

While I tend to shy away from the language of crisis, one must frankly admit that the priesthood has been in the throes of a major crisis for at least four decades (with subterranean rumbles long before that). Only in acknowledging a crisis can a way be found around it or through it. Truth be told, however, most vocations and professions are crisis-ridden these days. One need only reflect on how marriage and family life have been crumbling in the developed countries for half a century, as the foundation stones of those institutions—commitment and sacrifice—have become "dirty words" to generations raised on egoism and immediate self-gratification of all needs and desires. Future priests come out of such environments, and it would be presumptuous to imagine that they would be spared what the rest of the culture has imbibed. What I mean is that any renewal of the priesthood will have to be inserted into a much larger frame of reference, especially the Christian family and the Church-at-large, as well as the secular society whose air we breathe each day.

Just prior to priestly ordination, I took as my personal motto, from the Liturgy of the Hours, a line from a prayer recited on Fridays at Terce, as we are reminded that Christ died *"pro mundi salute"* (for the salvation of the world). In making that choice, I wanted to etch into my consciousness two important facts: First, that the world is in need of salvation; second, that the world is worth saving and can indeed be saved. Jesus Christ came for only one purpose—to save the world. It was not a "mission impossible," for "all things are possible with God," as the Evangelist says (Mk 10:27). The motivation for the mission of Christ is underscored by St. John: "God so loved the world, that he gave his only Son . . ." (3:16). And we men who share in Christ's priesthood must have the very same attitude as was in the Lord Jesus Himself (see Phil 2:5): a healthy realism, which takes account of the world's sinfulness while at the same time holding up the love and beauty that it can know, if only it allows itself to be transformed by the saving power of Christ's redeeming grace, made available through the Church and her sacraments. It is for this that we priests exist.

The title of this book, *Be to Me a Father and a Priest,* comes from a charming episode recounted in the Book of Judges (17:7–13), wherein Micah beseeches the Levite stranger: "Stay with me, and *be to me a father and a priest*, and I will give you ten pieces of silver a year, and a suit of apparel, and your living." The sacred author notes laconically: "And the Levite was content to dwell with the man; and the young man became to him like one of his sons." The final sentence declares a happy ending: "Then Micah said, 'Now I know that the Lord will prosper me, because I have a Levite as priest.'"

That passage is preceded by a telling verse: ". . . every man did what was right in his own eyes" (v. 6). Today we would say, "Everyone did his own thing." Micah knew that that was not good—which was why he knew he needed a priest. We could say that he fostered a vocation in the young Levite, and then he took responsibility for him, treating him like one of his family. That, I submit, is what must happen in the Church—the development of a realization that no one can do it on his own; that a priest is needed to do for us what we cannot do for ourselves; that a priest must be loved and respected. And then we can echo Micah's confident assertion: "Now I know that the Lord will prosper me, because I have a Levite as priest."

May this work of mine help bring about the renewal of priestly life and mission, so necessary for the renewal of the Church and "for the salvation of the world." May it also be seen as a thank-offering to the good God for allowing me to share in His Son's Priesthood and likewise a thank-offering to the countless sons and daughters of the Church who have supported me as I have endeavored to be "a father and a priest" to them.

Solemnity of the Most Sacred Heart of Jesus
June 19, 2009
The Beginning of the Year for Priests

ESSAYS AND REVIEWS

*The priest will not understand the greatness of his office
till he is in Heaven. If he understood it on earth,
he would die, not of fear, but of love.*

— St. John Vianney

The Priest, Youth, and Religious Education

(*Emmanuel*, January 1973)

So many priests have devoted a major portion of their ministry to religious education that we should surely be receiving some message. I believe the message is one of concern and near-panic, but little will be accomplished in this frenzied state.

This is indeed a vital issue, which must be considered from several angles. To say that youth no longer have faith questions the universal salvific will of God; to pass over the problem as transient is to bury our heads in the sand; to blame only parents or society is to disregard our own past negligences. Just what are the answers? Maybe they lie in the asking of the right questions. Have we failed really to get involved when confronted with a problem? Have we glibly or smugly refused to give answers and guidance? Recently there has been a regrettable tendency among many priests to indicate their distaste for being "answer men." I do not think today's youth are looking for a man who will think for them, but they are desperately seeking guidance. After all, they can legitimately expect us to be religious "experts"—after eight years' training! If a teenager asks a question, answer it; don't tell him to figure it out for himself—that's what they call a "cop-out." He may even get the impression that you don't care enough to help.

Have we given young people such major causes to battle and such a pessimistic, dismal world-view that they have given up in disgust and dismay? Let's instill in these people attainable goals and ideals, closer to home and more in keeping with their age. The situation in Vietnam may well be of great concern, and racial injustice is surely deplorable, but we should not teach youth to invest all of their Christianity in these two issues alone. We should not be training cynics. On the contrary, we should proudly point to the great social advances in two thousand years since Christ—a respect for human life and dignity, which never existed before Him. In other words, I think youth are tired of the incessant negativism and social breast-beating.

Have we presented what is really essential to the religious experience or have we exchanged them for more fashionable concepts? The Mass and the sacraments, personal prayer and contemplation, service to God through service to fellow man are perennial values, which are valid and necessary in every age. They cannot be betrayed for any reason!

Have we outdone ourselves in trying to "relate" better? Sports clothes and first names do not make for closer relationships—but a "Christ-image" does! Young people know the value of religious symbolism. By the same token, I am not surprised to find that the man who has a poor personality in a collar is usually the same without it, so let's not make inane excuses. Furthermore, our theological and sociological role is one of religious leadership, not camaraderie. Let's understand youth, by all means; but that does not mean we have to be one of them.

Have we fallen into the trap of "opinionism," which plagues so many today? One opinion is not as good as another. What we must present is *God's* "opinion," as it comes to us through His Church. It would never hurt to show our love and loyalty for the Church. No employee of IBM would hold his position very long if he made public statements against computer programming or machines. Some priests would do well to give that some honest consideration and evaluation. Have we turned the liturgy into one more social gathering? We are under a serious obligation (a rather unpopular notion today) to make liturgy prayerful and inspiring; to do less is to fail in our most basic and most priestly mission. We must give our young people a real appreciation and love for this wonderful gift of the Mass, which brings life and reconciliation—concepts which they understand well and fully appreciate. They are starving for real spiritual nourishment, as can be seen from the strong currents among them toward transcendentalism and mysticism. "What father among you would give your son a stone when he asks for bread?"

Nemo dat quod non habet. Is that the real reason why we may be failing? How can we hope to transmit a spiritual message if we have allowed ourselves to become spiritually desiccated? If we are to *be* truly "other Christs," we, like Him, must take time out from a hectic schedule in order to communicate with Him Who is the Source and Content of our teaching. Perhaps our Lord is letting us fail because we became too self-confident and self-assured, because we preached ourselves instead of Him, because we lost touch with Him. Were we to look through the annals of Christianity in search of the most successful teachers and preachers, we would also find the most prayerful men, men who realize the meaning of "without me you can do nothing."

All of this places a great burden on the priest, but he is the man of and for God and the task of the transmission of the Gospel belongs first and foremost to him. His is a divine commission to teach the tremendous mystery of God's love to all men—this present generation is no exception. We have at our disposal today the most advanced techniques of communication, the most nuanced understanding of learning theory and the most carefully researched methodologies. These are ideal times, and there is good cause for genuine optimism.

So, Fathers, like Christ, we must "be about our Father's business."

Religion, Relevancy, and Youth

(*The Priest*, April 1973)

Means of communication and instructional equipment have never before been so advanced, yet we find ourselves today with gaps which are widening into chasms. These gaps cross religious, political, racial and economic boundaries; no one seems exempt from the anguish and anxiety of a "gap-ridden" society.

As priests, teachers, or parents, no gap is so disconcerting as the "faith gap" of our youth. What follow are practical suggestions for all concerned with the religious education of youth. These are not merely nebulous concepts, but ideas that have been successful in a variety of situations. Not all are of equal value, nor is any one of them an infallible guide to "turning kids on" to religion.

I wish to share some thoughts which you may have already been thinking or to make explicit and vocal what you could only ponder in your mind but never execute in practice. This contribution comes from my experience in parish life, in the classroom, and in the homes of troubled, anxious parents.

The Priest

In spite of some current trends to de-emphasize the importance of the priest, there is no other man so influential in the religious formation of young people as is the priest. And we should be able to expect at least that much after his years of training. If a young person comes with a question, answer it; don't tell him to figure it out for himself. He came to you for help. Don't "cop out" under the guise of teaching him to think for himself.

If any image of the Church was ever poorly timed from the historical standpoint, it was the concept of the "Pilgrim Church." Just when secular society was involved in one of the most mobile, rapidly changing periods in history, the Church decided to pull up her "anchor" and let the "barque of Peter" be inordinately buffeted by the winds of change, flux, and fadism. I believe we, the clergy, must once again drop anchor and give youth at least one societal structure where they can experience comfort, relief and peace in a world bent on change for the sake of change. We do not want the Church to be an impenetrable fortress, aloof and unaware; but a weak structure, susceptible to constant change, is most undesirable sociologically, psychologically, or theologically.

Therefore, the priest must present the "constants" of the religious experience, those enduring values which are valid in every age: the Mass and the sacraments, personal prayer and contemplation, service to God through service of fellowman. Let us not go to bizarre lengths to "relate." Sports clothes and first names will not make us "one of the boys"—nor should we want to be such. In doing this, we are really at a loss to help and direct, since we have abandoned the role of leadership for a place in "the group." Quite often I get the impression that teenagers are saying: "Understand me, but don't imitate me!"

Let us not so stress our common Christianity as to forget our Catholic Tradition. This is crucial in establishing an identity in young people. When they have grasped the essence of their own religion, they can broaden their perspectives to encompass the ecumenical level. We see this principle operative in levels of child awareness and concern, from home to neighborhood to city, etc. The religious sphere should be no different.

Make liturgy prayerful and inspiring—this is the greatest builder of identity and community which we have at our disposal. Don't turn the Mass into one more social gathering! Recognize the strong currents toward transcendentalism and mysticism in youth culture today.

Never become so wrapped up in "dialogue" as to forget that you have a most valuable message to communicate—the Gospel of Jesus Christ, which has the power to be the leaven in the world to transform, vitalize, and sacralize human life.

The Teacher

You are the extension of the Church's Magisterium—a rather sobering thought—and your obligations are no less sobering.

There has been a rash of excessive "opinionism" in the Church today. We must remember to distinguish theology from religion. Theology is a science and, like any other science, has some definite formulations. No matter what I think, H_2O will always be water; so too with defined dogma. To debate dogma or interject your own faith problems is to do your class a great disservice.

Concentrate on the essentials of our Faith; other things can be learned in good time and as students are disposed to receive them. We would never attempt to teach all of a foreign language in one year; again, religion is the same.

Let's not make our religion classes big discussion clubs, which often simply result in shared ignorance. Content must be taught and internalized before it can be intelligently discussed.

Speaking of content, let's give our students some substance in their religion courses. A good elective program should offer classes on various levels of Scripture, liturgy, and morality. You'll find filled and interested classes!

Furthermore, truth must never be negated or "watered-down." Teenagers know what the Church teaches and really resent your "white-washing" attempts, since this actually says that you don't really believe yourself.

Parents

If your teenager has stopped going to Mass, give him good, solid reasons for going (and be sure you know them yourself). Do not resort to authority, pressure, or punitive measures. You will win the battle but lose the war.

Before preaching to your teens, be sure you believe what you say, and practice it. Never let them label you a "hypocrite."

Try to discover what they are really saying. Are they doing these things to "bug" you? To rebel because it is fashionable? Or do they really have faith problems?

You must similarly develop an ability to distinguish teenage fads and fetishes from genuine, enduring attitudes.

Finally, but most importantly, understand that your children are products of the times. Is it so surprising, in an age when scientism, secularism, and skepticism are glorified, that religion has been relegated to a notch above folklore or superstition? A patient, wise, and understanding parent is the greatest "salesman" for religion.

All of Us, Together

We must all redouble our efforts to combat eroding attitudes in our society and let our youth experience the joy and consolation of religion at its best.

Our youth say they are idealistic; let us give them the opportunity to prove it. Let us afford them the same opportunity to believe that we received ourselves.

Solving the Vocation Crisis

(*The Priest*, July–August 1973)

Each year, one of the greatest joys for a diocese is to be able to publish pictures of its newly ordained priests in the diocesan newspaper. Given the psychology and language of crisis we hear all around us, would we be surprised to find no such picture in our own diocesan newspaper in 1980? Such crisis-oriented thinking only nurtures doubts and confirms suspicions. What we need in the Church in the United States today is a resurgence of hope and the positive thinking that characterized our forefathers in the faith.

Just what do I mean? I mean that if we are ever to emerge from this present vocation crisis we must begin now to take positive steps to reverse the current trend. It will involve tremendous work to undo the damage of negativism, but a reversal is surely possible. And it must be the work of the whole Church, but especially of priests. All priests young and old, but especially the young!

What will attract young men to the priesthood? Perhaps the question to ask is, "What attracted me to the priesthood?" In all likelihood, many of the same things will draw boys to the ministry today. Let me deal with but a few of the qualities which seem indispensable.

The priest should be Christ-like. It's a truism; it's even "old hat," but really quite lacking in many instances. Can we be so confident of our "Christ identity" as to echo St. Paul, "Be imitators of me"? If a youth cannot see the Christ of compassion and love in a man who claims to represent Him, is it any wonder that he does not feel drawn to the priesthood?

We need happy priests. What kind of publicity agent for the priesthood is a man who exhibits a constant grimace? We often say with our lips that the service of the Lord is our greatest joy, while our lives often tell a completely different story. Let's not be afraid to communicate the happiness which comes from the ministry. One of the most disturbing statements I ever heard came from a boy who said that it took him fourteen years to find a man who was happy in the priesthood and who loudly proclaimed it!

A convinced priest is imperative—a man who really lives the Gospel message, a man who has no regrets, a man who loves the Church he serves. This type of attitude is contagious and inspiring; it sparks similar thoughts and actions in those who observe such a man.

A self-assured man elicits confidence in those who look up to him. He is not arrogant or proud, but he knows his tasks and performs them diligently, knowing that Jesus is with him. Who could not be impressed by a man who is a living witness to a vital and active faith?

I think we need priests who have a positive view of life. This does not mean Pollyannas who bury their heads in the sand to avoid reality, but it does mean the type of man who could say: "Some men see things as they are and ask why; I dream things that never were and ask why not?" This positive vision must also (and especially) apply to the Church. We cannot hope to attract young men to the service of a Church which comes under constant fire from her chief spokesmen.

Stable, balanced men are most important. If all the Church can demonstrate as examples of her priesthood are either eccentrics who belong to another era or pseudo-hippies who latch onto any fad, we are in bad straits. We must project an image which moves out of the arena of caricature into the real world of normal, healthy parish priests.

Finally, young people must see men who are involved, concerned, and serving. For the only sight of a priest to be the forty-five minutes on Sunday morning is extremely dangerous, especially today. Today's youth want religion to be a real part of life; we must let them see the man in the Roman collar at every opportunity possible in a multiplicity of circumstances. Surely the priest whose presence is constantly felt will make others ponder what satisfaction must be his, as well as what joy he must bring to his people!

In speaking of the priesthood, we should not be afraid to capitalize on the idealism of modern youth. Let's not be afraid to speak "sacrifice" to them, whether that involves celibacy or salaries. Let's not be afraid to use ourselves as examples of what we could have done or could have been but freely chose to forego for the sake of Christ, the Gospel, and the Church. No argument is so convincing as a personal testimony to the value and beauty of the priesthood.

Our speech and approach should convey an honest sense of urgency; it should provide boys with a concept of mission; it should establish in them a strong identity rooted in Jesus, our eternal High Priest.

We must never fear to affirm unequivocally: "We need you!" There is no room in Christianity for smugness or foolish pride. The priesthood is not demeaned by such a statement. On the contrary, it will be enhanced if we go on to explain why: We need you to make Jesus Christ present today; we need you to spread the Gospel; we need you to save immortal souls; we need you to heal men broken by poverty, injustice, and war; we need you to reconcile people to God and one another.

And then reiterate Christ's own promise: "Anyone who has given up home, brothers and sisters, mother or father . . . will receive in this present age a hundredfold . . . and in the age to come, everlasting life!"

The Parish: Crucible of Priestly Formation

(*The Priest*, November 1973)*

> *As he [John] watched Jesus walk by he said, "Look! There is the Lamb of God!" The two disciples heard what he said. and followed Jesus. When Jesus turned around and noticed them following him, he asked them, "What are you looking for?" They said to him, "Rabbi. where do you stay?" "Come and see," he answered* (John 1:35–36).

Once a man has recognized Jesus, he is compelled to discover where He "stays" (in the full biblical sense of that word). And Jesus encourages, even commands, them to do so. Those first men who were called to discipleship learned what it meant to follow the Lord in a very concrete way—they walked and worked with Him. They saw that He "stayed" with His people, even as He does today. They drank deeply from the cup of discipleship, with all its joys and sorrows. Those men were thoroughly prepared to make a final decision before eating that last Covenantal Meal with the Master; before being told to do the same thing as a remembrance of Him.

Our preparation of priests today can be no less all-encompassing, and yet it is commonplace to hear people on all sides decrying the woeful lack of proper training of seminarians. As solutions are offered, two general directions emerge: a tightening of discipline or an absence of structural limitations. The former view fails to take into account societal changes; the latter fails to recognize human nature as we encounter it. Furthermore, history indicates that a structureless preparation is dangerous; recent experience indicates that Tridentine training is inadequate today. Perhaps a cursory survey of current conditions would provide some helpful background.

The passage of centuries has a way of creating "hallowed institutions," and the seminary seems to be one of them. However, we should look back into the time of its establishment and discover its initial purpose. We must then ask ourselves if it is fulfilling its function, or whether an alternate structure could do as well, if not better.

When the Council of Trent established seminaries, the Fathers of that Council surely had many motives in mind, but their primary aim was to ensure careful and precise theological education for future priests. Given the obstacles to travel in that century, it is only

---

* Co-authored with Robert McBain.

logical that all the theological students would live under one roof. Today, such conditions do not prevail. Aware of the historical situation, then, we realize that the seminary as we now know it is by no means a strict necessity. Therefore, we should be able to make an objective evaluation of its effectiveness, open to the facts as they present themselves.

Those seminaries which attempt to maintain traditional forms of discipline indicate that they are not really aware of the societal changes of this century which have already influenced the candidate for priesthood until that point. We are not denying the need for discipline, but the kind needed for the diocesan priesthood is self-discipline. The seminarian should be gradually introduced to this concept, along with the idea of responsibility and accountability.

Those last two words were carefully chosen and are just as carefully neglected by the vast majority of seminaries. In the seminaries of the "old guard," responsibility means responsibility to the "Rule." In looser structures, responsibility is either to oneself or the "community." The former is entirely too egocentric; the latter creates many other difficulties, which we shall shortly discuss. For now, let us simply state that accountability must involve real life and not the artificial devices created to ensure conformity or good order. The future priest must be trained to handle the freedom and near-autonomy of his impending ministry, for there are very few external forces on the performance of a parish priest; his own interest, motivation, and good will are crucial.

Many seminarians learn to live the life of a professional "loafer," and they enjoy it. But it is not really their fault, for the present system not only allows it but fosters it. If a man is in a seminary where mobility is still limited, sleep can become the logical diversion and escape, an attitude that carries over into his priesthood. In seminaries where seminarians come and go at will, expensive, time-consuming, and often unpriestly habits are given time to develop. In short, the seminarian has entirely too much time on his hands.

We also find that seminarians are offered little challenge on any level. Originality is usually frowned upon, and the seminarian who gets involved is often looked upon as "pushy" or a "politician." Personal talents and assets are rarely given the opportunity to show forth, much less blossom. This is undoubtedly unfair to the seminarian and equally unfair to the Church-at-large, which is deprived of the benefits of creativity, resourcefulness, or individuality.

The amount of guidance that is given is minimal, and standards for acceptance seem to be lowered constantly. It is a standard joke (but sad and true) that nearly any man with two arms and two legs could probably be ordained today. Thus we are inflicting all varieties of eccentrics on our people. Just how much respect and credibility the priesthood will enjoy in future years is directly proportionate to the amount of guidance and selectivity operative now.

There seems to be no principle of integration in the training of the seminarian; each facet of his life is given token lip service while connections are rarely shown. Imbalances are in evidence depending on the seminary: One will produce social workers, another will send out recluses, while yet another ordains professional theologians. Rare is the seminary which sends out well-balanced, integrated parish priests. Why? Because the seminarian has been allowed to develop in a vacuum, which is the non-reality of seminary conditions.

The community life of many seminaries (which is more suited for contemplative religious than diocesan priests) stifles growth and precludes or hinders outside pastoral involvement. It provides a prep school atmosphere, with all the attendant athletic and social activities, as well as faculty paternalism. Such a concept of community induces game-playing to be passed on for Orders and encourages insincerity, "back-biting" and "squealing." Most dangerously of all, it equips the seminarian with the supports of a pseudo-monastic spirituality which he will never be able to live out in parish life.

We have just painted a rather dismal picture of the present seminary system. Where does that leave us? First of all, Father Eugene Kennedy recommends that all priests (and by extension, seminarians) be given greater opportunities for growth and personal development rather than relying on inadequate or protective structures. Father Andrew Greeley has little regard for careless experimentation in priestly training, but he also sees the need for real changes. Our proposal is to combine all the good features of the old system, make necessary adjustments, and refocus the seminarian's life from the seminary to the parish, which will be the central point of his life for the remainder of his active ministry.

Our system is not presented as a panacea for the difficulties of priestly formation, nor do we consider it the definitive structure or last word in seminary education. On the contrary, much more study and experimentation will be necessary. However, we do feel that two characteristics recommend our proposal: its moderation and its correspondence to real-life priestly ministry. We have attempted to avoid the pitfalls of other experimental programs, but we still see the need to be somewhat adventuresome and even confident of success.

The rationale, thrust, and direction of our program is well summarized in a statement of Father Kennedy: "For fuller preparation of seminarians, the Church needs teaching parishes, similar to teaching hospitals, in which the young men learn from well-developed and dedicated professionals" (see *St. Anthony Messenger*, December, 1972).

Therefore, our aim is to have every seminarian living in and working in a parish. This does not mean dabbling in pet projects one day a week or specializing in certain endeavors. Father Greeley has made a very astute observation on this point: "The latest fashion is the so-called clinical-pastoral training. This means that the seminarian hies himself to a hospital, prison or mental institution where he is supposed to get practical experience by dealing with kinds of people and the sorts of situations which he will almost never encounter when working in a parish" (see *Priests in the United States*, p. 30).

The seminarian would live in a parish with two or three others and work in close conjunction with one of the priests who would serve as his advisor or mentor. This mentor should be somewhat well-equipped theologically, as well as being an exemplary priest. Three days a week, the seminarian would attend classes at a nearby theological college. In frequent, planned evaluation meetings, all on the team would discuss their progress and parish involvements, thus teaching the seminarian to take good objective stock of his ministry. His duties could be as diverse as his abilities: liturgy, teaching, community projects, parish organizations, prayer groups, counseling. Furthermore. he would learn what rectory life is really all about, while also participating fully in the wider life of the total parish community.

Put on the spot each day, confronted with the reality of parish life, the seminarian should see all the more clearly the need for solid spiritual and academic formation. We cannot emphasize enough the necessity for real experience, which cannot be adequately replaced by any number of conferences, lectures, or homilies. *Experientia docet*.

Before we proceed to outline all the advantages such a program could offer, let us anticipate the most obvious objections and try to answer them.

Some will view this move as an iconoclastic action simply to raze one more ecclesiastical structure. This view is not correct; in fact, we are suggesting the creation of a new structure to do what is presently not being done. Perhaps a rather sobering reminder from a sociologist might be helpful here: "The old seminary system has collapsed, to be replaced by the present chaos" (Greeley, ibid.). Therefore, we are not killing the old system—it is already dead; we desperately need the resurrection of a structure which will train men properly for the needs of the Church in the twentieth and twenty-first centuries.

Others will say that the program's ramifications have not been thought out. They have been, and we are pleased by what we envision. If anything, considerable forethought and research have gone into this proposal, unlike many programs initiated since Vatican II. Once again, Greeley cites the nondescript, nomadic character of the American seminary to forewarn us: ". . . It is no exaggeration to say that American seminaries have not had the foggiest idea of where they were going, what they were for, or what they ought to be doing for the last ten years" (ibid., p. 29).

Finally, problems will be raised in regard to the seminarian's relationship to the parish and the rectory. Some will fear improper conduct on the part of the seminarian or bad example from one of the priests. In either instance, this would have occurred at a later date, anyway. Neither the seminarian nor the priest should be in the priesthood if his conduct is a source of scandal.

The advantages of this system are many and varied. We list only a few to indicate the direction in which this will take us. The first and most important is that a man will encounter the full and true parish ministry immediately; he will not be given any false sense of security, and he will not waste years of study preparing for a priesthood which exists only in his own imagination. He will not have to receive diaconate to discover parish life and will not feel as compelled to remain if he realizes the work is not for him.

The total integration of all aspects of a seminarian's life becomes a real and viable possibility, for the interplay of the spiritual, theological, and pastoral comes into perspective in this type of formational process. The need for both prayer and theology becomes immediately obvious when someone is confronted with his first pastoral problem. One's advice comes from thoughtful, prayerful reflection on certain data and constants, not a whim. Thus, all three facets of a priest's life are seen as crucial and indispensable.

The parish as a whole and youths in particular can be greatly edified by the faith and honest efforts of young men dedicating their lives to the service of Christ's Church. This is no slight contribution in the light of the bad press the priesthood has suffered in recent years.

The quality of academics could be immeasurably increased if we continued to phase out small diocesan seminaries in favor of provincial theological colleges or even ecumenical enterprises. It would be well to create a more academic, professional environment, one which is less protective, so that seminarians experience what their lay counterparts do in their academic pursuits.

Having removed seminarians from the closed-off, segregated culture which the seminary creates, they will react more maturely, more thoughtfully, and with more sensitivity, for they will be dealing with people on a daily basis who differ in age, theology, and background.

From a purely pragmatic point of view, we will no longer be spending thousands of dollars each year on fuel and utilities for buildings constructed for five hundred men with only fifty left. Surely, this money could be more wisely and profitably channeled in other directions.

The unnecessary tensions and anxieties of seminary life would be a thing of the past, for the abrasiveness of a pseudo-community would not exist. The seminarian would have too much to do to cause or become involved in petty arguments, especially if he were given the example by his older brothers in the ministry.

At the risk of sounding ominous, we must say explicitly what we have tried to indicate in so many statements throughout this paper: Priestly formation in America is in bad straits. If we leave the situation there, then there is good reason for glumness and despair. However, if we admit this reality and decide to work from there, we have good reason to be hopeful and optimistic, for we have extremely willing young men interested in the priesthood today. All they need is the support and guidance of other interested men and a system which will prepare them for the work they so much want to perform.

The Prophetic Priest Today

(*The Priest*, October 1974)

To speak of the priest as prophet may seem to illustrate an ignorance of the meaning of either vocation; to many persons, the two calls appear mutually exclusive. Throughout its development, the Catholic priesthood took on many ministries and characteristics which were not exercised by the apostles, but that does not imply infidelity to the apostolic patrimony. On the contrary, simply to mimic and reproduce apostolic structures could be a far greater infidelity. In our attempts to maintain continuity with the apostolic Church we must be most concerned with present needs—as were the apostles—as we bring the Gospel to this situation. That would be the best emulation of the Primitive Church.

We find ourselves today in desperate need of prophetic voices in the Church and in society, and the priesthood seems to provide a most appealing structure to carry out this function. We mentioned that some see the prophetic and priestly roles as separate, distinct, and even hostile to each other. This need not be so. Perhaps a caricature of both roles contributes to this image and understanding. Some people view the priest strictly as a "company" man, while the prophet is seen as antagonistic to any structure. This dichotomy is hardly necessary and does not find a solid basis in Scripture. In this article, we will suggest some prophetic characteristics and attitudes which would aid the priest in his ministry to his people, both in the Church and in society. For the sake of convenience, we will deal with these two aspects separately, while knowing full well that such a separation into religious and secular spheres would be most distasteful to the classical prophet.

The Prophetic Priest in the Church.

At the root of every prophetic vocation is a deep consciousness that the mission upon which one is embarking is divinely willed, that one is acting as God's mouthpiece: "Then the Lord extended His hand and touched my mouth, saying, 'See, I place My words in your mouth'" (Jer 1:9). In fact, a most powerful compulsion incites this kind of man to speak and act: "The lion roars—who will not be afraid! The Lord God speaks—who will not prophesy!" (Amos 3:8).

Because of his awareness of God's prompting him to speak, the prophetic man has a firm conviction and confidence that he will meet with ultimate success, not because of his own skill or cleverness but because he is working for God: "But the Lord is with me like a mighty champion: my persecutors will stumble, they will not triumph" (Jer 20:11); "The Spirit of the Lord is upon me" (Lk 4:18).

What the prophets experienced in their call is still valid for one called today. God's call is irrevocable, and His assistance never fails. This truth should bolster any person who believes he is speaking for God or is hesitant about his role and identity. God takes the initiative: "Prophecy has never been put forward by man's willing it. It is rather that men impelled by the Holy Spirit have spoken under God's influence" (2 Peter 1:21), but not everyone responds with the same generous, courageous, and spontaneous enthusiasm of Isaiah's "Here I am; send me" (Is 6:8). The classic example of the unwilling person called to do the Lord's work is Jeremiah. He resorts to excuses for his unwillingness: "Ah, Lord God! I know not how to speak; I am too young" (Jer 1:6). But God will have none of that and once more comes the assurance of God's presence and assistance (1:7).

And so, the individual has all this personal experience, but the question remains: How is the community to know the true man of God? First of all, the prophetic person must have heard the Word of God and interiorized it before he attempts to externalize it through his preaching. That is why Ezekiel is given that strange command to eat the scroll in 3:1. A German proverb reminds us that "a man is what he eats." In other words, the holiness and integrity of his life come from the Word he has received; these, in turn, present the most convincing testimony to the validity of his mission. Secondly, the prophet does not form a new religion; he builds on the foundation of the best in the Tradition. He takes the constants of the religious experience and transposes them into the contemporary idiom. He is not a slave to the past, nor is he so convinced of the "sacrament of the present moment" as to be unable to lead his people into the future to which God is calling the community.

As the institutional Church observes the prophetic priest at work, a certain skepticism may surface, but the New Testament contains two suggestions on how to deal with this type of dilemma: "You can tell a tree by its fruit" (Mt 7:20) and, "If their purpose or activity is human in its origins, it will destroy itself. If, on the other hand, it comes from God, you will not be able to destroy them without fighting God Himself" (Acts 5:381).

Therefore, both the individual and institution have some criteria by which to judge prophetic behavior. Ideally, the two perceptions of the reality should be the same, but such is not always the case. One basic understanding must be reiterated: The true prophet is not set against the Church or outside it; rather, he works for it from within.

In terms of his position in the community, many possibilities can be seen. The man of God is a sort of *rara avis*, neither fish nor fowl; the expression "man of God" aptly sums up the type of "schizophrenia" which is his life. He is a man, like all others, and so is conscious of how much he is like the people to whom he preaches. Nevertheless, he belongs to God and must be identified with God.

Because the prophet may speak against certain structures, those in authority may feel threatened, echoing the rage of the priests and people of Jeremiah's time: "You must be put to death!" (Jer 26:8). In today's Church, many topics are likely to bring tempers to a fever pitch, but the prophetic priest is one who is concerned to preserve Gospel values in preference to any other values. An unwavering commitment and an uncompromising posture result in alienation, and the kinship with one's people seems to be lessened. The feeling of rejection was so intense in Jeremiah that he even cursed the day of his birth (cf. 5:10ff; 20:18).

The man of God must be like Isaiah, who is overwhelmed by the holiness of God. He realizes that this holiness must be his goal and the goal of his people: "Be holy for I, the Lord your God, am holy" (Lev 19:2). Although both he and they fall short, they must continue. In the quest for holiness, the prophets stressed fidelity to God. Put negatively, they asserted that Israel would be betrayed by the very things for which she had betrayed God. Francis Thompson rendered that understanding poetically: "All things betray thee who betrayest Me." This is a very difficult concept to convey today, especially since Vatican II, when we went on record as supporting and praising modern man and his achievements. True religion does not despise progress, but many people do not make clear distinctions, so that the latest technological or scientific break-through becomes that week's idol. Simply because we do not burn incense before twentieth-century idols does not lessen the reality of the idolatry. This is what Hosea refers to in his account of Israel's infidelity represented as harlotry: "I will go after my lovers who give me my bread and my water, my wool and my flax, my oil and my drink" (2:9).

A perennial problem in religion is that of action vs. contemplation, and it is a hotly debated issue today. The prophets believed that both were necessary and absolutely indispensable. Today's priest must preach that same message. Some of our people believe that mere multiplication of Masses, novenas, or rosaries will bring salvation without concern and involvement on behalf of one's fellowman. Hosea puts it this way: "For it is love that I desire, not sacrifice, and knowledge of God rather than holocausts" (6:6). Love and knowledge lead to concrete action. Trito-Isaiah also stressed that prayer finds its fullest expression and value in positive action: "Then you shall call, and the Lord will answer, you shall cry for help and He will say: Here I am! If you remove from your midst oppression, false accusation and malicious speech; if you bestow your bread on the hungry. . ." (58:9l). The overriding and consistent message of the prophets may be summarized thus: "Without works, faith is idle" (James 2:20).

On the other hand, the prophet presumes a life of prayer and communion with God. It was once fashionable to present the prophets as anti-cultic, but such a position is quite untenable. Isaiah even receives his call while at worship in the Temple (6:1ff.). In his hyperbolic denouncement of one-sided religious observance, the prophet may seem opposed to traditional religious practices, but this passage is sufficient indication that the truly religious person needs prayer if he is to be effective in his work for man: "If you hold back your foot on the sabbath from following your own pursuits on My holy day, if you call the sabbath a delight, and the Lord's day honorable . . ." (Is 58:13).

Another problem confronting the prophetic priest is that of priests who do not measure up to the demands of their vocation. Correction is never easy, but the correction of a fellow-priest is most difficult. Yet this may be necessary if God's best purposes are to be served. Hosea spoke out against the corruption of the priests of his time: " . . . with you is My grievance, O priests! . . . they feed on the sin of my people. . ." (4:4, 8). Micah echoes the same complaint: "Her leaders render judgment for a bribe, her priests give decisions for a salary" (3:11). Jeremiah bewails the fact that "the priests teach as they wish" (5:31). Isaiah is forced to condemn the conduct of Israel's religious leaders: "Priest and prophet stagger from strong drink" (28:7). When Jeremiah prophesied against Israel, we already saw the reaction of the religious authorities—they wished to kill him. But why? While they would have been enraged at anyone's attack upon them, his was worse, because he belonged to a priestly family. And so, any priest presuming to attack the immorality or laxity of priests today can expect as hostile a reaction from his clerical confreres, since this action may be interpreted as traitorous. But once again, one recalls how misunderstood the prophet often is, especially by his own. As men call for reform and renewal (both interior and structural), their appeals may be viewed as iconoclastic. Their attitudes may seem disloyal; their visions, lacking in faith. However, the prophetic priest must raise the consciousness of those in authority to the startling reality of our crisis situation. Ezekiel challenged the traditional belief that Jerusalem was inviolate because God dwelt in the Temple there. While all Christians believe in the indwelling of the Spirit in the Church, it is not extreme to suggest that, at times, our structures and our refusal to listen make it difficult for the Spirit to do His work. The man who challenges the Church's confidence (because he sees presumption more than hope) is likely to be subjected to the same type of reprisal as Jeremiah.

In an age which, as some believe, has lost its sense of sin, the prophetic priest must proclaim that sin is possible. Sin is not our predominant preoccupation, but we must address ourselves to the whole of human reality, and sin is surely a part of it. Hosea offers himself as an apt example of a preacher who tried to stir his people to repentance, to return to the Lord. While using very strong language (4:4), he still was able to bring across the reason for repentance—because God loves us with an everlasting love: "How could I give you up, O Ephraim or deliver you up, O Israel? How could I treat you as Admah, or make you like Zeboiim? My heart is overwhelmed, My pity is stirred" (11:8). Hosea sets the perfect pattern: He calls for a change of heart, not through fear but through a recall of God's tender love. Such an approach would certainly meet with much success today.

In the priest's personal life, he is also called to reflect the prophetic. If any image or model is appropriate, it is that of the Suffering Servant. And both aspects are necessary: suffering and servanthood. As a group, the prophets were accustomed to physical and psychological suffering; hardship was a fact of life for them. If ministry is failing today, it may be because we have lost sight of the redemptive value of suffering. Every vocation entails difficulties, but very often the priest goes to great extremes to avoid this part of life. Celibacy seems to require more than enough, but if celibacy is lived grudgingly, it has no redemptive value, personal or vicarious. Life is a burden to many today, and we should be examples to our people of Christian life, a life which embraces the mystery of suffering.

The prophet is a servant. In the past, this was given hasty lip service. Today, it is given more prolonged lip service, for a new form of clericalism is emerging in which all the benefits of the former system are enjoyed without any of the inconveniences. In other words, many are seeking the best of both worlds without the worst of either. This attitude or life-style hardly speaks of servanthood. Flashy sports cars, winter and summer vacations, expensive clerical and secular wardrobes speak more eloquently than any pious meditation on the servant role of the contemporary priest. Taken from another angle, how available is the priest for service? Is he a priest only in the officially defined moments of cultic activity, or is his life one of total and unreserved self-giving? Is his life lived for the Church in the same manner as a husband's should be for his wife?

All of this may sound incredibly idealistic but that is our goal, or should be, and that is the expectation of our people. They are looking to us for an example and even heroic sacrifices. If they wanted an example of mediocrity and accommodation, our job would be superfluous. The task of the prophetic priest is to be an eschatological sign. Many of us are not signs of any description, let alone eschatological.

Like the Marcan Christ, the destiny of the priest is that of triumph through suffering. In Deutero-Isaiah, we see this pattern forcefully portrayed in chapter 52: "See, My servant shall prosper, he shall be raised high and greatly exalted" (13). And therein lies our reason for hope, optimism, and confidence. With the knowledge that we belong to God in a special way, we "consider the sufferings of the present to be as nothing compared to the glory to be revealed in us" (Rom 8:18).

The role of the prophetic priest in the Church, then, is most complex and multi-dimensional. Regarded in its full scope, the prophet should be a welcome member to the Body of Christ. If not welcome, he must be acknowledged as necessary. If he is not given the opportunity to exercise his charism properly within the institution, those in authority run the risk of compelling him to do so outside the structure, where it will do little for either the individual or the community. A delicate interplay between the institutional and the prophetic is crucial to the vitality, growth, and credibility of the contemporary Church.

The Prophetic Priest in Society.

If a Christian culture ever needed a prophet, it is twentieth-century America. And while the historical circumstances do change, human nature seems consistent throughout the ages. In fact, a reading of the castigations of the prophets makes one aware of the timeliness of their message. This verse from Haggai sums up the futility of modern American grasping after material things: "You have sown much, but have brought in little; you have eaten, but have not been satisfied; you have drunk, but have not been exhilarated; have clothed yourselves, but not been warmed; and he who earned wages earned them for a bag with holes in it" (1:6).

As one commissioned to preach the Gospel, the priest today cannot afford the luxury of retiring to the sanctuary. His thrust must be outward. He must show the relevance of the Gospel by his own life, by animating lives, by persuading others to action. Dogma does not exist for its own sake—it demands action. Put in another way: the indicative leads to the imperative. The prophets were keenly aware of this.

In a nation beset with economic depression, political corruption, and confused priorities, the Christian prophet is called upon to exhort, rebuke, threaten, cajole, and entice—like the prophets of old. He will use every literary, dramatic, and rhetorical device at his disposal: imagination, metaphor, parable, paradox, hyperbole, allegory. He, like the evangelists, will view an historical event and interpret it theologically. That is what Abraham Heschel refers to as "exegesis of the present situation from the divine perspective." Therefore, Amos does not hesitate to denounce the king (7:11), nor does Micah doubt that the Lord requires him to question the conduct and motives of the citizens (6:9ff.).

What issues in society today require a prophetic word? In an increasingly amoral culture, hardly any aspect would be free from scrutiny. In spite of laws on the subject, racial injustice is still most prevalent. The basic equality of all men was treated by Amos (9:7) and needs our attention once more.

Isaiah 11:6 still seems unrealistic to those who believe that war is good for the economy. The non-materialistic and the poor are still a thorn in the side of those whose only concern in life is wealth and prestige "because they sell the just man for silver, and the poor man for a pair of sandals" (Amos 2:6). In an age where sexual license is the order of the day, would it not be appropriate for the prophetic priest to accuse society of having abandoned God for harlotry (cf. Hos 4:11)?

When the government has become corrupt and self-serving, it is important to issue a warning: "Woe to those who plan iniquity and work out evil on their couches" (Mic 2:1). When a small minority controls the majority of the economic situation to the detriment of the poor and oppressed, can we be silent (Is 5:8)? No; our exhortation must be constant, uncompromising, and unwavering: "Learn to do good. Make justice your aim: redress the wronged, hear the orphan's plea, defend the widow" (Is 1:17).

Other areas of concern involve the high percentage of broken marriages, abortion-on-demand, anti-religious sentiment, secularism, complacency in the face of social and religious injustice, a certain national self-contentment and insularity.

The prophet's vocation is to announce the religious meaning of life, to affirm that God's law and morality are absolute, to declare that sin is possible, and to challenge the aphorism: *Vox populi, vox Dei*. And in spite of his constant challenging of their values, the prophet must reflect the compassion and mercy of God, Who never fails to love and forgive, so that the priest's efforts are also turned toward speaking a word to the weary and being a source of comfort (cf. Is 50:4, 40:1) to a people to whom God may seem distant, aloof, or unconcerned.

General Conclusions

As priests of the twentieth century, we are required, more than ever, to stand in and continue the prophetic tradition. In what does that consist? It is a spirit of religious optimism and hope, a belief in the Kingdom of God and the perfectibility of man who will bring about that Kingdom. They preached a God of providence and destiny in the context of a religion of spirit and truth. Rather than a series of answers or even approaches, it may be most beneficial to look on the prophetic tradition as a vision of life.

Prophecy is not just condemnation, but also edification, social reconstruction. In those moments when the prophetic and magisterial charisms converged, when dogmatic and moral teachings were mutually supportive, we find landmark documents like *Rerum Novarum*, *Pacem in Terris*, and *Populorum Progressio*. If prophecy is to become again an accepted charism in the Church and in society, we need to understand that criticism is not always negative in scope or intention, nor does it only come from people seeking to destroy or undermine. On the contrary, men speak out to correct because of interest and concern. If their justifiable criticism is not heeded, it will be to the loss of the institution.

Throughout its existence, however, no matter where it has appeared, prophecy has had one recurring theme, one which men must hear today and one which Micah enunciated most beautifully as the very essence of religion: "You have been told, O man, what is good, and what the Lord requires of you: only to do the right and to love goodness, and to walk humbly with your God" (6:8).

The Priest as Consoler

(*The Priest*, February 1975)

"Say only the good things men need to hear, things that will really help them" (Eph 4:29). Is this good psychology and good sociology, or is more involved?

While no single theory can account for all the variables, it is a common perception of many Catholics today that their priests no longer embody the characteristics of a Christ-like priest. Did priests ever really do this? Did the mystique of the priesthood in former years compensate for this? Whatever the answer, we cannot allow this view to persist. Perhaps the one attribute which most people find lacking in priests is an attitude of interest or understanding or consolation. In fact, without being overly simplistic, we could say that if we had these basic virtues, much of our work would be more fruitful and simplified.

The image of the priest as "*alter Christus*" seems to have fallen into disfavor, and that is really to our loss. Maybe in the past we did use the "other Christ" image to remove the priest from his people. If this is so, although I am not convinced that it is, it was cultural, not theological, for no one was ever more involved with or concerned about people than Christ. As men sent in His name, we can do no less. Besides the fact that Jesus exemplified these virtues, why are they important?

Because they present us to our people in a very human context, not as "professional religionists" but as fellow human beings who have a word to say to that situation, a word which is not our own but the one of Him Who sent us. One of the greatest lessons we can learn from the ministry of our Lord is the human concern He showed and used to illustrate a spiritual message.

If we find our spiritual message rejected today, it may be because our people think that is the only aspect of their lives which interests us, because that is our job. But our "job" is to save men by putting them in touch with the daring and exciting truth that God cares; that is the Gospel, the good news.

And St. Paul tells us to "say only the good things men need to hear." How often our message of good news gets overlaid with the bad news of our own personal problems and idiosyncrasies. How often we project our deficiencies onto our people. How often we add to the burden of their lives instead of trying to lighten that burden.

"Comfort, give comfort to my people" (Is 40:1). Do we take this injunction seriously? Life in the twentieth century is complex, baffling, and even overbearing. Oddly enough, our lives as priests are spared much of this suffering because of our celibacy and our "job security." And so, we find it difficult to understand how life can be seen in such negative terms. Whether or not we share that experience of life matters little; we do have to be understanding of it, however. Again, the example of the Master comes to mind.

In the Fourth Eucharistic Prayer, we acknowledge the mission of Jesus: "To the poor He proclaimed the good news of salvation, to prisoners, freedom, and to those in sorrow, joy." Jesus, then, is the answer to human suffering and privation.

As we look at the life of Christ, still another message comes across loud and clear: Suffering is redemptive. Our Lord never promised a cessation of suffering for His followers. On the contrary, the very invitation to follow Him was couched in the language of renunciation and self-denial. The Christian does not seek suffering, but he must realize that suffering not merely endured but accepted is a means of salvation.

Let us explain how Jesus prayed for a release from suffering but that He also saw doing the will of His Father as an opportunity for growth in communion with Him. If that is so for Jesus, it is much more so for us. In John's Gospel we get the impression that Jesus is never more kingly than in the time of His Passion. In fact, Christ's hour of glory begins not beyond the tomb on Easter morning but from the throne of His Cross, when the sacrifice of suffering and love is offered and accepted.

What does the parishioner who is lonely or sick or despairing need from his priest? He needs us to listen to him, to enter into his experience, to pray for him. He needs to be told to pray to the Lord for a release from his present difficulty but also to look to the Jesus Who transformed suffering into glory. Jesus holds out that possibility to all men because He was "a man like us in all things but sin."

As priests, we know a "God of all consolation. He comforts us in all our afflictions and thus enables us to comfort those who are in trouble, with the same consolation we have received from Him" (2 Cor 1:31). We have felt the power of God's love and mercy in our lives, and our mission to be "other Christs" requires us to assure others of this comforting good news. We are men charged to proclaim a word of hope and consolation; the Word is Jesus Christ.

Christmas Thoughts of a Celibate Lover

(*Pastoral Life*, December 1980)

Christmas joy.
Children's love.
Friends' warmth.
Festive days to recall when Joy and Love and Warmth
    first came to dwell among us.
I am asked to love dispassionately and passionately,
    at one and the same moment.
Called to love like a monk—and like Jesus.
Within the solitude of my personal cloister
    on cold, long nights in late winter,
    accepting friends help reincarnate Love.
Deo gratias!
A child would lead them, we were told—and so He did.
God in a Baby loving intensely then shows lovers the way today.
Gloria in excelsis Deo!

The Thorn Birds—Worth Watching, with Reservations

(*Our Sunday Visitor*, March 27, 1983)

The Thorn Birds, the ABC-TV mini-series based on the novel by Colleen McCullough, airs this week. But is it good or bad?

Some discussion of plot and technical aspects of the series is needed if sense is to be made of the more delicate issues to be raised, because *The Thorn Birds* is a sensitive portrayal of a priest caught among conflicting loves and desires.

Father Ralph, played with distinction by Richard Chamberlain, is an Irish priest exiled to Australia for offenses never revealed. He is befriended by a wealthy rancher, Mary Carson (Barbara Stanwyck), who has more than an ordinary parishioner's love and respect for her priest; she is, in fact, what was referred to in the old days as a "chalice-chipper," who wants to ensnare the unsuspecting and handsome young cleric in her web of lust. She fails, but is intent on discovering his Achilles' heel. She succeeds—his tragic flaw is ambition—and she uses her wealth, willed to the Church with him as administrator, to bring about in death the downfall she was unable to effect in life.

Mrs. Carson's brother and his family, with their little girl, Meggie (Rachel Ward), move onto the beautiful Drogheda ranch. Father Ralph watches Meggie grow and becomes her protector, taking the place of her parents, who have no interest in her. As the years pass, the cute little girl develops into a stunning young woman, whose childhood devotion to Father Ralph is transformed into sexual desire. The priest refuses the advances of Meggie, but she never really gives up on him—even after she is married.

In the midst of all this, Father Ralph comes to the attention of Archbishop Contini-Verchese (Christopher Plummer), the papal nuncio, thanks, of course, to the large Carson bequest to the Holy See. The archbishop's admiration for the priest's talents and drive eventually result in his elevation to the episcopacy and cardinalate.

Meanwhile, back on the farm, Meggie is most unhappy in her married life, so that, when the new bishop visits, she bares her soul to him, and they commit adultery. Unbeknownst to him, the child born to Meggie (Dane) is his son. That boy, in turn, loves the bishop-friend of the family so much that he wishes to emulate him completely—even unto the altar of God—ordained, of course, by his father!

On a future visit, Ralph (this time as a cardinal) again commits adultery with Meggie. Father Dane is drowned in an effort to save someone's life. Meggie tells Ralph that Dane was his son. Ralph dies in Meggie's arms.

Soap opera, not so pure and not so simple, with a very weak and dramatically disappointing ending.

It is important to recall that this is essentially a romance; it was not written to expound on points of doctrine—the Church and the priesthood are merely the backdrop (albeit a large and necessary one) for the action in this novel-turned-film.

Nowhere does anyone take jabs at the Church, although the papal nuncio to Australia does have a strong fascination for "king-making," which some Catholics might find offensive, sometimes giving the impression that spiritual realities and political considerations are of equal importance. The cinematography and soundtrack are exquisite. Details of liturgical and clerical life are quite accurately depicted, except for a strange switch of the Episcopal rings from the right to left hands in some scenes. In some scenes, John Paul II was flashed on the screen as John XXIII.

Sexual encounters are handled carefully, but still too overtly for good art. At the moral level, these liaisons are consistently justified as expressions of love and tenderness in a family history that reads like a genealogy of infidelity. Although Father Ralph and Meggie acknowledge their acts as a defiance of Divine Law, we never see or hear them go to confession.

Meggie subscribes to a rather childish belief that her human suffering is a result of God's vengeance heaped on her for her sins. Ralph is slightly more mature in that he can admit that he has "never made a choice for love," one way or the other, because he has always been half-given to Meggie and half-given to God.

Much of the controversy surrounding this work is centered on the priest's infidelity to his promise of celibacy—and this is good, I believe. Celibacy is meant to be a sign or a dramatic witness to the power of Christ's love in the life of an individual, a love so great that all human loves fade into insignificance. Thank God, the vast majority of priests are indeed most faithful to this commitment, and that is why we are justifiably shocked at unfaithfulness. However, we must also be realists, which means acknowledging the fact that men throughout Church history have sinned in this way (and in others). Perhaps a balanced perspective on the part of both Catholics and the media would be helpful. That is, that more priests probably sin against charity than chastity, and that it would be nice to see a film once in a while which deals with a faithful priest. And while we're at it, how come we rarely, if ever, are treated to a similar display of a minister's or rabbi's infidelity to his wife, for we know that that is just as real as our own Catholic problem.

Two aspects of the film are rather unrealistic. The first is that Father Ralph's landing of the Carson wealth would bring him notice in the Vatican. The implication is not only offensive, it is silly. In a universal Church of more than 500 million souls, that one young priest obtaining a few million dollars could attract so much attention strains the wildest imagination.

The second flight into fancy is that the priest who resists temptation so nobly for so long ultimately succumbs after he has been gone for years—and after he has become a bishop, no less. Possible but not probable. A final judgment: far-fetched fiction making for greater titillation of the viewing audience.

What message did the film really have? The conclusion I reach in regard to Father Ralph is that his successes far outweighed his failures, that he recognized his sinfulness and sought to amend his life, that God used his weak human nature, vessels of clay that we all are, to be an instrument of His love and His mercy. Father Ralph is a tragic figure in the classical sense of a person whose personal flaws lead to his downfall; the question is whether or not the grace of God for which he prayed overpowered the influence of evil at work in him. Our faith leads us to say that we are all saved in hope.

The Thorn Birds forces Catholics—whether we like it or not—to reflect on some realities that we take for granted: the Church, the priesthood, the charism of celibacy, God's grace for fidelity. Perhaps the best way to respond to this film—whether we view it or not—is to discuss these realities with those closest to us (friends, children, spouse). It is in that spirit the following questions are offered for prayerful reflection.

—What do you see as the underlying theme of this film? Is it broader than either the priesthood or "falling in love"?

—Meggie and Father Ralph are both examples of infidelity. What does it take to make a permanent commitment, to say yes, to mean it, and to live by it?

—How much of Meggie's problem can be attributed to poor parental acceptance and communication? Is this scapegoating, perhaps?

—Are you scandalized at the presence of sin in the Church? At political and sexual intrigue among the clergy? Why? Do we have a right to expect more from our priests?

—We have heard so much in recent years about a "vocation crisis." Why do you think this has happened? What is your own attitude toward the priestly vocation? If you are a young man, have you listened for the voice of God? If you are a parent, are you concerned enough about the Church's need for priests that you would support your own son in such a call and joyfully offer him to the Church? Or do you believe that this would be a wasted life?

—What is your attitude toward priests? Are you supportive and loving or critical and ready to believe the worst? Did you ever consider how much celibate priests need their people to be family to them?

—Was Father Ralph's only sin adultery? How did he handle all the temptations of life (not just the sexual ones)? Was he, in your opinion, a good priest?

—In our sex-saturated society, we are anesthetized by the frequency with which we are exposed to sex, and in such euphemistic terms ("fornication" becomes "making love," for instance). Did the sex scenes in the film upset you? Did you feel comfortable in pointing out to your teenagers that this was wrong and sinful?

—So many of the characters in the film were strong-willed individuals, some of them on a constant collision course with the divine will. Find examples of this. How do we discover God's will? How do we conform our wills to His?

Finally: Write to ABC (at 1330 Avenue of the Americas, New York City, N.Y. 10019) to let them know what you thought of *The Thorn Birds*.

The Priesthood

(*Our Sunday Visitor*, February 12 and 19, 1984) *

The priesthood of Jesus Christ encompasses far more than the administration of the sacraments. In a very real sense it is the perpetuation of Jesus' entire work here on earth. Far from being merely an earthly institution, the Catholic priesthood is a sharing in the priesthood of Jesus Christ, Whom the Scriptures describe as our heavenly High Priest (Heb 8:10). As Father John Hardon puts it, Christ "went out of His way to associate others with Him to learn His teaching, acquire His spirit, receive His powers, and thus continue His saving work for the human race."

Fundamentalists often say that nowhere in the New Testament does Jesus refer to the apostles, nor they to themselves, as priests. While the apostles certainly did not refer to themselves as priests, we know that they did share in the ministry of the High Priest, Jesus Christ.

There are two probable reasons why the term "priest" was not applied to the leaders of the early Church: first, there was a great deal of animosity expressed in the New Testament toward Jewish priests; second, there was undoubtedly a fear of confusing the apostles and their successors with pagan priests of that time. When the animosity waned and the fear of confusion subsided, the term "priest" began to be applied, quite appropriately, to those sharing in Christ's ministry.

A common legalistic criticism of the priesthood centers on the fact that priests are addressed as "father." Fundamentalists denounce this practice, citing Matthew 23:9 to support their position: "Do not call anyone on earth your father. Only one is your father, the One in Heaven." If we turn to the First Letter of John, however, we find that the writer of the epistle appears to have violated Jesus' injunction when he speaks to the elders of the community thus: "I address you, fathers, for you have know him who is from the beginning" (1 Jn 2:14).

In point of fact, what Jesus condemned was the giving to any human the honor or adoration proper to God. That same passage speaks of calling no one teacher, either; however, thousands of

---

* Co-authored with William Sweeney.

Protestant ministers are called "doctor," which means "teacher." Would Fundamentalists take this passage so literally that they would deny children the right to address their male parents as "fathers"? We must distinguish, then, between the letter of the law and the spirit of the law, as did the author of John's epistle.

A final point about the priesthood which must be addressed is the practice of priestly celibacy. In his letter to "his Catholic friends," Jimmy Swaggart claims that "Peter would have been ineligible to be a pope as he was married." This statement, while humorously erroneous, helps to illustrate the depth of misunderstanding which non-Catholics often have about the Church and its teaching. First and foremost should be the realization that priestly celibacy is a man-made law of the Church from which dispensations have always been possible. Second, married priests have always existed in the Church, such as those who belong to the Eastern rites or already married Anglican priests who enter the Roman Catholic Church. To contest Peter's papal role on the basis of his marital status is to misunderstand both the nature and source of priestly celibacy.

There are other misconceptions Fundamentalists have regarding priestly celibacy. They quote Paul's First Letter to Timothy, which warns against men "who forbid marriage" (1 Tim 4:1–3) to denounce the practice of celibacy altogether, charging that it "has caused untold immorality in the Catholic Church," offering no proof for such a charge. Despite these allegations, however, the practice of celibacy has significant foundations in Scripture.

In the nineteenth chapter of Matthew, Jesus' disciples ask Him if it is preferable not to marry. In response, Jesus tells the disciples that there are some men who are incapable of sexual activity, some who have made themselves deliberately so, and others who have renounced sex freely "for the sake of God's reign," adding: "Let him accept this teaching who can." Jesus' position regarding celibacy for the Kingdom is both positive and clear in this passage.

This statement is reinforced in Luke 18:19 as Jesus promises a plentiful life in this age and life everlasting in the next for all who have left wife and home, parents and children for the sake of the Kingdom of God. Renouncing sex for the Kingdom of God is indeed portrayed positively in the Gospels.

Another positive scriptural reference to celibacy occurs in Matthew's Gospel, as Jesus speaks with the Sadducees about the resurrection. Those who hold marriage as a necessary ideal because of the supposed "evils" of celibacy should closely examine Jesus' description of the life to come: "When people rise from the dead, they neither marry nor are given in marriage but live like angels in Heaven" (Mt 22:30). The life of celibacy is designed to emulate this situation, indeed to foreshadow it by reminding people of that life to come where "God is all in all."

Aside from the Gospels, Paul's First Letter to the Corinthians provides some final and significant support for the practice of priestly celibacy. In chapter 7, Paul advises men and women to marry in order to avoid immorality, but states that "given my preference, I should like you to be as I am" (1 Cor 7:7). Paul makes it clear that he is celibate, later explaining why such a lifestyle is preferable to marriage: "The unmarried man is busy with the Lord's affairs, concerned with pleasing the Lord; but the married man is busy with this world's demands and occupied with pleasing his wife. This means he is divided" (1 Cor 7:32–33).

St. Paul concisely describes the basis of priestly celibacy: to free priests from worldly cares to do the Lord's work and to provide a source of inspiration for the community to do so. If these points were understood, non-Catholics would come to respect and understand better both the priesthood and the practice of priestly celibacy, as well as the life and teaching of Christ, upon which they are based.

Holy Orders

(*National Catholic Register*, June 17, 1984)

When people hear of "ordination," their thoughts generally turn to the priesthood, because that is their usual contact with the Sacrament of Holy Orders.

However, the sacrament actually involves three ministries: the diaconate, priesthood, and episcopacy.

In all three orders, men are commissioned by a bishop's laying on of hands to serve the Church by preaching God's word "in season and out of season" (1 Tim 4:2) and by making present for God's people His saving mysteries.

A call to service in the Church comes from God and is acknowledged and validated by the Church. Like the prophets of the Old Testament and the apostles of the New Testament, once a man is consecrated by God for a special task, his ultimate meaning is bound up with that task. If he relinquishes it, his own dignity and personal meaning, as well as that of the Church which calls him, are threatened. Surely that is the heart of our Lord's comment that one who puts his hand to the plow but keeps looking back is unfit for the Kingdom (see Lk 9:32).

The diaconate, since Vatican II, has been restored to its original status as a distinct ministry. For centuries, the diaconate was regarded as a "stepping stone" to the priesthood. The Fathers of the Council, however, called for its restoration as a permanent state, especially for mission lands. This development has given rise to two categories of deacons: permanent (who usually have a secular occupation, are of a mature age, and may be married) and transitional (who are celibate and will become priests).

The liturgical functions of deacons include preaching, the distribution of Holy Communion, baptizing, and action as the Church's official witnesses at marriage. The Acts of the Apostles indicates that their primary function was to be works of charity (6:1).

It is interesting to note that some very reputable theologians, such as Louis Bouyer, question whether the diaconate truly belongs to the Sacrament of Orders. The rationale behind this line of argument comes from the fact that a deacon can do nothing after ordination that any layperson can do with proper delegation but without ordination. No dogmatic statement defines the diaconate as part of

Orders; nonetheless, the general theological opinion and practice of the Church would hold for its inclusion.

The priesthood exists for the Eucharist; this was certainly the mind of Christ as He instituted these two sacraments within the context of the Passover Supper (Lk 22:17–20). Fidelity to the Lord's command requires the continued celebration of the Eucharist which, in turn, requires a ministerial priesthood. Having said that, we must face up to the fact that the New Testament never speaks of the apostles or their successors as priests. Why so?

The first and most obvious reason was a fear that Christian ministers would be identified with either the Jewish or pagan priesthoods, and the early Church felt a strong need to distance herself from both. The second reason was concern that the unique high priesthood of Jesus Christ not be clouded over (Heb 8). Just as Christ's redemptive sacrifice was effected once and for all (never to be repeated), so too is Christ's priesthood unique. However, the Eucharist, which sacramentally re-presents the Sacrifice of Calvary, requires priestly ministers. Such ministers are not priests in their own right but participate in the priesthood of Jesus Christ. This point is sometimes lost on Protestant Fundamentalists, who think the Catholic notion of priesthood in some way nullifies the unique priesthood of Jesus.

The New Testament is also quite clear in describing the entire community of the Church as a "royal priesthood" (1 Peter 2:9). If so, why a priestly "caste" within the Church? The Hebrew Scriptures spoke of the Israelites as a royal priesthood (cf. Ex 19:6), but they still had a priestly class. If the Israelite community as a whole was to fulfill its priestly witness in the world, it needed the ministry of priests. The Church is no different: Having been ministered to by their priests, the people can then minister to the world.

No competition should exist between clergy and laity, because all Christians are called to serve both Christ and the world; it is not a question of who is better but merely of different ways to serve. It is ironic that, despite our contemporary understanding of sociology and psychology, we should experience so much role confusion as some clergy seek to run for public office and some laity seek to administer the sacraments. This situation is a result of poor self-understanding on the part of both clergy and laity. A careful reflection on Paul's theology of the Body of Christ might be very profitable (1 Cor 12).

An ancient tradition of the Latin rite calls for celibate priests. The priest's concern for the Church must be total, so that his individual attention and love are centered on his ministry (cf. 1 Cor 7). However, some misunderstandings about celibacy need to be clarified. First, celibacy does not depreciate marriage; its place in the priesthood emphasizes the fact that marriage and priesthood are vocations in themselves and that both deserve one's complete commitment. Second, the reasons behind celibacy are not simply pragmatic, e.g., greater priestly availability or economy. Celibacy is meant to be an eschatological sign which reminds people that "we have here no lasting city" and that our sights need to be set on that city "where God is all in all." The witness of celibacy for the sake of the Kingdom is all the more needed today precisely because we live in such a sex-saturated society. Third, the ecclesiastical law on priestly celibacy is not divine in origin, although surely the Lord's clear preference (cf. Mt 19:29; Lk 14:26; Mk 10:29). This means that the law does admit of exceptions. For this reason, the Holy See has recently granted special permission for married Anglican clergy who have joined the Roman Catholic Church to maintain their marital and family commitments and also be admitted to the priesthood.

A priest is a witness to the Gospel and a proclaimer of that Gospel. That Word then needs to take on flesh. Hence, a priest is ordained for two specific functions: to offer the Sacrifice of the Mass and to be an agent of reconciliation in the Sacrament of Penance. A priest must also do more than this; he must truly be a father to his people, standing as a constant sign of dedication to the Gospel and reflecting the mercy of Christ.

It is for this very reason that Catholics have always devotedly returned their priests' love by calling them "Father." Cardinal John Henry Newman observed that, of all the titles he had held in life, that of "Father" meant the most to him. This title should not create distance between priest and people but should serve as a reminder of the depth of the relationship that exists—a relationship which is essentially familial. Nor are critics on solid Scriptural ground who question this usage based on Matthew 23:9. The clear intent of this passage is to forbid giving to any human being the honor due God Himself. The same critics usually see no difficulty in addressing their male parents as "father" or in referring to physicians, professors, and ministers as "doctor" (teacher), a title likewise mentioned in the Matthean passage.

A bishop possesses the fullness of the priesthood. As such, he is the chief priest of his diocese and is capable of administering all the sacraments. He serves as a symbol of unity and continuity; a bishop provides the link with the apostolic Church, and his teaching authority rests on that fact and on his union with the entire college of bishops under the headship of the Pope.

I am writing these reflections about Holy Orders on the eve of my own seventh anniversary of priestly ordination. At this time each year I make a special point of thanking God for giving the Church the gift of the priesthood and for giving that vocation to me. Because a priest deals with intangible realities, it is often hard for him to calculate his own effectiveness. Most priests will never know the tremendous good they have done, even by their silent but visible presence on the street. Perhaps that is one reason why some priests hesitate to invite other young men to join their ranks. The solution to the so-called vocations crisis lies in a rediscovery of the meaning of the sacred ministry in the Church.

Or, as a French spiritual writer said: "If people could realize what the priesthood is, there would be too many priests."

Why Can't Our Women Be Ordained?

(National Catholic Register, June 17, 1984)

If it is true that the priesthood exists for the Church and the Eucharist, then it's entirely appropriate for us to reflect on one of today's most controversial questions: "Why only male priests?"

Of course, honesty requires us to note that the ordination of women is, for the most part, an issue only in the United States, Canada, and portions of Western Europe. It is also rather predictably derived from the secular feminist movement.

Both of these observations should give us reason to pause. Proponents of women's ordination maintain that the Church has no clearly articulated theology on this matter. Thus they come to the conclusion that this teaching is based on sexual prejudice. On the former point we might agree, but not on the latter.

A detailed explanation of the "male-only priesthood" does not exist, and with good reason: It has never before been a point of contention. The Church rarely works out a full-blown theology until it is called for by the circumstances of the times. Thus the Church always believed in and taught the doctrine of the two natures of Christ; however, until the doctrine was attacked, definitive formulations were not brought forth. That clear statement of the hypostatic union was achieved at the Council of Chalcedon as a response to the Monophysite heresy.

In the current debate, we should realize that the burden of proof rests on those seeking to change Tradition. This is standard debate procedure, and one not adhered to by many of the partisans of women's ordination. The best argument against the ordination of women is really the simplest but also the most easily caricatured: *It has never been done.* No other change resulting from the Second Vatican Council so clearly flies in the face of Tradition; a vernacular liturgy, permanent deacons, and even married priests all find precedent in Tradition.

The Holy Father has consistently said that the Church cannot ordain women; not that she also does not want to do it, just that she does not have the power to do so. To enter into dialogue on this issue is not necessarily to call the basic doctrine of a male priesthood into question, however, but to attempt to perfect *our* reasons for the teaching, in much the same way as the Council Fathers operated at Chalcedon in A.D. 451.

The basic reason why the Church ordains only men is that Jesus Christ, the Lord of the Church, chose only men. "But Christ was limited by his own culture, which had a low opinion of women," comes the retort. That might be true, at least in the sense that our Lord had to preach the Gospel to a people who were limited by their own cultural conditioning. However, we would likewise have to admit that Jesus never hesitated to break with other cultural patterns of His day (e.g., dining with sinners, talking to women, condemning divorce). How do we explain this apparent inconsistency, except to say that the all-male apostolic ministry is an expression of divine will?

Secondly, it's important to recognize that in the Christian faith sexuality is not a matter of indifference, for Christianity is an incarnational religion which takes the flesh seriously. In the early Church the Gnostic sects tried to say that sexual differences did not matter; the reader will recall that the Gnostics had problems accepting the humanity of Christ. The Church responded by asserting the symbolic value of the flesh, as well as its real meaning as part of God's Creation. In the Christian scheme of things, neither sex is better than the other, just different.

Thirdly, the reasons for a male priesthood are enhanced by Byzantine theology. When God chose to reveal Himself, He did so through the taking on of human flesh by the Second Person of the Blessed Trinity as God's Son. Anyone called to the priesthood since is called as a member of the one and unique priesthood of Jesus Christ. Just as Jesus was the icon (image) of the Father, so is the priest to be an icon of Jesus. This is also tied in with the so-called "scandal of particularity," which reminds us that God's ways are not our ways. For example, why did God call the Jews and not the Romans or the Greeks, who were certainly better educated and far more cultured? We do not know; nor do we know why men are chosen as instruments of sacramental grace, especially since the qualities they are expected to show forth in their lives are often looked upon as "feminine" virtues (such as patience, humility, kindness). Perhaps the paradox itself contains the answer: that God chooses whomever He wills to confound our human expectations and to show what an incredible new order of reality is being established. We must be comfortable in living with mystery.

Fourthly, we are not dealing with a question of rights here, for no one (male or female) has a "right" to ordination. If persons had such a right, the Church would not be able to set any prerequisites for Orders in regard to health or intelligence or moral living; all that would be necessary would be the assertion of a self-perceived inner call by the individual. No, a call to priesthood is one that comes from the Church and not from the individual. The biggest problem of all, however, is the strange idea that somehow sacramental ordination increases one's holiness or chances at salvation. Neither logic nor experience bears this out. Far from a question of rights, then, it is really a question of a diversity of roles and ministries in the Church—all of which are needed for the building up of the Body of Christ. In the natural order a man should not feel inferior to a woman simply because he is incapable of bearing children; his role is different—and so it is in the Church.

Finally, we must remember that the role of a priest in the liturgy is to stand in the person of Christ (the icon of the Father), not as part of the people but as their head. In the liturgy we witness a union between the bride (the Church) and the groom (Christ). That spousal union is made visible and sacramental through a male priesthood—and *only* through a male priesthood.

For those who understand and accept the sacramental nature of human sexuality, the issue is clear. For those who do not, debates on women's ordination will be to no avail. No short cuts or end runs are possible here. The *terminus a quo* (starting point) is not female ordination but the divinely established complementarity of the sexes.

Christus Dominus

(*National Catholic Register*, September 29, 1985)

The work of the First Vatican Council concluded on October 28, 1965, with the promulgation of *Christus Dominus*, Vatican II's Decree on the Pastoral Office of Bishops in the Church.

Pastor Aeternus (of Vatican I) dealt with the role of the Pope in and for the universal Church. But its reflections on the college of bishops were cut short by the siege of Rome, and that's why it is correct to see *Christus Dominus* as the second part of a diptych whose completion was finally achieved a century later—not unlike many of the great artistic works of the Middle Ages and Renaissance.

It's important to understand *Christus Dominus* in light of *Pastor Aeternus*, because they interface at many points. The Council Fathers were intent on maintaining a close linkage between the two. Extensive passages of *Pastor Aeternus* are even quoted verbatim in *Christus Dominus*. It is likewise necessary to relate *Christus Dominus* to Vatican II's *Lumen Gentium*, for the office of bishop is situated near the heart of the Church and has no reason to exist apart from the Church.

The bishops see the origin of their ministry in Jesus Christ: "Just as He Himself was sent by the Father, so He also sent His Apostles." These in turn passed on their mission to certain chosen men, "for the building up of the body of Christ, which is the Church" (no. 1).

Lest any confusion arise about the unity of the Church, the Council Fathers quickly and strongly reaffirm the papal ministry. Thus we read that the Pope "enjoys supreme, full, immediate and universal authority," and this "by divine institution." His is a "primacy of ordinary power over all the Churches." Then, and only then, do the bishops begin their analysis of the episcopal ministry, which is exercised "together with the Supreme Pontiff and under his authority" (no. 3).

"Bishops sharing in the solicitude for all the Churches . . . are united in a college." They "exercise this office individually in reference to the portions of the Lord's flock assigned to them . . . jointly providing for certain common needs of various Churches" (no. 3).

The bishops in the episcopal college, through "sacramental consecration and hierarchical communion," function on three levels then: First, as a universal body, which is the "subject of supreme plenary power over the universal Church," but "never without its head," the Pope. This collegial action is demonstrated "in a solemn manner in an ecumenical council," say the Council Fathers, quoting Vatican I (no. 4).

Second, bishops have jurisdiction over their own particular Churches or dioceses. A diocese lives "by adhering to its pastor [the bishop] and gathered together by him through the Gospel and the Eucharist in the Holy Spirit; it constitutes a particular Church in which the one, holy, catholic and apostolic Church of Christ is truly present and operative" (no. 11). A diocese, then, is not a "mini-Church" or a section of the Church *but the whole Church*, because of the union between people and bishop, and the bishop's union with the Bishop of Rome.

Third, bishops may collaborate on certain projects of a regional or national nature when this would be more effective, sometimes for social objectives or even for teaching.

The Council Fathers decree the establishment of the synod as an advisory body to assist the Pope and to show ecclesial communion by sharing insights from the Church throughout the world (no. 5). A synod is a gathering of a representative number of bishops to attend to certain matters of international Church concern. Paul VI called the first such synod, in fidelity to this conciliar mandate. These gatherings, which are held every three years, have dealt with a variety of topics: evangelization, penance and reconciliation, the Christian family. An "extraordinary" synod (i.e., not within the usual time-frame) will open in November 1985 to assess the effects of Vatican II, twenty years later.

Bishops are encouraged in *Christus Dominus* to have a broader vision of the Church than just their own diocese. They should promote evangelization, be concerned for the welfare of other dioceses, and "embrace in brotherly affection" those bishops "slandered or imprisoned for the sake of Christ" (no. 7). They are then reminded of the need to cooperate with the Holy See—both the Pope and the Curia—who "perform their duties in the Pope's name and with his authority for the good of the Churches and in the service of the sacred pastors" (no. 9). This admonition has become even more important today as some Catholics, attempting to forge their own path, malign curial officials unjustly. Usually this is just a cloak for attacks on the Pope himself, whose policies the Curia merely executes.

That said, the decree does acknowledge that the Curia should be reorganized and "better adapted" (no. 9) to modern times. Further, curial heads should also come from the ranks of diocesan bishops to give the Church's central administration a more pastoral bent, putting it in greater contact with "the real world." Finally, the decree notes the wisdom of involving lay people in the Curia to gain their expertise, so that "they will have an appropriate share in Church affairs" (no. 10). It fell to Paul VI to implement these wishes, a task he undertook with dispatch. The 1985 Curia is a far cry from 1962. The racial, national, and canonical characteristics of the personnel have drastically changed—all for the good of the Church.

The decree next takes up the teaching ministry of bishops, "which is conspicuously among the principal duties of bishops" (no. 12). In addition to their usual preaching of the Gospel message, they must also present, according to the doctrine of the Church, "the great values of these things: the human person with his freedom and bodily life, the family and its unity and stability, the procreation and education of children, civil society with its laws and professions, labor and leisure, arts and technical inventions, poverty and affluence" (no. 12). They should also address questions on the just distribution of material goods, and war and peace. It is also the task of bishops to oversee religious instruction "based on Sacred Scripture, tradition, the liturgy, the Magisterium and life of the Church" (no. 14), ensuring that catechists are properly trained both doctrinally and professionally.

In the American Church, a problem is sometimes created today by pressure group polarization. "Conservatives" don't like the bishops to speak on social issues. "Liberals" want them to speak *primarily* on social issues—as long as they pipe down about abortion, contraception and pornography. Both groups fail to understand the Council's clear teaching: The bishops must not and cannot be co-opted by partisan camps.

The decree goes on to outline the various responsibilities of local bishops, who are "the principal dispensers of the mysteries of God" (no. 15): concern for priestly and religious vocations; being shepherds who truly know their sheep; having "a special love" for priests, "ready to listen to them" and "solicitous" for their welfare (no. 16); providing for the special linguistic needs of various groups.

In terms of Church-state relations, the Council Fathers stress that the bishops "enjoy full and perfect freedom and independence from any civil authority" in discharging their apostolic office (no. 19). At the same time, they note the importance of bishops acting in harmony with public officials for the good of society. The decree also removes the right of certain governments in intrude into the process of ecclesiastical appointments, done in both so-called "Catholic countries" and, of course, in totalitarian states.

According to *Christus Dominus*, the diocesan Curia should see themselves as helpers of the bishop, who should also establish a pastoral council (including clergy, religious, and laity) "to investigate and weigh pastoral undertakings and to form practical conclusions regarding them" (no. 27). Such bodies are, obviously, consultative and not legislative in nature.

The Council Fathers also give commonsense advice to bishops on their relations with priests, pastors, and religious. In light of the tensions in recent years between hierarchy and religious in the United States, it's instructive to read that religious "should look upon bishops with devout respect and reverence, discharging their duties as active and obedient helpers of the bishops."

The decree concludes with recommendations for the establishment of episcopal conferences (usually at the national level) to facilitate "common effort" among bishops in a given area (no. 37); the erection of military vicariates (no. 43); the revision of Church law to reflect the principles of this document; and the drawing up of national directories on topics of special interest, particularly the field of catechetics (no. 44)—a project which the American hierarchy completed in the last decade.

Bishops often note how thankless a job they have today and how perplexed they've been by the postconciliar U.S. Church. But if *Pastor Aeternus* of Vatican I and *Lumen Gentium* and *Christus Dominus* of Vatican II are taken together, we find a clear mission statement for the entire believing community.

The bishops are our pastors and fathers in God. In the liturgy we pray that the shepherd will never lack his flock's loving obedience, nor the flock want for the shepherd's care. That is the sum and substance of *Christus Dominus*.

Optatam Totius

(*National Catholic Register*, October 13, 1985)

"The desired renewal of the whole Church depends to a great extent on the ministry of its priests," declare the Council Fathers in the opening line of the Decree on the Training of Priests (*Optatam Totius*, October 28, 1965). This is not hyperbole, nor wishful thinking, nor an insight gained through the modern behavioral sciences. The Church knows from centuries of experience that the sanctity of the whole People of God is directly proportionate to the sanctity of its priests. Further, the sanctity of priests results in large measure from the quality of formation offered to candidates for the priesthood. That's why the Council of Trent so stressed the importance of seminaries for bringing about the needed reforms within the Church of that time.

Optatam Totius lays out a detailed program of seminary education, gleaning the best from the Tridentine reform and bringing in adjustments necessary for modern life. Every aspect of the human personality and priestly life is touched upon in a convincing manner.

Priestly training should be "in tune with the particular needs of those regions in which the ministry is to be exercised" (no. 1). This comment is an obvious response to those who might argue that seminary formation can be uniform in all its dimensions on a universal scale, or that methods successful in one culture will automatically succeed in another. If the Church and its liturgy need to be adapted (within the bounds required by unity of faith) to specific cultural and ethnic situations, this is equally true for the preparation of the men who will serve as the Church's priests.

Fostering vocations is the work of the whole Church, note the Church Fathers, but especially that of families, teachers, priests, and bishops. Such encouragement is brought about by prayer, fasting, reminding the faithful about the need for vocations and good planning. While these suggestions may seem like truisms, it's fair to say that too little of our recruitment in the United States has these elements, overemphasizing Madison Avenue techniques (which do have their place) and sometimes failing to invite young men *personally* to consider a priestly vocation.

Contrary to popular impressions, the Council Fathers did not call for the elimination of minor seminaries. Rather, their concern was that formation should correspond to the needs and psychological make-up of such candidates. Hence, they warned: "Nor should the fitting opportunities be lacking for social and cultural contacts and for contact with one's own family" (no. 3). While many priestly vocations blossomed to full maturity from minor seminaries, statistics also show a disproportionate number of priestly defections from the same quarter, perhaps due to the lack of "social and cultural contacts" during formative years. However, two extremes must be avoided. The first simply declares minor seminaries obsolete; the second makes them no different from other schools for young men of the same age. Balance is the needed ingredient here.

As far as major seminaries are concerned, the bishops assert that "wise laws" are crucial, with "qualified educators" who instill in their charges a "deep joy" in their vocation (no. 5). This is a far cry from the rigidity of pre-conciliar priestly formation and the confusion of many post-conciliar American seminaries. Furthermore, truly qualified educators would never engage in petty psychoanalysis of more "traditional" students with whom they theologically disagree. Even more so, if these same professors had deep joy in their own priestly vocations, they would not misinterpret seminarian zeal for the priesthood as a sign of "clericalism" or "emotional insecurity"—a problem quite a few seminarians would attest to in recent years.

Of course, many of these problems have surfaced because of the failure of some American bishops to be "a true father" (no. 5) to their priestly candidates, having delegated responsibility in this matter to others, so that some bishops only meet their future priests on the day of their ordination.

According to the decree, seminarians should be "saturated with the mystery of the Church" and "bound to the Vicar of Christ" (no. 9). Yet American seminarians, over the past 15 years, have sometimes come to this posture not because of their formal training but *in spite of* it. This is likewise the case where education in celibacy is concerned, which should be done "with great care" (no. 10). Seminarians must be prepared for the dangers to chastity and should be "aided by suitable safeguards, both divine and human." Too often, this is not adequately done.

In listing virtues to be cultivated, the bishops speak of "sincerity of mind, constant concern for justice, fidelity to one's promises, refinement in manners, modesty in speech coupled with charity" (no. 11). They also emphasize the need for discipline which is not mindless and lockstep—as was often the case in "the old days"—but rather which leads to personal conviction and trains men "to use freedom wisely" (no. 11).

As is now common in the United States, the Council Fathers note the wisdom of having seminarians exercise the diaconate for some time (usually six months to a year) before priestly ordination. This enables the candidate to engage in full-time ministry before the priesthood, giving him good experience and an accurate picture of what he can expect as a parish priest.

In offering an appropriate curriculum for priestly candidates, the bishops include: humanistic and scientific studies, Latin, the languages of the Bible, philosophy of a perennial value, Scripture studies, dogmatic theology (especially Aquinas), liturgy, canon law, Church history, the study of other religions, as well as psychology, pedagogy, and sociology. They also advocate pastoral training and experience both during vacation periods and throughout the academic year (a practice now commonplace).

In other words, the bishops ask for the development of a true "Renaissance man." Unfortunately, this is still seldom realized in the life of the average U.S. seminarian.

Of course, men whose past training was inadequate should not view themselves as irremediably lacking in education, because one of the important points of *Optatam Totius* is the continuing education of the clergy, which is to be an ongoing and lifelong process, according to the decree.

Because the ideals set forth in *Optatam Totius* have been unsatisfactorily achieved in some American dioceses and due to various complaints in this regard, the Holy See has mandated a study of U.S. seminaries. Alarmists have seen this as a renewed "inquisition," but the intention of the Holy See is really quite clear: the healthy desire that seminaries do what they are charged to do, according to the mind of the Church as expressed by the Second Vatican Council. Those who object to Roman "interference" should know that if they had handled the problems as they arose, Roman action would not have occurred, because it never would have been needed.

It should be the prayer of every U.S. Catholic that the implementation of this decree will do for the seminaries of our day what a similar plan did for the Faith at the time of the Counter-Reformation—an age which enabled the Church to flourish with saints and scholars for nearly four centuries.

Review

Theology of the Priesthood, by Jean Galot
San Francisco: Ignatius Press, $15.95
(*National Catholic Register,* November 24, 1985)

In Bishop James Malone's September report for the Extraordinary Synod on Vatican II, submitted on behalf of the American hierarchy, he noted the need to re-establish a clear sense of identity for the ordained priest if the vocation shortage is to be reversed. He is absolutely on target. And in that regard, Ignatius Press and the National Conference of Catholic Bishops deserve hearty thanks from every U.S. Catholic for collaborating to bring this book (first published in Italy) to the States.

Father Jean Galot has performed a hugely valuable service in producing this work, which synthesizes the Council's theology of the priesthood. A few chapter headings alone demonstrate the thoroughness of the project: "The Definition of the Priesthood"; "The Witness of Jesus Concerning His Own Priesthood"; "The Institution of the Ministerial Priesthood"; "The Priesthood of the Faithful and the Ministerial Priesthood." The tone and content are completely in tune with the Council—which is to say that the book is faithful to both its letter and spirit, and is rooted in the revealed Word of God. In fact, Galot's handling of Scripture may be the strongest aspect of this work, especially on some of the more controverted points, like the failure of the New Testament to speak of the apostles and their successors as "priests."

The first ten chapters offer a calm, dispassionate discussion of every significant aspect of priestly ministry. In the last two chapters, Galot takes on topics that other authors might avoid: secular occupations and the political involvement of priests; celibacy (done with a very strong scriptural base); and the all-male priesthood. Even these issues, however, he treats in a scholarly, non-polemical manner.

"The Mission of Women and the Priesthood" alone is worth the price of the book. The author is not content with a statement of the Church's clear and constant tradition on this matter. Rather, he examines every angle and possible objection. Most importantly, he situates the question in the broader context of conciliar teachings on the universal call to holiness, the interrelatedness between the priesthood of the faithful and the ministerial priesthood, and the diversity of roles and ministries in the Church. He never patronizes women, but rather encourages authorities to promote a genuinely feminine mission in the Church.

The translation and editing enable the book to flow easily. Quality printing, which we have come to expect from Ignatius Press, is thoroughly in evidence here. One minor criticism, however, is the placement of end notes at the conclusion of each chapter, making a less-than-enjoyable search for the excellent material contained therein.

If you're looking for a Christmas gift for your favorite priest or seminarian, consider this book. If you know a priest going through an identity crisis or a young man struggling with a decision regarding a priestly vocation, put him in touch with Galot's book. You'll do him and the whole Church a big favor.

Presbyterorum Ordinis

(*National Catholic Register*, December 1, 1985)

Priests "are signed with a special character and so are configured to Christ" (no. 2), causing them to be "set apart in some way in the midst of the People of God" (no. 3).

They "fulfill their principal function" (no. 13) at Mass, should "cherish [the] precious gift of priestly celibacy" (no. 16) and are bound to their bishop "with sincere charity and obedience" (no. 7), refusing ever to be "servants of any human ideology or party" (no. 6).

With these emphases on cultic and other-worldly dimensions, are we face to face with yet another attempt by the "reactionary" team of Wojtyla and Ratzinger to "turn the clock back" to a pre-conciliar model of priesthood? Hardly! These are but a few of the key points contained in the Decree on the Ministry and Life of Priests (*Presbyterorum Ordinis*), promulgated on December 7, 1965.

In Bishop James Malone's report for the Extraordinary Synod, submitted to Rome on behalf of the American hierarchy this past September, he noted our need to re-establish a clear sense of identity among ordained priests. Only in this way would current tensions be resolved and the vocation shortage reversed. Of course his approach is right on target, and there is no better starting place than *Presbyterorum Ordinis*, which describes the precise nature of the priestly vocation. In fact, if the renewal of the whole Church desired by Pope John XXIII is to become a reality, it will occur *only* when a renewal of the priesthood materializes, because the Church in any age is only as holy as its priests. St. John Vianney went so far as to say: "After God, the priest is everything. Leave a parish twenty years without a priest, and they'll worship beasts." With that in mind, just what does this decree have to offer?

The Council Fathers turn their attention first to the various functions priests perform both for the Church and for the world at large. Since, as St. Paul noted, "faith comes through hearing," it is "the first task of priests . . . to preach the Gospel of God to all men" (no. 4) as they apply "the eternal truth of the Gospel to the concrete circumstances of life." Inasmuch as the proclamation of the Word necessarily leads to the celebration of the sacraments, the decree next takes up the role of priests as ministers of the sacraments, especially of the Eucharist, in which "is contained the whole spiritual good of the Church" (no. 5). Finally, as "rulers of God's People," priests must attend "to the formation of a genuine Christian community" (no. 6), doing so "with the greatest kindness—leading souls to Christ."

How should priests relate to others in the Church? First and foremost, they are collaborators with the bishop (no. 7), who should, in turn, look upon them as "brothers and friends." The collaborative nature of this relationship is expressed liturgically through concelebration and institutionally through a consultative body such as a council of priests, now mandated in the revised Code of Canon Law. Among themselves, priests should be seen as members of a "brotherhood" (no. 8) concerned for the welfare of one another and never acting out of rivalry, since they all serve the one Christ. Priests should interact with the laity as "brothers among brothers" (no. 9), in "appreciation and promotion of laypeople's dignity." For their part, the faithful should treat their priests "with filial love as being their fathers and pastors."

On a pragmatic note, the Council Fathers discuss the proper distribution of priests throughout the world. They encourage priests from areas with a surplus of clergy, after having secured the approval of their bishops, to offer themselves to places in greater need (no. 10). The bishops also call for the revision of the rules on excardination and incardination (the process of leaving one diocese and joining another), so that the needs of individual priests and the wider community of the Church can be better served. The new Code of Canon Law reflects that mandate, now making it easier for a priest to leave the diocese of his ordination when necessitated by changed circumstances. *Presbyterorum Ordinis* then reminds all Catholics that attention to priestly vocations is the task of every member of the Church, but especially of priests, teachers, and parents (no. 11).

In describing the life of priests, the bishops observe that "every priest in his own way assumes the person of Christ" and hence receives a unique call to perfection (no. 12). "For this reason the daily celebration of [the Eucharist] is earnestly recommended . . . even if it is impossible for the faithful to be present." Priests must likewise be available for the Sacrament of Penance "whenever it is reasonably requested by the faithful." They must pray the Divine Office or Liturgy of the Hours for the good of the Church as part of an intensive prayer life, all the while "renouncing their own convenience" and developing the gifts of humility and obedience (no. 15).

A strong statement of support for clerical celibacy follows, as the bishops ask "that all . . . would beg of God always to lavish this gift abundantly on His Church" (no. 16). Since priests should strive to imitate the obedient, virginal, and poor Christ as completely as possible, they are "invited to embrace voluntary poverty," thus further freeing them to serve the advancement of the Gospel and to be a clearer personal sign of the Kingdom.

The decree then suggests some practical helps in living the priestly life with joy. Pre-eminent is the fostering of a healthy interior life (no. 18). Also needed is study on a continuing basis, leading to the acquisition of effective pastoral knowledge (no. 19). Lest a priest have inadequate resources to meet his temporal needs during his active ministry and in retirement, the decree notes the obligation of bishops to provide for such necessities (nos. 20–21).

With pastoral sensitivity, the Council Fathers conclude their reflection on the priesthood today by acknowledging that many priests today "feel themselves estranged from" the world because of changing values and mores (no. 22). The solution to this problem lies neither in aloofness (since the world is loved by God, redeemed by Christ and to be saved by the ministry of priests) nor in conformity to any secular agenda (for then the priest would be failing in his mission to bring about the conversion demanded by Christ). The solution will come from the attainment of a secure self-image on the part of priests, for only then can they effectively minister to others.

To obtain that identity, a good point of departure would be a prayerful re-reading of this decree, allowing a genuinely Vatican II model of the priesthood to form a genuinely Vatican II model of the whole Church.

A Cry for Help

(*National Catholic Register*, June 1, 1986)

Pedophilia isn't a polite topic for discussion; and it's particularly disturbing to discover among clergy, especially Catholic priests. To address the question in the Catholic press isn't a sign of disloyalty but a sign that we are good, loving members of the family of the Church, trying to understand a problem affecting some of our brothers in Christ and hoping to find some helpful solutions.

Let's begin by dispelling some myths. First, pedophilia is not a clerical epidemic. About 40 cases are currently in litigation, out of approximately 57,000 priests serving our country. Granted, unreported cases exist. Granted, too, that even one such case is one too many. However, hysteria has never resolved anything and surely won't in this instance.

Second, although most of these cases involve young boys, many psychologists argue that these priests are not necessarily acting out homosexual tendencies, since boys at a tender age are often not distinguished from girls. The issue is sexual, not homosexual, and perhaps in some cases not even sexual but a matter of grossly misplaced attempts at experiencing intimacy.

Third, data on pedophilia among the general population suggests no causal link between celibacy and such activity. Married clergy of other denominations appear to be every bit as prone to the difficulty as are celibate priests.

With the air thus cleared, I'd like to address the matter from two different but related angles: the general moral confusion of our time and the nearly complete collapse of a clerical culture.

Twenty years ago, American society was torn in many directions in regard to moral issues. That situation has spawned a generation of young people who can honestly be classed as "amoral" due to invincible ignorance. Twenty years ago, the Catholic community of the United States was an anchor of moral certitude in the sea of moral chaos. The past two decades have seen that stance sabotaged from within by dissenters who prefer to present themselves as the "loyal opposition." The result has been the intimidation of priests and bishops alike, so that sexual matters are rarely, if ever, discussed. Aside from Pope John Paul, when was the last time you heard a Catholic cleric speak of birth control, lust, fornication, or adultery?

Hugh Hefner was counter-cultural when he began his Playboy philosophy. Today, Catholics in America are weary of being counter-cultural and have generally given into the "sexploitation" of this age. It has been a vicious cycle: Clergy stopped preaching on the question because they sensed less than enthusiasm from their people; the laity continue to be sold a bad bill of goods on sexuality by society because their clergy are silent.

While many people see this first aspect rather clearly, the next eludes them. Up until the late 1960s, priests enjoyed a camaraderie with other priests that could only be seen as a unique clerical culture. Clergy conferences, Confirmation dinners, Forty Hours Devotions—all brought priests together regularly for spiritual, intellectual, and social interaction. When priests had "duty days," other priests could count on their being home and so visited each other in their rectories. It was nothing more or less than a support system, not unlike that of other professions, but at a much deeper level.

Misguided implementations of Vatican II's theology sought to rout out any semblance of a ministerial priesthood, making priests feel guilty for enjoying their vocation. Priests were told they were emotionally insecure for not broadening their horizons and exchanging priestly companions for lay friends (forgetting that most situations in life are not either/or but both/and).

The decline in the use of the Sacrament of Penance certainly has been an influence. With very little preaching on sexual sins, very few are confessed. This prod to the priest's conscience is absent and acts he might otherwise avoid because he would be asked to absolve others of them, he finds himself committing. Hearing few confessions, he frequents the Sacrament seldom, as well.

Contrary to popular impressions, I believe most priests either have too much time on their hands or are engaged in useless activities which do not bring about job satisfaction and personal fulfillment. Very often priests run from committee to committee for endless debates on ridiculous topics. Meanwhile, the very things for which they were ordained and which could bring them meaning and strengthen their priestly identity—Communion to the sick, for example—they have delegated to laity.

Finally, I think the excessive discussion of celibacy over the past two decades has had an unhealthy and demoralizing effect on our priests. Celibacy should turn us outward for service, not inward for narcissistic introspection or self-pity.

Corruptio optimi pessissima—the corruption of the best is the worst. Thus did Lucifer fall from the realms of glory to the depths of

Hell. One could expect the same for priests who fall from grace. Maybe the dramatic fall of pedophilia is itself a desperate cry for help to be restored to grace.

That restoration will come when the Catholic community-at-large, together with her priests, rediscovers the meaning of our Lord's very sobering thought: "And if your light is darkness, how dark will the darkness be!" (Mt 6:23).

"Father, Did You Lose Something?"

(*Southern Nebraska Register*, January 2, 1987)

Some weeks ago I visited a parish and celebrated Mass there. At the Creed, the altar boy dutifully held the sacramentary in front of me. At the words which recall the Incarnation, I bowed—as is my custom and as the rubrics require. The boy became flustered, started looking down at the floor and up at me. Finally, he stammered: "Father, did you lose something?" Obviously, he is unfamiliar with this gesture of reverence of the central mystery of the Christian faith.

That incident set me to thinking about how careless many Catholics—laity and clergy alike—have become in their worship and most especially, how many of us fail to worship as body-soul unities. Our physical actions should reveal our inner thoughts and should aid our interior reflection.

In my boyhood, the Sisters in school stressed the appropriateness of bowing one's head at the sacred Name as a practical way of heeding St. Paul's injunction: "At the name of Jesus, every knee must bend."

Interestingly, both the line in the Profession of Faith and the name of Jesus point to the same cardinal doctrine, namely, *our salvation*. So often we succumb to a soupy sentimentality around Christmas but forget its meaning the rest of the year. The Church tries to forestall the development of just such insipid piety precisely by encouraging her sons and daughters to acknowledge the Incarnation all year round. One of the most positive ways to do that is through this gesture of love and devotion.

When the server asked, "Father, did you lose something?" I was tempted to say, in my exasperation: "Yes, the Church has begun to lose her sense of the sacred." However, we were at Mass, and he wouldn't have understood, anyway. Most importantly, the sense of the sacred is not totally lost, and it is most certainly worth saving.

The Priests We Deserve

(*National Catholic Register*, January 4, 1987)

Throughout high school I was exposed to "vocation days," during which various religious communities came to school to encourage us toward a priestly or religious vocation.

On one such occasion, a student asked a visiting Sister what she thought about the "vocations shortage." Without batting an eyelash, she replied: "We can't say there is a vocations shortage, because God always provides the exact number of vocations His Church deserves."

"The exact number His Church *deserves*." A very wise response.

In recent years we've heard some people use the vocations shortage (especially of priests) as a tool in pressing for major Church changes, as though celibacy and obedience are responsible for today's so-called "crisis." The argument usually runs like this: "If we don't get more priests soon, whole communities will be left without the Eucharist."

My first reaction is to shrug this off as alarmism at its worst. My second is a variation on Sister's answer of 1967: If a diocese cannot produce enough priestly vocations, those people need to look at the root causes of why this is so. They may not "deserve" the Eucharist until some adjustments are made.

Let me suggest some points for reflection:

1. *Priestly identity must be clear and positive.* When everyone and his grandmother distribute Holy Communion, what appeal does the priesthood hold for the average youth? When priests look and act like everyone else, why bother to study for eight years—and for what? When priests are unavailable or joyless, where's the attraction?

2. *The priesthood should be seen as a normal vocational choice.* As such, vocations should be fostered—dare I say it—beginning in grammar school. Although many young people today delay career decisions, most seminarians note that their first interest in the priesthood began back in grade school. This work of fostering devolves upon the entire Church, but especially parents, teachers, and priests. Children should also be taught how to support their classmates in a priestly vocation.

3. *The contraceptive mentality and its behavior should cease.* Refusal to

accept God's will in marriage offers an overall environment of rebellion in a home—subtle but real. Will a young boy be ready to sacrifice his life if he knows his parents are unwilling to sacrifice certain luxuries, so that another child can come into the world?

4. *Catholic schools need to be used.* My reading of the biographies of the newly ordained over the past ten years in a dozen dioceses confirms Father Andrew Greeley's data. There is a direct correlation between attendance at Catholic schools and the pursuit of a priestly vocation. In fact, the current Catholic school population (about 30 percent of all Catholic youth) has supplied approximately 90 percent of the clergy over the past decade. This should come as no surprise to those who understand the debilitating effects of public schools. This should also force bishops to look carefully at the urgency of opening schools in the suburbs and of ensuring that those schools remain within parental reach financially.

5. *Esteem for chastity has to return.* This not just a vague societal problem; it is fundamentally a domestic one. Children are not impressed when parents tell them not to have sex before marriage, especially when they see their parents using porn magazines and videos for personal entertainment. If parents live marital chastity and expect pre-martial chastity of their children, a celibate lifestyle will not appear at all bizarre.

6. *A turning away from materialism is necessary.* Where things and dollars outrank persons, it's no wonder that the Church loses potential vocations. Human worth in our culture has become equated with the size of a paycheck and not the meaning or beauty inherent in a calling. Often, people discover too late that today's values are flawed. The loss to both the individual and the ecclesial community has already occurred.

7. *Young people must be trained to make choices and to stick by them.* Permanent commitment is a frightening thing for adolescents today because they have so little experience of it. Some 60 percent of the students in one suburban school where I taught came from broken homes. While they instinctively know that saying "yes" forever is a good thing, they honestly don't know how to do it.

Now, some readers will respond that I've buried my head in the sand if I think any of this is possible. Not at all. In ten years as a priest, relying on just such a program, I've sent at least eleven young men off to the seminary, with the oldest among them now being ordained. Simply to wring our hands in despair is not only unproductive; it is also un-Christian. This is surely what John Paul had in mind when he told the clergy of France: "This resignation [to the vocations crisis] would be a bad sign for the vitality of the Christian people and would put its future and its mission at risk."

A few years back, a Midwestern bishop sent his diocese into a tailspin by initiating a new personnel policy: When an assistant is transferred, no replacement will be given to a parish which has not produced a priest in the past ten years. I like that idea because it officially recognizes the fact that the Church always gets the priestly vocations she *deserves*.

The Role of the Deacon

(*National Catholic Register*, January 11, 1987)

"It is not right for us to neglect the word of God in order to wait on tables" (Acts 6:2). So concluded the Twelve, with the resulting appointment of seven men to attend to the infant Church's works of charity. This passage is generally regarded as the *locus classicus* for the institution of the diaconate. But interestingly, the individuals on whom the apostles "imposed hands" (Acts 6:6) are not referred to as *diakonoi*. In fact, the word appears only five times in the entire New Testament (and never in the singular), four of which occurrences are found in the First Epistle of St. Paul to Timothy, where no duties are detailed.

The historical record shows that very soon deacons were assigned liturgical roles along with the exercise of their social-ministry. Today, deacons may baptize, witness marriages, distribute Communion, proclaim the Gospel at Mass, and preach. But in listing these roles, Pope John Paul II, in a recent talk, immediately added that deacons exist *"above all* [emphasis added] for bringing the testimony of charity in many sectors in the life of society."

Careful analysis will lead us to see that not one of these diaconal functions requires ordination, strictly speaking, so that any layperson could perform them under certain circumstances with appropriate episcopal delegation. And this fact has led some theologians to question whether the diaconate is truly a part of the Sacrament of Orders.

The Council of Trent passed over this matter silently, while Vatican II merely noted that "at a lower level of the hierarchy are to be found deacons, who receive the imposition of hands not unto the priesthood, but unto the ministry" (*Lumen Gentium*, no. 29). The common theological opinion is that deacons do participate in Holy Orders. That notion is reinforced by *Lumen Gentium*'s reference to the assistance provided deacons through "sacramental grace." Nevertheless, no dogmatic definition stands ready at hand, and the unsettled state of the question poses some identity problems for deacons themselves and for all who are touched by them.

The ancient Church knew of the diaconate only as a permanent ministry, but gradually this died out. In our own day, Vatican II opened the way "to restore the permanent diaconate as a proper and permanent rank of the hierarchy" (*Lumen Gentium*, no. 29). Every candidate for the priesthood is ordained to the diaconate as a transitional order. Of course, a man does not lose one ministry upon receiving another. Therefore, a bishop is at one and the same moment a priest and deacon, too; this point was made in former days by having a bishop wear vestments proper to lower orders under his episcopal garb.

Permanent deacons do not aspire to the priesthood. They may be married men of a mature age (at least 35), but cannot re-marry should they become widowed, on the venerable principle that while a married man may be ordained, an ordained man may never marry. They do not have the same degree of responsibility for the recitation of the Liturgy of the Hours, as do other members of the clergy. They generally hold secular jobs, thus making their diaconal ministry part-time in nature. Although clerical garb is not required for permanent deacons (aside from the vestments needed for liturgical services), dioceses occasionally allow it to facilitate deacons' work in the Catholic community.

Ironically, the renewed diaconate has not worked out quite as planned. Twenty-five years ago, supporters saw it as a potential godsend for the priest-starved developing world. But today, more than 80 percent of the world's permanent deacons live in the United States, perhaps because some people saw it as a "wedge" in their push for a married clergy or as a means to "declericalize" the priesthood. In typically American haste, some dioceses jumped headlong into diaconate programs, so that poor training was provided (which was a disservice to the candidates themselves, as well as to those they were to serve). Too many deacons were ordained in some places; hence they had little to do, intruding on both priests and laity with the awkward ambiguity of their roles.

An unfortunate percentage of permanent deacons have put aside their ministry after only a few years, maybe because of identity questions already alluded to. And due to these difficulties, some dioceses have declared a moratorium on accepting candidates until a better evaluation can be made of the basic concepts undergirding the diaconate.

Essentially, the permanent diaconate is a bridge between the clearly defined functions of the priesthood on the one hand and the laity on the other. Perhaps too much has been made of a deacon's liturgical ministry, often at the expense of the scriptural intent noted in Acts 6. The main purpose of his work should be evangelical charity; in fact, it seems entirely correct for the diocesan head of Catholic Charities (or its equivalent) to be a deacon. In that capacity, he can serve as a personal example of, and impetus for, Christian outreach to the laity, providing a special witness in the world.

The key problem with the permanent diaconate (as presently constituted) is twofold. First, it diverts priestly vocations; young men may prefer to take advantage of what they perceive as the "best of both worlds" (clerical and lay). Second, the permanent diaconate often diffuses lay activism, because it gives the impression that "real" ecclesial activity requires ordination, thus losing sight of Baptism as the catalyst for all Christian witness. Therefore, instead of a bridge between the unique apostolates of clergy and laity, the diaconate has sometimes deepened the chasm.

Hopefully, the upcoming World Synod on the Laity will look closely at this development. We should pray that some concrete suggestions will emerge, "restoring" the diaconate once more.

The Priesthood and Celibacy

(*National Catholic Register*, January 25, 1987)

If every priest in the country would ask his congregation why they think he should be celibate, I believe he'd be told it is so that he could be more available to them or so that the congregation could save money by not having to support a priest's family. And to those responses, I would say, "Not on your life!" So what *is* the reason?

Because priests are called to imitate the pattern of Christ's life as closely as possible, an ancient tradition of the Latin rite calls for celibate priests. The priest's concern for the Church is to be total, so that his love and attention are centered on his ministry. However, some misunderstandings about celibacy need to be clarified.

First, celibacy does not depreciate marriage; its place in the priesthood emphasizes the fact that marriage and priesthood are vocations in themselves and that both deserve one's complete commitment. Second, the rationale behind priestly celibacy is not simply a pragmatic solution for greater availability or economy.

Celibacy is meant to be a sacred sign which reminds people that "here we have no lasting city" (Heb 13:14), and that our sights need to be set on that city where God is all in all. It seems to me that the witness of celibacy for the sake of the Kingdom is much stronger today precisely because we live in such a sexually oriented society.

In Matthew's Gospel, Jesus' disciples ask Him if, given the tremendous demands of marriage, it is preferable not to marry. In response, our Lord tells them that there are some men who are incapable of sexual activity, some who have made themselves deliberately so, and others who have renounced sex freely "for the sake of God's reign," adding: "Let him accept this teaching who can" (Mt 19:12). Jesus' position regarding celibacy's place in the Kingdom is both positive and clear in this passage.

This statement is reinforced in Luke 18:28–30, as Jesus promises a plentiful return in this age and life everlasting in the next for all who have left wife and home, parents and children, for the sake of the Kingdom of God. Renouncing sex for the Kingdom of God is obviously portrayed in a most positive light in the Gospels.

Yet another clear scriptural witness to celibacy occurs, again in Matthew, as Christ speaks with the Sadducees about the resurrection, when He describes the life to come in these terms: "When people rise from the dead, they neither marry nor are given in marriage but live like angels in Heaven" (22:30).

The celibate life is meant to reflect that situation, indeed to foreshadow it. When people see a man in a Roman collar, then, they should immediately have their thoughts directed to that aspect of reality which transcends our present experience. That is what the Church intends when she asks her priests to serve as "eschatological signs."

In *Sacerdotalis Caelibatus*, Pope Paul VI referred to celibacy as the "jewel" of the priesthood, a poetic encapsulation of the New Testament message that a celibate clergy is to be preferred. The Catholic Church makes this preference a norm, and it is a tradition that has served the Gospel and the Church very well throughout her history.

Interestingly, this isn't the first time that the wisdom of celibacy has been questioned. And just as interesting is that all the arguments advanced against it today surfaced in the crises of the fourth and sixteenth centuries; the Church heard those objections and responded to them with an affirmative judgment on celibacy. At Vatican II and in the pontificates of Paul VI and John Paul II, she has repeated the pattern.

Gandhi saw the purpose of celibacy, leading him to declare that "because of her celibate clergy, the Roman Catholic Church will remain eternally young." Precisely because her sights are always fixed on eternity does the Church cherish so highly the charism of celibacy.

Reviews

Churches Respond to BEM: Official Responses to the "Baptism, Eucharist and Ministry," Text 2–3. Edited by Max Thurian.
Geneva: World Council of Churches, 1986, 1987.

Faith and Renewal: Commission on Faith and Order, Stavanger, 1986.
Edited by Thomas F. Best, Geneva: World Council of Churches, 1986.

Catholic Perspectives on Baptism, Eucharist and Ministry.
Edited by Michael A. Fahey. Lanham, Md.: University Press of America, 1986.

Who in the World? A Study of Ministry.
Dover, N.H.: EDEO-NADEO Standing Committee, 1986.

(*Theological Studies*, April 1987)

The past two decades have been regarded as an era of ecumenical good feelings, but a trip for the heart or pleasant attitudes are not enough; the present documentation indicates the direction taken by the head once the heart has been touched.

At Lima in 1982, the World Council of Churches embarked on a major effort in the multilateral conversations, tackling the weighty matters of Baptism, Eucharist, and ministry. Volumes 2 and 3 noted here contain the official responses of the various member bodies of the World Council of Churches, to which the Roman Catholic Church does not belong for a variety of reasons. Catholic representation does exist, however, on the all-important Faith and Order Commission. Reactions to BEM clearly demonstrate how far the ecumenical journey has taken us, as well as the distance yet to be traveled.

Although Roman Catholicism does not have a formal voice, its position is generally well reflected by the several Eastern Orthodox interventions. The Russian reaction views the agreed statements thus: "Not sufficient for pursuing now the question of restoration of the Eucharistic communion and *koinonia* between the churches," but "a step towards greater catholicity" and a "promising path." Cardinal Jan Willebrands would probably concur in that judgment. The Bulgarian Orthodox questioned the dual categories of "infant baptism" and "believers' baptism" as though there were two kinds of Baptism, with infant baptism not corresponding to believers' baptism, an objection also voiced by the Lutheran Church of Australia.

The connection between original sin and Baptism was raised by the Anglican Church of Canada and the American Lutheran Church, and implicitly noted by the Lutheran Church of Australia, which missed the mention of Baptism as a "means of grace." The Protestant Episcopal Church of the U.S.A. was joined by the ALC in expressing concern that the statement "does not sufficiently stress Baptism as God's own saving act," while Anglicans of Canada were interested in a "gender-free form" for Baptism.

The description of the Eucharist as the central act of Christian worship was problematical for the United Methodist Church of Central and Southern Europe. At the other end of the spectrum, the Russian Orthodox called for clearer language on the who and how of the Eucharist, a point highlighted by the Church of Norway, which specifically asked how the member bodies see the Real Presence being effected: the *epiklesis*? the words of institution? the total Eucharistic prayer? In very probing style the Presbyterian Church in Canada asked: "Does an umbrella term such as 'real presence' indicate meaningful consensus or does it simply conceal radical differences which are not being honestly expressed?" Equally penetrating is the Bulgarian Orthodox query: All well and good for frequent Communion, but what about the Sacrament of Penance? Similarly, the ALC observes that the "forgiveness of sin is absent" from the Eucharistic discussion, and the LC of Australia wonders about the one-dimensional view of the paschal mystery (namely, the Resurrection alone) which is presented in regard to an understanding of what is commemorated in the Eucharist.

Reaction to the ministry document is particularly strong, with the Orthodox Churches consistently questioning the ordination of women and the apostolic succession and calling for a clear definition of the ministerial priesthood. The fact that Holy Orders is nowhere precisely spoken of as a sacrament is cause for concern for the Bulgarian Orthodox, while the ALC just as strongly asserts that "we take exception . . . to a three-fold order." Interestingly, PECUSA asks how any serious reflection on order in the Church can take place without reference to the Petrine ministry.

Catholics may not see the totality of the deposit of faith in these documents, but an appreciation is essential for the other perspective. Undoubtedly, many "separated brethren" had significant difficulties with these attempts at consensus, most notably the United Methodist Church of Central and Southern Europe, which view all this as "too sacramentalist," and the Seventh Day Adventists, who could not help but consider the ministerial statement as "too

Catholic in intent." The reader will notice, however, a tendency in the responses which might well indicate the more profitable dialogues in which to engage in the immediate future, at least if organic unity is a goal.

Volume 3 has a splendid introduction by the late Orthodox theologian Nikos Nissiotis, in which he identifies three issues "skirted" by BEM, matters which can cut both ways: how sacramental churches should regard non-sacramental churches; the status of the Petrine office; the apparently irresolvable matter of the ordination of women. If the ecumenical movement is to progress, can the hard questions be avoided?

Catholic Perspectives was commissioned by the Catholic Theological Society of America to offer summaries and reactions to the Lima papers. At times the volume is less than helpful in advancing ecumenical progress, since it often gives the impression of a desire to dialogue with the Magisterium rather than with the various churches and ecclesial communities. Because the contributors note that they represent neither the Catholic Church nor the Catholic theological community-at-large, one is led to ask: If that is so, *cui bono?* An outstanding exception is Edward Kilmartin's evaluation of the Eucharist document.

Who in the World? is not directly related to the multilateral documentation; rather, it serves as a barometer for the bilateral conversations between Rome and Canterbury in the United States. This study of ministry contains the results of a questionnaire responded to by 89 Episcopalian and 94 Roman Catholic ecumenical officers, revealing "a consensus of astonishing dimension and great significance." In spite of the consensus, important divergences between Roman Catholics and Anglicans surface as to what constitute "minor" or more serious problems. Even though the ecumenical officers may not reflect the grass roots, J. T. Ford reminds the ecumenists of their prophetic obligation to stress to all "that the ecumenical pilgrimage is not an optional side-trip, but an integral part of their Christian vocation."

Faith and Renewal rounds out this ecumenical potpourri with the official record of Faith and Order's 1985 meeting at Stavenger, Norway, in which the Commission reviewed BEM's reception by the member churches. As such, it is an important series of papers of an introspective or self-reflective nature. Not at all self-congratulatory, they are objective, honest, and realistic assessments. Also included are areas other than BEM for future exploration and evaluation, especially for united/uniting churches. Thomas Hopke's presentation is extremely insightful, setting the tone for the long road ahead with a spirituality to undergird the arduous process: "We are dealing here with words. This is our peculiar calling and craft. Theological words are always words of confession; words 'adequate' and 'proper' to God, born of prayer, adoration, service and sacrifice in imitation of Christ and empowered by His Spirit. They are words which God Himself provides for His people, for His glorification, and for theirs. May the Lord give us His words, anointed and inspired, as we now take up our task."

Review

Old Testament Priests, and the New Priest According to the New Testament,
by Albert Vanhoye, S.J.
Petersham, Mass.: St. Bede's Publications, $24.95
(*National Catholic Register*, April 5, 1987)

Nearly two decades ago, Raymond Brown caused a stir simply by noting that the word "priest" is nowhere applied to a Christian minister in the entire New Testament.

Making such a mild observation created a furor because it hit a Catholic nerve that's been raw since the Reformation, when the priesthood was first questioned. Today, the attacks have been renewed by Fundamentalists and even by some Catholics.

It is against this backdrop that Jesuit Father Albert Vanhoye, rector of the Biblicum in Rome, takes objections to the priesthood seriously and engages in a fruitful study of the scriptural data, not unlike Brown's effort of an earlier era, but in much greater depth. The present *magnum opus* is divided into three parts: the place and meaning of the Old Testament priesthood; Christ's priesthood; and, what it means to be a priestly people.

For the busy person, Vanhoye thoughtfully offers his conclusions right in the title of the work: Whereas under the Old Covenant there existed a multitude of priests, in the New Dispensation, Jesus Christ is the sole Priest. Was Luther right then, after all? Hardly, for "the priesthood of Christ is fundamentally open to participation." That provides the rationale for the whole Church as a "priestly people" (*à la* First Peter), but Vanhoye also astutely notes that "the Epistle to the Hebrews places the 'leaders' of the community *at the side of* Christ the priest" (emphasis added).

How are the priesthood of the faithful and the ministerial priesthood interrelated? Vanhoye tells us that "the common priesthood is personal *offering*, [while] the pastoral ministry is a tangible manifestation of the priestly *mediation* of Christ." Thus are the two aspects of priesthood made visible in different ways by the laity and the clergy, respectively. This complementarity reflects the basic unity of the priesthood in Jesus Christ.

The practical implications cut in two directions. Those who argue that the New Testament abolishes a ministerial priesthood fail to understand the scriptural evidence in a sufficiently nuanced manner. At the same time, a man who shares in the mediating aspect of Christ's priesthood must studiously avoid expressions like *"my priesthood,"* lest he convey the impression that he believes he's a priest in his own right, rather than merely a sharer in the saving action of the only Priest known to the New Testament Church.

Who will profit from this work? First, this should be a required text in every seminary. Second, retreat masters for priests would do well to digest its main points and use them as topics for a series of reflections. Third, lay people and religious with deeper theological tastes could gain a better understanding of the vocation of service which is at the heart of the Sacrament of Holy Orders.

This translation (from the French) flows well. The layout is appealing, as St. Bede's releases always are. The only drawback is the price, which may prevent some from making the purchase.

Pastors and Money

(National Catholic Register, June 19, 1988)

For the first ten years after ordination, I never really engaged in full-time parish work. As a weekend assistant, I often listened to the financial woes of pastors and sometimes ventured advice to these crusty veterans—who, not infrequently, would dismiss my suggestions as the unrealistic musings of an ivory tower academic.

Well, over the past eighteen months, this "ivory tower academic" has had pastoral responsibility for a struggling Lithuanian parish of his own. I certainly have a better grasp of pastors' woes. And a lot more respect for their patience and charity. What I've learned is this:

1. *Catholics talk with their purses.* If people aren't coming to church or aren't giving, they're sending their priest a message. Is he celebrating the liturgy properly? Is he preaching the Gospel in its fullness? If not, he'll have to change. If he is, *the people* must change, so as to accept the truth of Christ he's presenting; otherwise, to be biblically blunt, he should shake their dust from his feet.

2. *The parish belongs to the people.* I always ask: "Do you want a parish? If so, respond accordingly. If not, we've lost the necessary ingredients for a parish, and it should close." This approach places the burden where it belongs.

3. *The people must be informed of needs.* If the faithful don't know what needs to be done, they can hardly be expected to act. That means more than simple announcements regarding the necessity of a new roof on the school, with its attendant second collection; it means total fiscal responsibility and honesty, that is, full disclosure to the whole parish at least once a year.

4. *The parish community must be catechized in a spirituality of sacrificial giving.* I always remember what our pastor told us as grammar school students: "When you give to Christ's Church, you must give sacrificially. How do you know you've given sacrificially? You give till it hurts—and then you give some more!'

Priests shouldn't be intimidated by people who say, "All Father does is talk about money." After being sure it's not so, the priest might answer: "If you gave the first time I asked, I wouldn't have to mention it again."

5. *The whole parish community has to be involved.* Canon law man-

dates a finance committee, to which the pastor should appoint individuals for reasons of competency (both spiritual and financial), rather than as signs of favor or because of their potential for being manipulated.

The entire parish, regardless of means, needs to participate in the giving program by works of prayer and penance. This reinforces its spiritual goal and enables all (young and old, rich and poor) to play a part.

6. *Parishioners should be encouraged to look beyond their own parish.* Parochial concern or pride can be a wonderful thing, but the priest must emphasize that this particular community doesn't exist in isolation. Parishes must also support their diocese and the Church Universal.

7. *School finances must be reintegrated into the total parish budget.* The decision made in the 1960s to separate school expenses from the rest of the parish was a mistake. If the school is indeed "the heart of the Church," as John Paul II argues, that should be reflected in the accounting procedures.

Pastors have to function in a society where "money talks." They shouldn't be embarrassed to make that connection very clear for their people. The spiritual reason for being generous to Christ's Church is a recognition of the truth in His words: "For where your treasure is, there also will your heart be" (Lk 12:34).

Ministry and Priesthood

(*National Catholic Register*, November 27, 1988)

The expression "lay ministers" has been tossed about a lot in recent years, and many now describe themselves as active in the "ministry of hospitality," the "ministry to the sick," or a "social justice ministry."

Some wonderful Christian work is being done under those headings, but there's a cost. Those terms can lead to confusion of roles and ministries because of their theological imprecision.

On the recent occasion of the Pontifical College Josephinum's centenary, Cardinal William Baum, prefect of the Congregation for Catholic Education, urged seminaries to employ "the language of ministry in a more disciplined, theologically informed manner." He was merely echoing the concerns raised by dozens of bishops who spoke at the Synod on the Laity in Rome last year, citing the identity problems for clergy and laity alike which arise when every act of Christian outreach is regarded as "ministry."

When this happens, a certain flattening of reality occurs. Distinctions are lost, and the word "ministry" no longer has any meaning. Furthermore, what becomes the possible responsibility of everyone ends up as the responsibility of no one. And a lack of interest sets in when this kind of undifferentiated consciousness takes over.

This is particularly true when the common priesthood of all believers conferred in Baptism is confused with the ministerial priesthood conferred in Holy Orders. The very different roles of the clergy and the laity then appear to be interchangeable, and the ordained priest is reduced "to being merely the animator, facilitator, or coordinator of other people's ministries," as Baum put it.

When this distinction is blurred, the ministerial priesthood will also tend to be viewed as what a priest *does* rather than who a priest *is*—namely, a man who has been "configured" to Christ through the imposition of hands, to quote Vatican II.

By a winding path, we shall have found ourselves embracing a concept of the ministerial priesthood which is merely functional or utilitarian and not ontological (that is, grounded in a changed identity) and, therefore, at odds with the Christian traditions of both East and West.

Furthermore, this kind of thinking usually leads the laity to look excessively to the clergy for standards of holiness and action. But, according to Vatican II, a Christian vocation lived out at home or in the world is every bit as good as one lived out in the sanctuary.

This is because a healthy lay spirituality should consider Baptism (not Holy Orders) as the basic sacrament. And Baptism itself is sufficient for living a proper Christian life.

Fuzzy language breeds fuzzy theology; and that, in turn, fosters confused and confusing vocational lifestyles for both clergy and laity. Therefore, if Baum is correct in cautioning seminaries to use "the language of ministry advisedly," the same advice would be worthwhile for all of us.

How would that translate into daily usage? Following the lead of Vatican II and the many interventions at the Synod on the Laity, I believe that the activities of the laity should be described as apostolates or services and that the term "ministry" should be restricted to the work of the ordained.

This is neither clericalism nor snobbishness; it's simply the recognition that our language should reflect as accurately as possible the reality it attempts to convey. As in a biology class, the student dissects a body into many parts in order to appreciate the whole; so too in the theological enterprise, there should be a careful analysis of the distinctions between the ministerial priesthood and the priesthood of the faithful.

This will produce a clearer understanding of the one Body of Christ under Whose headship and from Whose fullness all service has its source and meaning.

Smearing Future Priests

(*National Catholic Register*, October 15, 1989)

Notre Dame's Father Richard McBrien has often used his nationally syndicated newspaper column to engage in *ad hominem* attacks on people with whom he disagrees, including Pope John Paul II and Cardinal Joseph Ratzinger.

Recently, he veered off in a new and particularly venomous direction. With all the dogmatism of a medieval pontiff, he facilely generalized about what "all the surveys" say about the present crop of seminarians: namely, that they are "passive, dependent, rigid and authoritarian. And more and more candidates are gay and/or sexually immature."

As a vocations director, teacher, and priest who has been responsible for at least eleven young men entering the seminary in the past dozen years, I think I've read "all the surveys" of seminarians. And I don't find McBrien's conclusions in any of them, except perhaps for one which is flawed by its overt left-leaning agenda.

McBrien's language shows him to be locked into the peculiar time-warp which existed during the silly sixties and savage seventies. I was a seminarian then. And when we were labeled "passive, dependent, rigid and authoritarian," it meant we were submissive to the authority of the Holy Father and courageously opposed to dissenting faculty members, whose goal was to form us as priests for a brave new Church which would have little connection to the one founded on the rock of Peter.

Because of our fidelity to Rome, many of us were sent off for psychological counseling. This was the ecclesiastical equivalent of the gulag and its psychiatric hospitals where those in the Soviet Union who refused to toe the party line used to be banished.

Putting my own spin on McBrien's prejudicial language, I agree with him that today's seminarians are increasingly loyal to the Magisterium, joyfully and proudly orthodox, and unafraid of consequences. This is a cause for celebration. It means that the Holy Spirit is indeed bringing about a true renewal in the post-conciliar Church.

McBrien is afraid of this development. He senses that these "young Turks" aren't likely to be tolerant of his brand of "Catholicism," which was expounded in his book of the same name. (This volume also received a reproach from the National Conference of

Catholic Bishops' Committee on Doctrine.) McBrien's glib generalizations about the seminarians' sexual proclivities are especially shocking. They simply aren't true.

Isn't it ironic that a man who has consistently called for "compassion" toward those who don't accept Church teaching on birth control and homosexuality, must now resort to "fag-bashing"? He obviously wants to destroy the credibility of future priests who don't share his ideological agenda, and he's willing to use any means necessary to achieve that end.

Interestingly enough, McBrien may discover that this generation of seminarians is not as "conservative" as he thinks. Word has it that some of them are banding together in a class action lawsuit against him for defamation of character.

McBrien's approach reflects the terror and terrorizing techniques of those who realize they've lost "the battle for the American Church." Understood from that perspective, his smears and recriminations become comprehensible and, yes, even a source of delight.

It means that our side is winning.

Review

Transforming Parish Ministry: The Changing Roles of Catholic Clergy, Laity and Women Religious. Edited by Jay P. Dolan. New York: Crossroad, $27.50

The Meaning of Christian Priesthood, by Gilbert Greshake Westminister, Md.: Christian Classics, $10.95

(*National Catholic Register*, November 12, 1989)

There ought to be a law against writing Church history until a hundred years have passed, and *Transforming Parish Ministry* could be used as Exhibit A in advancing the legislation. This book crudely imposes its biases on historical events whenever the facts prove inconvenient.

The subject matter is important: the role of parishes in the American Church throughout its history. Editor Jay Dolan divides his study into four major sections with chapters by different authors. The concept is excellent; the results, disappointing.

A good example of the book's prejudices can be found in R. Scott Appleby's, "The Transformation of the Roman Catholic Parish Priesthood," which presents a sad caricature of preconciliar theology, particularly in regard to Christology and the priesthood. It leaves the impression that the ever-resilient laity did well during the pre-Vatican II period, despite the "institutional" Church and its "brick-and-mortar" priests. He leaves no room for the fine parish priests who influenced so many vocations in the 1950s and early 1960s.

Matters of theology are judged by the principles of contemporary sociology and psychology. And ontological categories are rejected out of hand. Thus "ministry" is not who a man is by the power of divine grace, but rather what he (or she) does.

After stripping away everything unique to the priesthood, except for consecration and absolution, Appleby concludes that "Catholic parishioners continue to esteem and to require his [the priest's] presence as a radical expression of their own rootedness in God and in the divine work of redemption."

If Appleby believes that the people in the pews really think this way, then he's spent too much time talking to those who share his own curious ideas.

As bad as the priesthood section is, the one on women religious is even worse. First, Sister Patricia Byrne limits her historical review to only six congregations of Sisters, none of which are either the largest, the most influential, or the most representative.

In her examination of pre-conciliar convent life, Byrne mocks the "remnants of Victorian mores." But unsavory developments since the 1960s make some of those earlier self-imposed restraints seem remarkably wise. Byrne tries to discredit those benighted women of yesteryear by speaking of the "deceptive unity" of that period. Their courage and faith are barely acknowledged. It suits her purposes to stress only the negative aspects of that time.

The period from 1970 to the present is described as a time of "diminishment, disillusion and discovery." The first two terms are certainly accurate; but "discovery" is only possible if the genuine renewal envisioned by Vatican II is finally allowed to take root. In this country, many of its true intentions have been confounded.

Debra Campbell then leads the reader through "the lay apostolate to the ministry explosion." Everything that happened before 1970 is painted as bad, and everything since then is called the wave of the future. But the facts she marshals could be interpreted quite differently: A careful reading of those events could lead to the conclusion that a more fruitful lay involvement in the American Church existed sixty years ago than does today.

The cure for the problems described in Dolan's book comes in Father Gilbert Greshake's small volume on the priesthood. Part One seeks to provide "a theological definition of priesthood," while Part Two looks at "the spiritual life of the priest." Clear thinking and precise language in touch with the sources of Catholic theology make this enjoyable reading—a must read for priests, seminarians, and any who wish to be supportive of the priestly vocation. Greshake is a thoroughly post-conciliar theologian, offering balanced insights into the nature of the priesthood.

Perhaps the best line in the book, and worth the purchase price alone, is the following: "The Catholic Church of the West, in setting celibacy as a precondition for ordination, is proclaiming with the utmost clarity that, for its office-bearers, it wishes to have only 'charismatics,' that is, men who have received particular gifts of grace from the Holy Spirit, and are striving for more." So much for those who fret about the "imposition" of celibacy.

In contrasting these two books, one thing becomes very clear: Catholic Tradition—the real record of our life as a believing community—is the best guide for those who seek to make sense of the present and then chart a course into the future.

Questions of Identity

(*The* [Sioux City, Iowa] *Globe*, January 11, 1990)

"I don't know who I am" was a sentence frequently uttered in the confused and confusing sixties. Often these people found their way to a psychiatrist's couch because questions of identity are so important that when they go unresolved, personal disorientation and disintegration result. The Scripture readings for this Second Sunday in Ordinary Time (Cycle A) provide answers to two critical questions of identity: Who is Jesus? Who am I?

Speaking through John the Baptist, Almighty God reveals the identity of Jesus: He is "God's chosen One," who "ranks ahead" of John because He was before him. In other words, Jesus is—as the Creed puts it—"eternally begotten of the Father, God from God."

Those insights tell us Who Jesus is in Himself; but, Who is He for us? He is "the Lamb of God who takes away the sin of the world." There is an intimate and necessary connection between those two aspects of Christ's identity: His ministry in regard to human sinfulness is effective only because of His divine nature.

Jesus is acclaimed by the Baptist not as a prophet or a social reformer or a teacher but primarily as one "who takes away the sin of the world." If we want to benefit from a relationship with Jesus Christ, then, it must be on those terms, which leads directly to the second question: Who am I?

First and foremost, I am a sinner in need of salvation. The bad news of the human condition without Christ is our sinfulness. Once that state is understood and admitted, the cure is close at hand, for the very name of Jesus means "Savior." He saves me from a fate worse than death when I allow Him to liberate me from my natural desires to control and manipulate persons and things. That, of course, is just another way of describing sin, isn't it?

When I go to Christ acknowledging my sins, He not only takes them away through the Church's sacraments; He provides me with a new mode of existence—the life of grace, which confers on me a new identity. Like Isaiah, I receive a divine commission to be the Lord's "servant" and then "a light to the nations."

The honest servant of God realizes that he or she is in the Master's debt and so lives in a grateful manner. Furthermore, like John the Baptist, one who has come to know Jesus in this new way is called to testify before the world regarding the meaning one has experienced by responding to the invitation to salvation.

That is what the prophet has in mind when he speaks of the saved or redeemed servant as "a light to the nations." One who is redeemed has been "bought back" from slavery to the self, to the world, to the Devil; he or she replaces the yoke of slavery to sin with the gentle yoke of Jesus Christ. And the wonderful irony is that a true servant of Christ knows a greater freedom than any king.

Jesus, the eternal Son of the Father, reveals His identity to us. In so doing, He also reveals our identity to us—in two stages: first, as sinners in need of salvation; then, as servants privileged to point Him out to others as He was first pointed out to us—as God's Chosen One and God's Lamb.

"I don't know who I am" can never be said by a believer; he or she has been delivered from that sad statement by Christ and because of Christ.

Personally Responding to God's Call

(*The* [Sioux City, Iowa] *Globe*, January 17, 1991)

It's always interesting to ask people what made them go into a particular field of endeavor, because the answers are as varied as the people themselves. The Scripture readings for the Second Sunday of the Year (Cycle A) provide us with what might be called a study in personal responses to the call of God.

In the First Reading, we meet young Samuel who heard God's call but didn't know what to make of it; he was confused, but willing. The Gospel presents us with the disciples who were invited to follow Jesus and responded quite readily.

Do you recall the circumstances that brought you to the decision to become what you have become? I do.

I received no major revelation that God wanted me to be a priest, but that does not mean God did not call me. On the contrary, I remember the event that got me thinking about the priesthood as vividly as can be. It wasn't profound; it might even be considered kind of silly, but God works in strange ways.

It was the first day of kindergarten; our pastor came into class. He was a monsignor, and I was very impressed by his red-buttoned cassock. When I got home that afternoon, my mother asked me how everything had gone and, to her surprise, I said, "Great! I want to be a monsignor when I grow up." I hope my appreciation for the priesthood has grown since that first spark of interest, but that's how it all began.

The Scriptures show us time and again that once a person has experienced God's call and given an affirmative response, that person's life is completely changed. Young Samuel was anointed. Simon got a new name. St. Paul tells us that Christians have to live a life worthy of the vocation to which they have been called. All the while, we realize that if God has called us to a particular way of life, He will give us the help we need to follow through on His invitation. Nor is God's call limited to the priesthood and religious life. Every Christian is asked to do, in the words of Mother Teresa of Calcutta, "something beautiful for God," and it is most important to see whatever your vocation is as God's personal call and your acceptance as your reply.

Let me direct a few points to my readers.

You, young people, have you ever prayed and asked the Lord to help you know what He wants you to do with your life? As a high school teacher, I saw so many teenagers so incredibly confused by all the choices modern life holds out to them. Try to discover what makes you happy and how you can make others happy by using your talents to the fullest. And while we're at it, have you ever thought about the priesthood and religious life? Give full-time ministry and permanent commitment a chance. This year several young men have come to me for direction and guidance to enter the college seminary in the fall. What about you?

Parents, do you ever talk about your children's future with them? Or do you simply worry in silence? Help your children come to understand themselves and what they have to offer. Give them guidance in making choices that are in line with God's will for them.

All of us need to seek out God's will and way every day of our lives, not just in the broad picture of vocation selection but in the day-to-day living out of our fundamental Christian commitment. God's call, the divine will, the human response: These are the really big issues in life.

A Broadway play put the question in this way: "What's it all about, Alfie?" Jesus confronted His future disciples with the direct question: "What are you looking for?"

Those same questions are applicable to every one of us today. Even though we may not have the answers on the tips of our tongues, we can imitate the example of little Samuel who had the good sense to say, "Speak, Lord, your servant is listening."

We all need to listen to that silent, inner beckoning, which is nothing other than the voice of God.

Helping Priests Be Celibate

(*National Catholic Register*, October 6, 1991)

Many have complained that adequate Catholic marriage preparation is lacking. And while Pre-Cana programs and the like could be improved, they are often light-years ahead of the preparation many seminaries offer to men who have made a lifelong commitment to celibacy.

Not a single course, workshop, lecture, conference, homily, or class was ever totally devoted to a consideration of celibacy during my eight-year training for the priesthood. Of course, it was whispered about in small groups during the sixties and seventies that by the time we were ordained, celibacy would be optional. But more than a dozen years into the priesthood, we know otherwise, and several of my classmates were unprepared.

The former prefect of the Congregation for Catholic Education, Cardinal William Baum, called attention to this regrettable gap in an address at the Pontifical College Josephinum's centennial and urged those charged with priestly formation to do something about it. Baum noted the pressure exerted nowadays on the Church to ordain married men but wisely placed things in historical context: "Each time the Western Church has encountered the crisis of celibacy in the past, the solution to the crisis has not been to authorize a married priesthood, but to rediscover the meaning, the worth and the discipline of celibacy." He indicated that the greats of the Western Church, from Augustine and Dominic to Ignatius Loyola and Vincent de Paul, had all faced the question squarely by recovering the foundation of celibacy "in the personal example of our Lord, its theological motivation, its asceticism and spirituality."

How can this be done today? By a healthy combination of theology, psychology, and spirituality. If the Father decreed that "it is not good for the man to be alone," did the Son contradict Him when He counseled celibacy for the sake of the Kingdom? Of course not. Therefore, it is essential to help young men see how being alone doesn't necessarily make one lonely; how celibacy creates a necessary and holy emptiness for God; how the joys and sufferings of celibacy complement the joys and sufferings of marriage; and how spiritual fatherhood can and must be fruitful.

Modern psychology has given us a deeper understanding of the human person. And if its insights are properly employed, today we may be in a better position than ever to explain to candidates for the priesthood the unique values of celibacy. Seminarians deserve this kind of preparation, and, as Baum observed, they have so often expressed "how much they appreciated programmed conferences and workshops which treat [celibacy] constructively."

Because celibacy is a gift for the whole Church, dealing with it should not be the task of seminary faculties alone. Affirming its importance is everyone's responsibility. Bishops need to be fathers to their priests, offering them a sense of purpose and identity. Priests must recapture the sense of fraternity in their vocation. And the faithful should provide their priests with a support system which makes celibacy not only tolerable but also a joy.

If priests receive this kind of commitment from the entire Church, they will be better able to live out their promise of celibacy. And the brilliance of this special charism, which Paul VI called the "jewel" of Western Christianity, will shine forth with great beauty.

Review

Last Priests in America: Conversations with Remarkable Men, by Tim Unsworth
New York: Crossroad, 1991, 281 pp., $29.95
(*Pastoral Life*, February 1992)

They say you can't tell a book by its cover. In this case, the title says it all. Be seated. Put on your seat belt, and get ready for a rollercoaster ride which will destroy not only your confidence in the priesthood, but perhaps even your faith. Tim Unsworth purports to have written a work dealing with normal, everyday-type priests who love the Church and the priesthood. What we are treated to, however, is a cast of characters right out of a Fellini film. Add to that a clear leftward orientation (e.g., not one of the men interviewed has a positive word to say about Pope John Paul II; all but two or three dissent from Church teaching on *Humanae Vitae* and a male priesthood, as well as the discipline of clerical celibacy). Almost all the priests come from the Midwest (indeed, mostly Chicagoans or long associated with Chicago). We meet a melange of priestly malcontents, even men in their seventies, who were unhappy with the Church forty years ago and have just grown in their dissatisfaction over the decades. The rancor toward the "institution" borders on the pathological, leading one to ask why they have remained.

Now, one need not expect Unsworth of *National Catholic Reporter* fame to produce a paean to the traditional model of the priesthood, but some fairness and decent research would be welcome and expected. Several errors have found their way into the text. For instance, we read that Pope Paul VI's encyclical on artificial birth control was published in 1965, rather than 1968. One of the priests asserts that none of the eucharistic prayers of the Roman Rite has an epiclesis; three of them are quite explicit, and Prayer I is implicit. John Tracey Ellis, of all people, even underestimates the enrollment of New York's theologate by 60 percent (in an effort to paint a bleak picture of things in a traditional environment?).

Who are the clergy of the book? The usual names pop up: Andrew Greeley, Richard McBrien, Joseph Bernardin, Raymond Lucker, William McManus, and others. One fellow astutely and candidly describes himself as "a non-denominational Buddhist." Most of them read the same books and magazines, go to the same workshops, have the same heroes, take the NCR for the Bible, hate the past, and fear the future. One interesting point that comes across repeatedly is that although we might say that priestly formation today is somewhat lacking, it was certainly problematic in "the good old days," producing a crop like this, almost all of whom note grave reservations about the education and lifestyle they led in the preconciliar period; now, of course, they are unhappy, too.

Am I calling for a book on the priesthood which is thinly disguised hagiography? Hardly. After twenty-three years of priestly formation and ministry, living with saints and sinners alike, I know the weaknesses all too well. But this is an incredibly distorted picture, not in the least rising above the level of advocacy literature for a married clergy, ordination of women, relaxation of traditional moral norms, temporary commitment—in short, the Protestantization of Catholicism.

The bottom line is simple: Don't waste your time or money on something so shallow and transparent. As Fulton Sheen reminded us so often, the priesthood is a mystery; none of it is in evidence here.

A Few Good Men

(*National Catholic Register*, May 3, 1992)

For more than two decades now, the Church has focused her attention on special prayer for vocations and their promotion on Good Shepherd Sunday—this year, May 10. A fitting preparation for this observance is the release of John Paul II's document, *Pastores Dabo Vobis* ("I Will Give You Shepherds"), his apostolic exhortation on the formation of priests, growing out of the 1990 synod. As usual, the Pontiff's work contains a wealth of material for reflection for everyone in the Church, but especially for those charged with encouraging priestly vocations.

Experience shows that many seminarians have several things in common: They're bright and orthodox; have a deep devotion to the liturgy as it should be celebrated; and love the Pope and our Lady. And, they have one additional common element—they are often the victims of institutional harassment, either from vocations directors or seminary professors.

Until we decide what to do with this unpleasant fact, there's little point in weeping about vocational recruitment. The right candidates are out there but, in too many instances, they're deliberately steered away from the "system" or weeded out once in. As a result, bishops need to have a very clear picture of the type of priests they want, and what qualities they should embody, before looking for future priests and certainly before appointing a vocations director or team of such directors. Once a proper image is in place, and only then, will we all know what our seminarians should be and do.

Typically, today's average Joe who has gone to a Catholic high school and thought about the priesthood since grammar school will be referred to the diocesan director of vocations. If Joe belongs to an average diocese, the priest he meets will be in his late thirties or forties; he'll have had little parochial or teaching experience; he's theologically ambivalent and influenced by various lobby groups within the diocesan bureaucracy, often including feminist nuns; and, he's had just enough psychology to be dangerous.

If he's wearing clerical clothes at all, the collar may be open with studied informality. He may encourage the potential seminarian to "just call me Tom." His mannerisms may be weak or indecisive; he may repeatedly stress how little will be required of the candidate and how "open" he needs to be, particularly if the young man seems to know exactly what the priesthood is about and what he senses he should do next. If the boy has been exposed to good, solid citizens in the priesthood at his parish or high school, he'll of course wonder what's going on, unless he's been warned in advance what to expect and how he should behave—that is, with an appropriate degree of indecisiveness and politically correct jargon.

When he is quizzed by "Tom" about liturgy, priesthood, celibacy, the Pope, and women priests, the uninitiated youth may well give the "wrong" answers, causing him to be dropped or resulting in his being entered into a year's worth of group activity for "growth," which generally means digesting discredited seventies notions of ecclesiology and priestly life and ministry.

Some bishops actively seek out a vocations director like the one just described; most, however, don't know what goes on behind the scenes in the candidate-discernment process. But if a bishop really wants candidates impressive both in quality and quantity, he needs the right public relations man.

The individual should be fiercely loyal to Christ and His Church, unabashedly orthodox, spiritual (given over to prayer), hard-working and zealous, proud to be a priest (as evidenced by his attitudes and actions), manly (not necessarily John Wayne or a former high school quarterback, but clearly a man), and sensitive but not emasculated. This sort of vocations director will ensure that future priests will be attracted and then given appropriate formation all along the road to the altar.

What should we look for in a seminary candidate? Ideally, a young man, not much past his college years and preferably right out of high school (while we are not ruling out older men, it is good to note that no corporation builds its future on second-career people; nor should we), and one who has no ax to grind and simply knows the meaning of *sentire cum ecclesia*. Thus, he doesn't run after either Tridentine Masses or avant garde liturgical events.

He should not be any more Catholic than the Pope—but no *less* Catholic, either. He should be a cultured gentleman, or at least open to becoming one. We should be on the lookout for a man who is theologically clear-headed and well-adjusted, both socially and sexually. He should also have an intense desire to be a priest—even a holy anxiety; which is why seminaries which discourage their students from looking and acting like priests are so curiously off-base. He also needs the psychic grit to endure the "head games" which he will too often encounter in the still problematic environment of many U.S. seminaries.

He has a right to feel needed, wanted, and accepted in a seminary, in the parish where he works (and not simply as one of a thousand other lay workers), in his diocese or religious congregation. He should likewise recall the wise words of Pope Pius XII that one does not have a vocation to the seminary but to the priesthood.

It all seems so simple and self-evident, that one's tempted to ask what the problem is: *Why isn't this the norm?* Some will argue that the downward vocations spiral is continuing—although they often fail to note that this is true mainly for secularized Western Europe and North America—and that the suggestions outlined here will simply drive away even the few applicants we do have. On the contrary, the difficulty is that too many people in the past twenty years have *not* been trying to form shepherds after God's own heart (cf. Jer 3:15), but after their own. Young people, willing to commit their lives, want to model their existence on Christ and not on some transitory human deformation of that powerful reality.

The Holy Father's exhortation ends with a call to prayer "for an extraordinary outpouring of the Spirit of Pentecost." Indeed, today's "extraordinary" vocations crisis—unparalleled since the Protestant Reformation—requires both extraordinary prayer and extraordinary effort. To those willing to respond with faith, God promises the increase.

Another Modest Proposal

(*National Catholic Register*, June 28, 1992)

A Midwestern diocese recently announced a strong policy on sexual misconduct by diocesan workers (clerical, religious, and lay alike). Virtually airtight, it has detailed procedures for reporting such incidents and for correct diocesan responses.

There is an obligation to report problems to local Church officials, including the vicar general, who then informs the bishop of allegations or documented incidents. When evidence indicates that misconduct has in fact occurred, the perpetrator will be relieved of all diocesan responsibilities. Appropriate records will be kept of accusations and substantiated occurrences.

Aggrieved parties, meanwhile, will be ministered to by diocesan officials. If the guilty party is a priest, the process for his removal from the clerical state may be initiated; minimally, he will be required to undergo medical and psychological treatment before being allowed to return to active service.

I've spent some time on these details because the reader needs to know them in order to evaluate my own modest proposal, which I'd like to have piggyback on this sexual misconduct policy: When will we see one of our bishops set a policy for liturgical misconduct or doctrinal error for his clergy, let alone religious and laity?

Such a policy might say things like the following:

—All the faithful should make known to the dean and vicar general any improvisations in the liturgy or other mishandling of approved rites.

—Instances of the wrongful use of extraordinary ministers of Holy Communion should be reported to the bishop's office.

—A priest accused of such freelancing will be invited to confront the facts (tapes, witnesses, etc.). If he is guilty, he will be suspended from the exercise of his priestly office for a minimum of three weeks; if he persists after restoration to priestly service, more substantial canonical penalties will be pursued. Examples of wrong teaching and preaching should be conveyed to appropriate diocesan authorities, with necessary documentation. When the same is proven, perpetrators will be deprived of any diocesan position, unless and until a clear intention is shown to change behavior.

—Parties whose faith (or whose children's faith) has been injured will be personally visited by the bishop, who has the ultimate responsibility for safeguarding the worship and doctrine of the local Church.

Of course, I doubt that any such policy will ever be enacted. Yet, until we see action like this taken on the doctrinal and liturgical fronts, all our talk about sexual misconduct will sound hollow, because the average person has already concluded that our real interest in that issue is limited to saving face and saving money—when our main concern should be saving souls.

Vocations and Visibility

(*Catholic Twin Circle*, August 9, 1992)

As we try to discover where things went awry with vocation recruitment—an admittedly complex situation—I go back to the moment when bishops in the nineteen-fifties began to appoint vocations directors. "What's wrong with that?" you ask. "Doesn't that reflect a bishop's concern for future priests?" Surely, the motivation was praiseworthy, but the underlying—and probably unconscious—philosophy was bad, and the results were even worse.

At root, the vocations director in every diocese is the bishop: It is he who should do the calling forth of young men to consider a priestly vocation; it is he who, during his parish and school visitations, should surface potential candidates and interview them; it is he who should be intimately involved in the formation of seminarians. At least one bishop in this country sees that; and, therefore, the priest he has appointed to deal with vocational matters is called the "vicar for vocations"—to make clear that the bishop is truly the director of vocations, and that the priest-assistant is the nitty-gritty handler.

Having vocations directors also caused a further problem, namely, that priests in parishes, schools, and other institutions thought they were "off the hook." After all, there was a full-time priest dedicated to that work. But, in truth, the most important man in any diocese for vocations, next to the bishop, is the local priest, and many of them simply gave up the ghost in that regard.

The purpose of this reflection is to arouse priests to a deeper appreciation of their role as "vocations directors" in the concrete circumstances of their daily ministry and to offer some simple suggestions on how that can be done effectively and painlessly.

1. *Invite and encourage boys and young men to consider a priestly vocation.*

Some years ago, *Our Sunday Visitor* surveyed boys in Catholic high schools around the country. A remarkably large percentage had given serious thought to becoming priests, but only one-fourth had ever been asked by any adult to think about such a prospect. Imagine what might happen if we did our job?

Yet another issue of concern is that when young fellows approach a priest with interest in the priesthood, all too often priests do not demonstrate genuine interest or actually tell them not to channel their lives so directly so soon—and to "play the field."

Boys, no matter how young, don't need or deserve that kind of treatment from clergy; they can easily get that from society. In other words, our task is to make the priesthood seem as natural a vocational choice as becoming a lawyer, doctor, teacher, etc., and to show that by our wholehearted response.

2. *Use Catholic schools to advantage.*

The natural and most effective "seedbed" for priests is the Catholic school. If we check out the biographical sketches of the newly-ordained each year, we find that as many as 90 percent of them are products of Catholic schools—even though fewer than 25 percent of our youth attend Catholic high schools.

That fact should lead priests to spend time in both elementary and secondary schools—teaching, on the playground, counseling, going to games and dances, being a "priestly presence."

3. *Let people see you do "normal" things.*

One of the sadder developments in the post-conciliar period in this country is that so many priests feel the necessity of going incognito when "off-duty," as though one can ever be off-duty from the priesthood. Taking God off the streets of our cities and towns has made the priesthood unreal: out of sight, out of mind. If the only time a priest is seen is on church property, what kind of image is being conveyed?

While such a scenario might be understandable for the Church in the catacombs, it is hardly in keeping with a Church that is truly a part of the fabric of a society. It is healthy to let people know that priests—precisely as priests—enjoy movies, dinner, and shopping, like everyone else.

4. *Pray for vocations.*

The priest himself must pray fervently for vocations and make personal sacrifices. If he is doing that, then he can honestly ask his people to do the same.

No parish Mass should be celebrated in which a petition of the General Intercessions is not directed toward the intention of an increase in vocations to the priesthood and religious life. Aside from the prayer-power involved, it is also an effective means of raising the consciousness of the congregation to the need. Regularly scheduled holy hours are likewise important, as well as using Mass formularies for vocations when no specific feast occurs.

5. *Be kind and generous to seminarians.*

Some priests are good about getting candidates, but once they're in, they're forgotten or even maltreated. Seminarians require constant affirmation and consideration; the interest and good example of the elder brethren is most encouraging.

Sometimes that means just a friendly phone call. It should always mean that the young man knows the rectory door is open. It may also mean the expenditure of parish or personal funds—to help meet some extraordinary expenses or simply to celebrate a feast day or anniversary. Unless a seminarian is independently wealthy, no self-respecting priest should let him pay for dinners or movies "until the stole hangs straight." After all, these fellows are our sons in a way that no one else can ever be.

Seminarians should also be invited to participate in clergy gatherings in parishes and rectories, introducing them to the fraternity of the priesthood. They should also know that their services are needed and wanted, not as lay men but as future priests.

6. *Be a source of moral support and even more, when needed.*

Nothing is so demoralizing to a seminarian or a future seminarian as to be abandoned to "the system." When a candidate is applying to a diocese or is awaiting an assignment or has gotten a "raw deal" from the seminary, he should be able to count on his priest-friends to give him wise counsel but also to go to bat for him, if that is necessary.

Priests who are not willing to do that should not bring men into the pipeline, to begin with. The role of a father is not just to beget and let go, but to accompany a son along the way, in spite of difficulties and even especially so during them.

7. *Be joyful.*

Cardinal Joseph Ratzinger has a wonderful book on the priesthood, *Ministers of Your Joy*. Some priests have made a religion out of being and looking miserable—hardly an apt advertisement for one assigned the task of proclaiming the Good News by word and deed. As Nietzsche remarked, "If Christians wanted me to believe in their God, they would have to look more redeemed."

Our demeanor should be such that no one, but especially potential priests, could ever doubt that we love the Church and the priesthood and, yes, would do it all over again. Who wants to go into a "business" in which everyone looks so glum? Joy is not hilarity or silliness; it is a peaceful and calm approach to life, which communicates satisfaction and fulfillment.

What I have been suggesting is nothing earth-shattering. Much of it is basic common sense; none of it is incredibly time-consuming. All of it taken together, however, bespeaks an attitude and mindset that can refocus concern for priestly vocations in the right direction, setting a tone and establishing an environment in which God's call can be heard and answered.

Leader of the Parochial School

(*Catholic Twin Circle,* August 16, 1992)

Life is full of ironies. Last century, the Catholic laity were so opposed to the notion of a separate school system that bishops and pastors had to threaten parents with excommunication for placing Catholic children in government schools. Now, in all too many instances, clergy want to close schools, while the laity wish to maintain them at all costs.

As a priest who has also spent the lion's share of his ministry in the classroom, I have a somewhat unique perspective. Shamefacedly, I have to admit that many (perhaps the majority) of my brother-priests have no idea of the purpose of Catholic education, of how and why the system needs to exist, and of what they should be doing to foster the growth and development of Catholic schools.

For those who do not understand the rationale behind the Catholic school system of America, I can only refer them to the crystal-clear statements of the Second Vatican Council, the Code of Canon Law, and the many utterances of the present Holy Father on this subject.

Secular data coming from the fields of education, psychology, and sociology is completely supportive of our historical option for such a method of educating our youth. Nor should we neglect the input from the ecumenical front, especially evangelical Protestants and Jews.

Suffice it to say that I am convinced for a host of reasons that the future of the Church in the United States is directly related to the number of children who have the opportunity to attend Catholic schools. With that in mind, what should the priest be doing to advance the cause of Catholic education?

What I have to suggest is a list that is aimed primarily at parochial elementary schools; appropriate adaptations can be made for inter-parochial institutions and high schools, as well.

1. *Be present.*

A very fine Sister-principal of a large interparochial school told me recently that of the five pastors whose parishioners' children attend her school, she cannot get one to "just visit." Several of them (but not all) are willing to come to celebrate Mass for the children or to hear confessions, but not one is willing to "waste time" by simply dropping into the classrooms to chat with the children.

Some of my strongest and fondest boyhood memories of priests come from the casual calls paid to the school by our parish priests. Hardly a day went by when one of them didn't pop into the cafeteria at lunchtime or play ball on the playground at recess. We thus came to regard our priests as normal, happy, interested, and interesting men.

Youngsters appreciate the presence of priests at their games, plays, and dances. If a name is needed to justify the activity, let's call it a "theology of presence."

2. *Teach religion.*

One large eastern diocese (until only a decade ago) assigned all newly-ordaineds to a five-year stint as a high-school teacher. While one can argue that not all priests are born teachers, there was a wisdom to the practice, for several reasons. It made a strong institutional statement about the diocese's commitment to Catholic education; it taught priests how to deal with youth (and their parents); and it provided a stable body of competent religion teachers.

It seems to me that from junior high on, students should be exposed to priest-teachers—at least for religion class—at least once a week. It would also he helpful to have priests participate in (if not directly teach) preparation programs for First Penance, First Holy Communion, and Confirmation.

Some priests will object that they can't teach kids. Not every priest is a Socrates, but that's not what's being asked. What's needed is a willingness to impart the Catholic Faith with integrity and joy, precisely as a priest.

In days when clergy and religious are in short supply and religion must be taught by lay people (who might not always have the best training), the priest can add an important dimension to the total religious-education picture.

The pastor has a particular responsibility for catechesis in the parish school, one that cannot be delegated. It is not by accident that the Roman congregation concerned with catechesis is the Congregation of the Clergy—not the Congregation for Catholic Education.

Therefore, the pastor needs to know who is teaching religion, how that is being done, and with what texts; those tasks cannot be shunted off onto a parish DRE or principal. A logical corollary is that the maintenance of a truly Catholic-school atmosphere is the pastor's special duty and right.

3. *Raise community consciousness about the school.*

The way Catholic education has been presented over the past two decades is as though it is merely one option (albeit a nice one, in most instances) among many for the development of the next generation of Catholics. But it isn't; it is the necessary option. And if the parish priest does not say that at every opportunity, he shouldn't be surprised that few people take the option.

The parish priest should also be a voice for the school in the community-at-large: in civic associations, in ministerial groups, etc. He should use public moments to let everyone know the contribution being made to the general population by his parochial school. In short, he should be *the* public-relations man for Catholic education.

4. *Keep the school within reach of everyone.*

Nothing grates on my nerves like hearing priests say that "the school is a drain." What a negative way of looking at what Pope John Paul II has called "the very heart of the Church." It's like saying that Granny is a drain.

Do schools cost money?

Obviously, but "drain" implies useless or unwarranted expenditure of funds. Furthermore, I doubt if there's ever been a school in history that actually made money; the nature of the beast is that a school costs and does not generate funds. Once that notion is in place, then we are ready for two other policies.

First, tuition must be affordable. We are presently pricing ourselves out of existence and turning our schools into institutions for the elite—in direct contradiction to the intentions of those like St. Elizabeth Ann Seton and St. John Neumann, who intended a system for the general Catholic population.

Because we have failed to demand our rights from the government, because we have allowed costs to get out of hand in some places (ridiculously competing with government schools in all the wrong ways), because we have not engaged in creative fund-raising, because we have not treated the school as the financial and moral responsibility of the entire Catholic community (and not just of parents whose children attend), we have come to rely on tuition to balance the books. This has to stop, or else we'll find ourselves out of business in short order.

Second, no Catholic child should ever be denied a Catholic education for lack of money. Such a cold-hearted judgment could never expect God's blessing on an institution. If we do not believe that God will provide, then we shouldn't be running a school, begun under the banner of Divine Providence and committed to teaching children to live in that awareness.

Similarly, if we hold to the doctrine of *Humanae Vitae,* we should never charge tuition by the child but by the family. In other words, we need to put our money where our mouth is.

5. *Serve as a faculty resource.*

Catholic-school teachers and administrators should feel comfortable with the parish priest, seeing him as an ally, a colleague, and a spiritual director. They should be able to approach him with questions about the Faith and about their own wonderful apostolate. Therefore, he should be as present to them as he is to the children of the school, attending faculty meetings and parties, and being a part of significant events in the lives of the teachers.

Some priests will look at the "job description" given about inspiring Catholic schools and say they don't have time for it all. To which, I ask, "Can you think of a better way of spending your time?"

Others will argue that it is based on a pre-conciliar model of pastoral leadership, to which I respond, "Has anything else since been so effective?" After all, the priest is not simply a sacramental magician; he should be actively involved in the formation of young Catholic lives. Only then can sacraments and ritual make sense.

Yet others will say that they would like to do these things, but the principal won't let him. To which, I say, "Assert your rights as a priest to incarnate Christ in a unique way for our youth." Any principal who does not want a priest in the school should not be the administrator of any Catholic institution and probably has other problematic "hang-ups," as well; time to cut one's losses, in my opinion.

Many observers of Catholic education have noted that the success formula seems to be linkage and cooperation between home and school. And that is true, but one other house has to be entered into the equation: the rectory.

Scholars and Intellectual Explorers

(*Catholic Twin Circle*, August 30, 1992)

Not long ago, waiting on a supermarket line, my mother and two other women engaged in conversation about their children. When they learned that her only child was a priest, the Catholic lady expressed horror that "he could do something like that to you." The Jewish lady said: "How wonderful! A scholar!"

Ideally, priesthood and scholarship should go together for two reasons: First, we priests represent the God of all truth; second, we represent the Church that gave birth to the university system and, indeed, the largest educational system known to man.

In recent years, however, a subtle kind of anti-intellectualism has crept into the ranks of the clergy, leading some to adopt the mentality of one medievalist who commented that he would rather experience compunction than be able to define it. In reality, of course, there is not and never should be a dichotomy.

If the truth be told, the Church in the United States never produced great scholars. We were expending our efforts on building an ecclesial home for millions of immigrants. Scholarship wasn't highly valued and was often enough caricatured as "eggheadedness."

Another aspect of this problem, unique to seminaries of the 1940s and 1950s, was the generally unspoken but clearly conveyed notion that a young man could emerge from those hallowed corridors fit to minister to God's People for the rest of his life with the knowledge he had obtained over the previous eight years. And many priests actually believed that—with some being bold enough and foolish enough to boast that they never read a whole book from that day forward.

Fifty years ago, the priest was the modern equivalent of a Renaissance man, having a gentleman's acquaintance with a broad spectrum of knowledge; he was also, in most cases, the best educated man in his parish. Today, it is not uncommon to discover that the priest might be among the least educated in his parish.

Nothing less than a wholehearted commitment to lifelong learning will turn this situation around. Let me suggest but a few components of such a program for seminarians and even for priests, who are young at heart.

1. *Gain an exposure to the liberal arts and an understanding of them.*

Centuries ago, someone asked, "What docs Athens have to do with Jerusalem?" His point was that knowing Church doctrine was sufficient, without the necessity of secular data.

The Catholic Church has historically responded to that myopic view by asking her future priests to be firmly grounded in the intellectual and cultural tradition in which Christianity took root and blossomed. Was it sheer coincidence that caused the God-Man to come on the human stage at the very moment when civilization had reached a pinnacle worthy of the event?

The old pagan Cicero knew that the man who is ignorant of the past is doomed to repeat its mistakes. Much of the silliness we have witnessed in the Church for two decades must be laid at the door of blissful ignorance of where we have been as a Church. Much of the terrible liturgical music and bizarre forms of experimentation arose from a lack of connectedness to the cultural achievements of two millennia.

2. *Cultivate a love of knowledge and truth for its own sake.*

The truly wise person believes that it is better to know than to have never known. In other words, knowledge makes one a better and more fulfilled human being.

I am not referring to a grasp of useless trivia, but information that can be integrated into a system of knowledge, which in turn issues forth in wisdom—that virtue by which an individual is able to live life to the fullest. This kind of thirst for knowledge has one other practical effect: It helps cultivate a broad grasp of human reality.

A person can gain information (as distinct from knowledge) in three ways: schooling (which is simply time spent in schools): training (rote memorization of discrete moves designed to perform particular tasks); and education. The last is a process of humanization; it combines information, facts and experience, head and heart.

Although one need not look for a "payoff" in learning, there is always one; for the believer, it begins to affect relationships, starting with God.

Intellectual curiosity is that sense of awe and wonder at God's creation and our place within it; it is a desire to know the truth and the acknowledgment that all truth is one because it comes from the God of truth and ultimately leads back to Him. Jews have always realized this, which is why even those most observant of the Sabbath rest still permit the study of any sphere of human knowledge—because study, at base, is prayer.

3. *Develop the habit of reading for fun.*

No priest should be too busy for novels, plays, and poetry. They expand one's horizons; they enhance one's preaching, teaching, and counseling. It goes without saying that a priest must stay on top of the unfolding of the progress of theology, keeping up with the latest insights of the Magisterium and of theology.

I would be remiss if I did not include travel in this category. If one puts aside the usual American desire to import our culture wherever we go and if we allow ourselves to experience the life and history of another people, we come to see things in a new light.

The importance of travel was accented by none other than St. Augustine. He declared that "the man who has not traveled is like the man who has read only one book!"

For priests, the experience of travel is crucial to remind us that Catholic life is not limited to this continent or even this hemisphere. International travel rescues us (and eventually our people) from the worst forms of theological and ecclesiastical imperialism, whereby the Church in this country becomes the measure of ecclesial existence.

4. *Seek professional, ongoing, structured education.*

Every true professional is interested in plumbing the depths of his or her field of expertise. How impressed (and comforted) we are to hear that our family doctor will be off for a week to attend a seminar on the latest procedures dealing with preventative medicine.

Priests should be no different. We have to keep up with theological and pastoral journals; we should participate in worthwhile courses, which will make us better and more faithful stewards of the mysteries of God. Men who have the ability and the opportunity should not discount degree programs, which have the effect of keeping one on track in the intellectual life.

5. *Obtain an exposure to and an appreciation for the classics.*

It is inconceivable to me that for more than twenty years we have been ordaining men to the priesthood who don't know a word of Latin, Greek, or Hebrew. As a result, these men will have the fate of either disregarding (of necessity) the great patrimony of thought that is available only in those languages or being held hostage for life to translators (remember, an Italian proverb teaches that every translator is always a traitor!).

The Scriptures, the liturgy, the Church Fathers provide a bottomless well of life for those who can read them as they were written. Furthermore, learning a language introduces a person to a culture, a mindset, a particular frame of reference. The classical languages plug a student into the tradition of Rome, Athens, and Jerusalem, sources of both Christianity and Western civilization.

6. *Develop an appreciation for nuances.*

Nuances are those distinctions and fine points of human conversion. One should never forget that God is found in the details; if the details are missed, the entire picture cannot be comprehended, except in the most superficial manner. Having just the right word or turn of phrase is a real blessing and boon for communication, taking much work and practice. But it's worth the effort.

Someone may be tempted to say: "Who cares about minutiae? It's all just words, anyway." But words are powerful conveyors of truth. As long as you're living in a house, does it really matter whether you're called the "tenant" or the "owner"? You bet it does! Just as it made a world of difference whether Nicaea would say that Jesus was "homoioousios" (similar in nature to) or "homoousios" (of the same nature as) the Father. Sloppy thinking and imprecise expression are disastrous for humans in general and priests in particular. After all, we are commissioned to preach to the world about the Word made flesh.

To set as a goal of priestly life the movement toward becoming a scholar is not snobbery; it is simply the realization that our vocation is to drink deeply from the mystery of the God of all truth and to put others in touch with Him.

Serving as Visible Public Witnesses

(*Catholic Twin Circle*, September 6, 1992)

"Be a *witness*." . . . "I'm interested in the *witness* value of that action."

Isn't it a little bit ironic that, at the very moment when talk about "witnessing" has become so important to so many, the visible witness of priests in clerical garb should be on the wane? Isn't it a shame that the world has been missing out on the simple, eloquent, and silent sermons of priests in this country for the past twenty-five years?

Practically speaking, it's left the Catholic Church without a voice in the public forum, with no reminders of Christ in the secular city.

So often we hear priests respond, "But I'm not on duty!" And therein lies one of the most detrimental effects to the clergy—the creation of an on-duty, off-duty mentality in reference to priestly life and service. Does a married man take off his ring when he's away from home? If he does and his wife finds out, she'll surely have some questions.

Why would a priest want to be "incognito"? "I need to relax," comes one response. But a priest who cannot relax in a collar would seem to have some real identity problems, and perhaps a bit more. Others argue that the collar is used as a sign of privilege or power by many. Granted, that's an abuse, but as the old Latin proverb reminds us, abuse does not abrogate use. The priest should commit himself to the collar's use, both when convenient and inconvenient.

In a more positive vein, however, what is accomplished by wearing clerical garb?

First, it is a sign of availability. I think I have done more good for Christ and His Church on streets, planes, and trains than I have in rectories, classrooms, and pulpits.

The identifiable priest is an open invitation to all to come to Christ. People—even practicing Catholics—who might never go near the neighborhood priest with certain problems approach a priest on the street with complete confidence. It gives outsiders the opportunity to raise questions, to level challenges, or to get straight answers to thorny problems.

The stranger in the Roman collar is often seen as a potential friend, confidant, even father, but certainly an emissary of the

Church for some who may never encounter the Church in any other way.

Second, clerical dress ensures that a priest looks like someone who bears a dignity beyond his own, precisely as the personal presence of Christ today.

How often people remark that priests (like religious in general) are such bad dressers when they wear secular outfits. They frequently display poor taste and out-of-style clothing; and they are usually a bit more casual than everyone else in a crowd. The priest or seminarian who is attired according to his vocation is never embarrassed, nor does he embarrass the Church he represents. While it is true that we carry the Gospel in earthen vessels, that is no reason for us to do so without dignity or decorum. Nothing is too good to communicate God's Word in a way that is effective and proper.

Third, the collar is a twofold reminder: to the man himself, as well as to others.

The latter point is frequently made, and it is certainly valid. Clerical garb does let others know that this particular man is set apart or consecrated to the service of God and His people. All too often, however, the forgotten truth is that ecclesiastical dress is a potent reminder to the cleric himself.

Speaking for myself: I know that, because I always appear in public looking like a priest, I am always very conscious of acting like a priest, especially in terms of courtesy toward others in lines or in traffic. I also effectively remove myself from some of the more glaring temptations posed by contemporary secular society.

Fourth, being a visible public witness to Christ spares the priest from being a witness to materialism, consumerism, and fads. How much money is wasted by clergy who maintain dual wardrobes, and to what end? To be part of the shallow fashion show of modern life?

When people see a priest, their thoughts automatically turn to Christ and the Church. I cannot count the number of occasions when I have walked into a restaurant or store and, moments later, hear nearby folks talk about their parish or their youthful experiences of religion. God knows that could never happen with priests who function like "plainclothesmen" or secret service agents.

Fifth, wearing the collar in public allows people to see priests doing "normal" things—as priests and even as happy priests. When was the last time you saw a priest in a movie theater or at a play, or shopping in the mall? Did you begin to wonder if they did such things? How good it would be for young people to see priests doing these very normal things, thus projecting a natural and well-adjusted image of priestly life. Is it any surprise that so few youngsters are interested in the priesthood when the only sight they catch of a priest all week is at Sunday Mass? Too many priests have made themselves and the priesthood invisible—out of sight, out of mind.

What I've been saying could be summarized thus: If the priesthood is more than a job or the performance of a function, then the priest and the priesthood need to be seen together all the time. One of the most concrete ways that occurs is by the regular wearing of clerical garb.

In other words, the normal garb of a priest is the Roman collar. He should have a reason to dress otherwise (playing racquetball, for instance). Unfortunately, many of the brethren have turned that around, so that they think they need a reason to look like priests.

All people (priests included) need signs and symbols. One of the most precious signs for the Catholic community is the visible public witness of its clergy. Those who have this vocation should be proud of it, in a humble way, grateful that Christ has called them to be extensions of Himself to the world He loves and which He wishes to redeem.

The Priest and Prayer

(*Catholic Twin Circle*, September 13, 1992)

Our venerable and witty seminary spiritual director once said: "Gentlemen, I pray never to die in chapel. My body wouldn't be found for days!"

As unpleasant as it might be, one must admit that one of the surest practical results of the post-conciliar period in the United States was a dramatic cut in the quantity and quality of prayer offered by priests. While we know that for a secular priest to spend twelve hours a day before the Blessed Sacrament is an aberration, and just as assuredly can we assert that trying to finish the Divine Office by headlight before midnight is foolish, we must equally declare that we have gone to the opposite extreme, so much so that the laity all too frequently express pleasant surprise to find a priest engaged in private prayer.

What can be done about this regrettable lapse in clerical life? Nothing less than going back to the drawing board and returning to the time-tested and approved forms of priestly prayer.

1. *The Mass.* Few priests have ever gained reputations for being devout during the liturgy—in the "old days" or now. But the slovenly behavior and cavalier attitudes have reached epidemic proportions today, especially as clerical failings are now visible and audible in this regard. The Mass is not something to be rushed through in twelve minutes, nor a Broadway show; it is the pre-eminent prayer of Christ's Church. And that means it must be the first and best prayer of the priest.

As a seminarian, I came across a plaque in the sacristy of a small country church: "Priest of God, say this Mass as if it were your first Mass, your last Mass, your only Mass." Familiarity can and does breed contempt—even with the Eucharistic Sacrifice. A priest who is forewarned is forearmed.

2. *The Liturgy of the Hours.* At the risk of scandalizing the faithful, I am going to let a cat out of the clerical bag. The vast majority of priests no longer take seriously the promise they freely and solemnly made on the day of their diaconate (or subdiaconate for the elder brethren)—namely, to pray the Divine Office on behalf of the Church.

Now some priests will quickly defend themselves (or others) by saying they don't find the Liturgy of the Hours "meaningful." To which, several responses are appropriate. First, one's personal opinion doesn't matter here; the Church requires it, and we pledged to do it. Secondly, if one doesn't find the Sacred Scriptures a source of prayer, indeed the very psalms used by Christ Himself, then what else is there? Third, for the sake of argument, if a priest cannot "relate" to the prayer of the Breviary, with what has he replaced it? The sad truth in most instances is: nothing.

Aside from his unique role in offering the Eucharist, the priest is never more the intercessor of the community than when praying the Divine Office in the name of the whole Church and for her intentions. No wonder, then, that priests who "cheat" on the Office so often end up confused about their priestly identity.

3. *The Sacraments*. When the priest baptizes, distributes Holy Communion, absolves from sin, anoints the sick, he should be conscious of *praying*. Some will suggest that this should be self-evident. It should, but people in all professions run the risk of becoming functionaries, slot-fillers, cogs in a wheel—and the priesthood is not spared the pitfall. Nothing less than a conscious effort to make these into personal moments of grace and prayer will suffice. Prayer before the administration of a sacrament is also a valuable way of reminding oneself of the awesome task about to be accomplished through the earthen vessel who shares in the priesthood of Jesus Christ.

4. *The Sacrament of Penance*. Reception of the Sacrament of Penance is down among even the most faithful Catholics for a variety of reasons (lack of encouragement, loss of a sense of sin, etc.), but one important reason is that priests do not avail themselves of this important means of grace and Christian perfection.

Humbly submitting to the ministry of another man is a good and holy medicine for a priest. Even if serious sin is not present, it presents him with an opportunity to grow in sensitivity regarding his sacred duties and vocation: prayer, pastoral zeal, love for one's flock, growth in purity, etc. The priest who is a faithful penitent becomes a better confessor. Prayer for mercy for self makes one a better channel of mercy for others.

5. *The Rosary*. For many years as a seminarian and young priest, I had practically abandoned the rosary, because we had been trained to consider it as the prayer form of ignorant and even superstitious old ladies. Falling flat on my face on a few critical occasions convinced me that I needed the faith of some old ladies and especially the maternal assistance of the Woman who has a special love for her Son's brothers in the priesthood.

Years later and now the wiser, I find the rosary a beautiful way to pray with and to Mary about the mysteries of our Catholic Faith and to clear my head of a "conceptual" approach to reality (for at least fifteen minutes a day!), attempting to get to "the heart of the matter"—for which most men require a woman's help and direction. The seemingly interminable hours of driving have become the occasion for the rosary, thus redeeming the drudgery.

6. *Personal Devotions.* So often people whose parishes still have novenas and holy hours remark about the smugness or condescension of the clergy who rather grudgingly preside over them. I have often said that anyone who is too "grown up" to say with conviction the prayer to one's guardian angel is too "grown up" for the Christ Who called us to become "like little children." And that is likewise true about devotion to the saints, having "favorite prayers," and being awed and touched in the presence of the Blessed Sacrament exposed on the altar for adoration.

The Second Vatican Council was surely correct in declaring that the Sacred Liturgy is the "source and summit" of the Christian life, but that more than implies the necessity of other, lesser forms of prayer which lead toward and flow from the liturgy proper. Those forms are largely neglected by the laity today and almost universally so by priests, leading to liturgical sterility.

7. *Spiritual Reading.* We priests are human, and all too human at times. Which means that we need to be built up or edified by holy thoughts and heroic examples. Reading the lives of the saints and the reflections of the great spiritual masters aids us in deepening our relationship with Christ and our love for His Church, as well as our holy vocation. A wonderful side-effect is that it provides us with great material for preaching, teaching and counseling.

8. *Theological Study.* An old priest once bragged to me that he had never picked up a theology book since the day he left the seminary. His assistant expressed a doubt if he had ever read one while in the seminary, either!

Attending lectures, reading theological journals and books, following closely magisterial documents is not a luxury; it is essential for a priest who wants to be of maximum service to his people. Why do I include this under the rubric of prayer? Because seeking to gain a greater knowledge of divinity is an act of prayer, if properly embarked upon. Nothing is so desiccated as theology uprooted from the context of faith; nothing is so shallow and saccharine as spirituality divorced from solid theology.

With all the pressing obligations of a priest today, one is often tempted to "cut corners," especially in areas where deficiencies won't show. Foolishly, many priests have thought prayer could be treated that way; the result has been disastrous: loss of personal power and magnetism, confusion and disorientation. Ironically enough, the priest who has made such a decision ends up actually having less time for his pastoral ministry and even less to offer. A fitting if sad punishment for one who has forgotten the Master's words: "Without Me, you can do nothing."

The Priest as Preacher

(*Catholic Twin Circle*, October 11, 1992)

The French Modernist priest Alfred Loisy once quipped: "Can you imagine that in Paris each Sunday more than 10,000 sermons are preached? And the people still believe!" Setting aside the snideness of the remark, one would have to admit that Catholicism has never been known for the quality of its preachers, for any number of reasons. Not least of which, however, is that for us Catholics, the total worship experience does not rise and fall with the sermon; no matter how bad (or good!) the homily is, the best is yet to come in the celebration of the Liturgy of the Eucharist. That is both a humbling and consoling reflection, but not one which should allow us priests to become complacent or careless.

What is necessary for a good homily to emerge? One old-timer said it takes three ingredients: preparation, preparation, and preparation. I would reduce it to two components: preparation (remote) and preparation (proximate). No secret recipe is going to be given, just a few helpful hints from a short fifteen years of doing the job every day, both Sundays and weekdays.

If I might put in my oar at this point for weekday preaching, let me note the following. Although the Church does not *require* a homily at daily Mass, she strongly encourages it and even more so during Advent and Lent, but other reasons can also be brought forth. First, getting a brief homily (one to two minutes) ready for daily Mass is spiritually good for the priest. Second, it should be of benefit to the congregation. Third, it helps nervous preachers get more accustomed to public speaking in a usually smaller and less than threatening environment than on Sundays.

But back to preparation—remote. The priest needs to be a well-read man. The Scriptures and the Fathers of the Church should trip off his tongue. He should be in touch with current events, reading secular newspapers and magazines. He should be familiar with great literature, as well as music and drama. All these become sources for homilies, either in terms of a poignant story or to develop the priest's own sensitivity and sensibility. The good preacher is a keen observer of people and human affairs.

Now we look to laying the groundwork for a particular homily; it should go without saying that the most important preparation is prayer, preferably before the Blessed Sacrament. What follows is a series of procedures which I have found helpful, but there is no substitute for trial and error. I am no Fulton Sheen, but I have been reasonably successful in the liturgical presentation of the Word of God—and I think just about any priest can be, too.

1. *Where does this set of readings fit into the lectionary as a whole and in the liturgical season?* When I was first ordained, I readied myself to preach on one of the eucharistic passages in John 6; I labored mightily to include every aspect of eucharistic doctrine possible, only to discover later that this chapter would be continued for several more weeks, causing me to repeat myself after having "crunched in" too much, to begin with.

2. *Where does this passage fall in the Bible and within a particular book of the Bible?* In other words, what is the context? Is this selection from an historical book, the wisdom literature, the Sermon on the Mount? Or, does this passage reflect a consistent theme of the sacred author? Such determinations will influence the way a text is treated.

3. *KISS (Keep it simple, Sam!).* Simple is not simplistic or insulting to the intelligence of one's listeners; it is just the recognition that complicating reality does no good and obfuscates one's message. Believe it or not, all the bases needn't be covered in one homily. One clear thought offered every Sunday and holyday produces fifty-eight clear thoughts for the year; that is far better than expecting people to work their way through a maze, hoping they'll be able to sift out what the preacher considers "the main point."

4. *Have a regular schedule for sermon production.* This enables homily preparation to form an integral part of one's weekly ministry. For years, I have followed a schedule like this: Sunday evening—garner ideas and jot them down. Monday and Tuesday—draft the text. Wednesday—revise. Thursday and Friday--re-edit and type. Saturday—take ownership of the text. Aside from the daily celebration of the Liturgy of the Hours and Mass, I cannot think of an activity more worthwhile than homily preparation; after all, it is the one block of time that the average priest has to reach the majority of his people in one fell swoop.

5. *Make connections.* By that I mean, we shouldn't restrict ourselves to exegesis (textual interpretation) or to parenesis (encouragement to live the message of the Scriptures), as good and essential as they are. It is crucial to demonstrate linkages between the Scriptures of the day and Catholic doctrine and practices. Without constant reinforcement, even well educated Catholics tend to forget the

basics. While a Sunday homily is not an adult education class, and should not be handled like one, it does present a significant chance to educate or re-educate a congregation. One thing to be avoided at all costs, if the laity's comments mean anything, is the boring and deadly re-statement of what was just proclaimed in the Gospel; presumably the people heard the passage already and now await the ordained minister's application of it to their daily lives.

6. *Have a written text.* I cannot stress this enough. Some men cannot preach from a written text (Fulton Sheen said he could never work that way and actively discouraged others from doing so!). Whether or not the paper is used or even brought into the pulpit, the exercise of writing out the homily provides the structure necessary to deliver a coherent sermon. It allows me to guarantee a crisp, no-fat, no-frills homily in three to five minutes; that realization makes a congregation willing to listen. If a man is not comfortable with a complete text in front of him, I would counsel at least the opening and closing paragraphs since they are critical for grabbing attention and then clinching the main point in a memorable manner.

7. *Don't try to be a great orator.* No one is interested in a lot of shouting, whispering, or gesticulations. That may provide a show or entertainment, but it is not necessarily meaningful communication. If a priest has a well-thought-out homily, steps up to the microphone, speaks into it clearly without garbling his words, the people will be plenty satisfied.

Catholics consistently give their clergy bad marks for preaching, all too often with good reason. But the laity should also tell priests when they do well, if for no other reason than it lets the priest know when he has hit stride.

If the homilist makes homily preparation a top priority of his ministry, Loisy's sarcastic remark will no longer have the ring of truth about it: People will not believe in spite of our preaching, but because of it.

Bring Back the Black

(*National Catholic Register*, November 1, 1992)

A few weeks ago, as I walked into a local church-supplies store, the saleswoman pulled me to one side. "We've got something I think you might be interested in. All the young guys are ordering it," she confided. Flattered that she considered me to be a "young guy," I followed her to a back room, where I beheld a full Gothic black chasuble. She was sure I'd want to purchase one in time for All Souls Day. But I told her that, being older than "all the young guys," I already had a couple of black sets of vestments and had, in fact, been wearing them for All Souls Day (November 2) for nearly fifteen years. (I prefer purple for funerals, as is the usage almost everywhere but in the United States.)

Several things in the conversation amused me, however, and a few provided some real food for thought. First, what must "the older guys" in parishes be thinking when the newly ordained appear in freshly crafted black vestments, not unlike the ones they irreverently tossed onto the garbage heap or burned twenty years ago? It must be a trifle disconcerting to wake up and discover yourself a dinosaur in your own lifetime.

Second, I can envision any number of rectory battles around November 2 between "young guys" and "old guys' as the latter tell the former that "black is out" or "black is forbidden." To which the former will reply that black is still a liturgical color and is specifically noted in the *Ordo* for the day as one of the three acceptable options.

Third, at a more substantive level, I hope some of these conversations get around to discussing the need to allow people to grieve in an appropriate manner. White vestments for All Souls' Day just don't cut it, as a rule. If people aren't permitted to express their sorrow over a loss in the safe bosom of Mother Church, where can they do it? On a psychiatrist's couch?

Whatever the real or perceived faults of the old funeral rites, one thing they did do was give people permission to be human—no contrived "Alleluias," no decrees of canonization from the pulpit for a deceased relative the family knew could hope for Purgatory at best, plus a healthy acknowledgment of the pain of separation. If the liturgy is to perform its task for the whole People of God, it must take seriously the human condition; that was certainly one of the most important insights of post-conciliar reform. The way the Church in this country has handled death over the past two decades has been woefully inadequate, arguably because the signs and symbols were invented in a vacuum, often by those who had little experience in ministering to people burdened with grief. The Church needs to help mourners move from sadness to joy—which consists not in manufactured smiles but with calm and peace in the face of tragedy by taking into account death's gritty reality first.

White vestments and alleluias simply haven't achieved that; if the "older guys" can't go for the black, let them at least try purple. A more sober funeral liturgy could actually bring folks to a more profound experience of peace than we ever thought possible.

The Greek Orthodox Church and Celibacy

(*The Priest*, May 1993)

One of the issues I wanted to explore on a recent trip to Greece was the relationship between optional celibacy and priestly vocations. For the past two decades in the United States and in most of Western Europe, we have heard that: (a) Celibacy is the reason for the dearth in vocations; (b) Celibacy causes priests to fall into immorality; (c) Celibacy attracts an inordinately high percentage of men with a homosexual orientation.

Conversations with Greek Orthodox clergy and laity revealed many interesting facts. Despite centuries of optional celibacy for priests (bishops are chosen from the ranks of celibates), the priesthood has the same basic problems for Orthodoxy as for Roman Catholicism. None of what follows is intended as an attack on the Orthodox Church; on the contrary, it is intended to show that we're basically in the same boat.

(a) Even though priesthood candidates can marry (no marriage after ordination), the Greek Orthodox Church is suffering from a severe shortage of priests, with the average age of their clergy far exceeding ours in the United States.

(b) Many Greek Orthodox—clergy and laity alike—expressed their dismay over priests who were unfaithful to their wives, so much so that public scandals are all too common.

(c) Reports indicate that large numbers of married priests are homosexually involved as well. This would seem to destroy the apparent essential connection between celibacy and homosexuality.

I was not really surprised to learn these things; in fact, they confirmed data I already had from ecumenical work with Anglican and Protestant clergy for more than a decade. When people allege that one matter is the cause of all one's woes, I suspect either ill will or a simplistic mentality.

Celibacy has been with the Church for two millennia—an apostolic tradition—carefully documented as such in Jesuit Father Christian Cochini's new book from Ignatius Press, wherein he shows that while the Early Church had married priests, strong evidence demonstrates that these men lived as brother and sister with their wives after ordination.

In eight years of priestly formation, I was never exposed to a single course, class, retreat conference, homily, or day of recollection dealing with celibacy. Rather shocking, when you think about it!

We need a strong statement from our bishops that celibacy is here to stay and strong encouragement to assist young men in living celibate lives after the example of Jesus Christ—for the sake of the Kingdom.

Priest—A Year Later

(*National Catholic Register*, June 23, 1996)

"Distance creates perspective" is an old saw from art appreciation, and I have recently found it very useful in evaluating a controversial film. A little over a year ago, *Priest* made its grand entrance onto the big screen amid much hullabaloo. Since I did not want to increase any potential box-office receipts for it, I refrained from viewing it at the time; not having seen the work, I therefore refrained from commenting. Having seen the video, I now feel competent to offer some reflections. Some of the instantaneous reviews were uninformed and, hence, not helpful; others were so laudatory as to tax the limits of credulity.

Allow me to begin by making a few observations. First, I think the film was a bad idea, largely spawned by the anti-Catholicism of the producer and director, both of whom have an ax to grind against the Church. Second, while having certain merits, the film was seriously overdrawn and melodramatic—in short, bad drama. Third, anyone who thought the piece concerned homosexuality and the priesthood was grossly deceived; the issue was much broader and much more sinister. One final disclaimer: In no way do I wish any reader to assume that I am diminishing the significance of homosexual "acting out" in the priesthood; the teaching and discipline of the Church are clear—celibacy obviates any kind of genital activity (heterosexual or homosexual). However, that was not the main point of the film, just the hook on which to hang the real centerpiece. It is this latter matter which will occupy us now.

What good can be said about *Priest*? Whoever the technical advisors were, they knew what they were doing—in far more than a perfunctory way. For example, they had a profound understanding of signs and symbols, realizing how one's theology/ideology affects our use of symbols. At the outset, we meet Father Greg always in clerical garb (often even in cassock); at the same time, we encounter a young priest who, although "with it," is an articulate spokesman for the Church's positions and for the more basic argument on behalf of the existence of objective truth. As he becomes derailed, emotionally and spiritually, his daily dress and liturgical style begin to mirror his own internal confusion. Priestly identity, liturgy, and doctrine all form a unity for Father Greg. And likewise for his middle-aged, radical pastor. Father Matt never wears a collar, is slovenly and casual at the altar, and preaches a warmed-over sixties liberalism; this makes sense, of course, because we already know that he is living in concubinage with the rectory housekeeper. In other words, his external comportment is also a mirror image of his internal dispositions.

Throughout the film, the director and producer would lead us to suppose that proponents of traditional Catholic teaching and mores are benighted, cruel, intolerant, and inhuman; their foil characters, on the other hand, are made to appear warm, loving, compassionate and human to the point of being God-like. But the fail-proof categories failed with me. In short order, I found myself incredibly drawn to Father Greg and equally repulsed by Father Matt; indeed, even after his first sexual tryst, Father Greg is clearly remorseful (I guess the film-makers would say "guilt-ridden") and, most remarkably, rejects Matt's attempts to soft-soap his actions. Hence, even in his own regard, he refuses to call sin virtue; which is to say that he asks no more of his flock than he expects of himself—an honest and essentially good man, albeit a sinner.

The issue behind the issue, in my estimation, is not clerical sexuality but dissent from Church teaching. Poor Greg gets dragged into that vortex, little by little. Although on several occasions he informs Matt that he will not allow himself to become a pawn in his pastor's political chess game with the Church, it does eventually happen. And we're supposed to be delighted when it occurs. I was not; I was saddened. In truth, Father Greg loses his charm when he loses his verve and his capacity to see clearly and objectively.

For all the film's inadequacies, the one point (probably made unwittingly) is that priestly life in general and celibacy in particular cannot be lived without support. When Father Greg has no one to turn to for encouragement in being a loyal son of the Church and faithful expositor of her doctrine; when he discovers his pastor is living in sin; when the parishioners themselves demonstrate no interest in his full-throated proclamation of the Gospel, the young priest escapes into illicit sexual experiences. Truth be told, he does not really seek sex for its own sake; in fact, he detests it—and the man who provides it for him. He personifies the message of the God Who addresses us in Francis Thompson's "Hound of Heaven": "All things betray thee, who betrayest Me."

Whether or not the film-makers would agree, I maintain that *Priest* teaches us that priestly life and ministry demand a support system, comprised of bishops, priests, and lay faithful. And that support is in short order today. Therefore, the only surprise ought to be that there are not many more Father Gregs in our midst.

Catholic Higher Education as a Source of Priestly and Religious Vocations

(*The Turnabout*, April 1998)

Historically and to the present moment, one of the impressive facts about Catholic elementary and secondary schools is that they are "seminaries," that is, "seed-beds" for priestly and religious vocations. Although, unfortunately, less than half the Catholic population of our nation currently has the advantage of a Catholic school experience, the vast majority of ordinations continue to come from that one single source.

And if that is the case for Catholic schooling at the lower levels, ought we not expect the same at the higher levels? Regrettably, I often find myself sharing the opinion of the late, great Archbishop Fulton J. Sheen who counseled parents, by all means, to use Catholic elementary and secondary schools but to avoid at all costs Catholic colleges and universities for their children, that is, if they wanted the life of faith to grow or even merely to survive.

However, Catholicism is, by its very nature, interpersonal and communal, which means that doing advanced studies in a Catholic environment should be the logical conclusion to the learning experience of a Catholic. The syllogism could run something like this: If it is true that the Church expects all her sons and daughters to avail themselves of a Catholic education; and if it is true that one of the prime effects of a Catholic education is the promotion of priestly and religious vocations; then, Catholic colleges and universities should be known for the quantity and quality of their alumni who choose to serve God and His People as clergy and religious.[1]

As a seventeen-year-old college seminarian entering Seton Hall University in 1968, I was incredibly impressed by the number of priests on the faculty (interestingly, Seton Hall still has the largest

---

[1] I believe that, ideally, a high school graduate who has had the blessing of a Catholic-school education and perceives a priestly or religious vocation should launch out into a program of formation immediately. Not infrequently, however, calls are not clearly heard or are even discouraged in some quarters. Attendance at a Catholic college, then, takes on a significance that would have attached to a Catholic high school in previous generations.

percentage of any diocesan presbyterate assigned to a single apostolate), but especially by the fact that nearly every department of the School of Arts and Sciences was chaired by a priest. Clearly, this put the lie to the theory that priests had "tunnel vision" or that the Church was anti-intellectual or an opponent of science and progress. Aside from that kind of persuasive empirical data, what else does a Catholic college have to offer in terms of fostering and nurturing vocations?

Catholic colleges should:

1. *Offer good liturgy.* It was not an accident that Isaiah received his call to be God's prophet in the context of a splendid and impressive Temple liturgy. The Church is never more the Church than when she celebrates the Eucharistic Sacrifice of Christ, for it is there and then that the Lord performs His most powerful work. Surely, a full and wholesome liturgical life for the college community will enable young people to fine-tune their hearing to the call of the Master. When the Church's rites are done with dignity and decorum, they become automatic (shall we say *ex opere operato?*) invitations to "do this in memory of Me."

2. *Provide contact with clergy and religious.* Seeing priests and religious on a regular basis in the daily affairs of life is an important element in making the choice of such a vocation seem normal and natural. If a Catholic college has seminarians, novices, and others in formation on campus, as well, that too adds to the "normalcy quotient" of the entire process. The availability of clergy and religious, their visible presence, their commitment to Christ and the Church, and their joyful living of the consecrated state—all constitute touchstones for vocational awareness.

3. *Develop the philosophical and theological knowledge of students.* As children, we learned that we need to know, love, and serve God. But notice: Knowledge precedes love and service. Beyond that, when St. Paul spoke of the transformation of the human person into a Christian, he did not say that one must adopt the heart of Christ; no, we are to put on the *mind* of Christ, he said (cf. 1 Cor 2:16; Rom 12:2). Most people fail to do the good they could and to avoid the evil they should, not because they are unloving or selfish but because they are ignorant, in the root sense of that word. They just don't know what they ought to know—about themselves, about the world, about God, and about how all those realities interface—or should. Only when that kind of information has been communicated and assimilated can one begin to expect intelligent life choices to be made, let alone those calling for heroism and virtue.

4. *Afford an integrated understanding of human learning.* The greatest disaster of post-Enlightenment education has been the "compartmentalization" of the various disciplines and the sundering of faith from the fabric of human existence. It is no surprise that Pope John Paul II has repeatedly called for a re-integration of faith and life or faith and culture. Living life in dichotomous ways is unhealthy, indeed, abnormal. The modern university was born back in the Age of Faith, *ex corde Ecclesiae* (from the heart of the Church). In truth, the very word "university" means "turned toward the one," that is, that each and every science is part of the total truth which man must always seek, that Truth Who is God Himself. Young people who have been exposed to that kind of synthesis will never again be willing to live a schizophrenic existence—and will want to ensure that no one else does, either.

5. *Make available possibilities for apostolic work.* We know that a child has begun the maturation process the first time he says, "Mommy, can I help you with the dishes?" A college education can never be simply a matter of taking or receiving; it necessarily involves giving. Tutoring youngsters in local Catholic schools; serving as moderators of parish youth groups; working in a soup kitchen; doing door-to-door evangelization or street-preaching; these are ways of exposing students to the many avenues of pastoral outreach which call for their time, treasure and talent. The Moonies and the Mormons have no hesitancy whatsoever in challenging their youth to serve—and the response is truly impressive. We neglect to ask for even minimal effort and then claim to be shocked when far more dramatic calls go unheeded.

6. *Be places where young people witness to their faith and are witnessed to.* The Second Vatican Council in the Decree on the Apostolate of the Laity stressed the centrality of an apostolate of peers. The most effective witness to an inebriated student is not a priest residing on a dorm corridor (although there is certainly a place for such an intervention); it is the reaction and testimony of a fellow student who, lovingly but firmly, gives fraternal correction. Nor can the often silent but powerful witness of committed faculty be gainsaid. In truth, the entire academic community must serve as a united voice of Christian witness to the world, to academia, and to one another. Teaching young people about the importance of this aspect of a Christian vocation and about being comfortable with it is an essential component in developing any vocation—lay, religious or clerical.

7. *Extend opportunities for spiritual direction, retreats, days of recollection, and the Sacrament of Penance.* When such activities are woven

into the fabric of college life and are seen as much a part of the tapestry as basketball games and exams, we are well on our way toward creating a climate of openness to spiritual realities. Spirituality is like candy; when we have some, we generally want more. For some, at least, that "more" will consist in responding to a priestly or religious vocation.

The reader will notice that very little in this "laundry list" is earth-shattering. In fact, nothing suggested here should require the addition of a single staff member or the establishment of a single new committee or the expenditure of a single dollar. Oddly, it's all so simple, so obvious, so transparent that it appears so complicated to most. However, all that is needed is a comprehension of a Catholic understanding of education, coupled with a love for the Church, and a program of action immediately begins to form.

A trite hymn of the sixties shouted out that "they will know we are Christians by our love." It would be no exaggeration to say that "they will know we are a Catholic college by our vocations!"

Can Anyone Say "Forever"?

(*Lay Witness*, March 2001)

The title of our essay was the name of a book that was very popular in the late nineteen-sixties and -seventies, in a moment of civil and ecclesiastical history when many people would have presumed a negative answer to that very probing and incredibly critical question. In truth, if one went by simple empirical data, the question probably would have been perceived as rhetorical. Marriages were breaking up at an unprecedented rate, in a country where not fifteen years earlier divorce among friends or family was discussed in hushed and embarrassed tones. Having graduated from high school in 1968, I discovered that within two years two of the four priests and seven of the eleven nuns who had taught me had turned in their collars and veils. Shocking by any standard, but comprehensible nonetheless when one places the phenomenon within the overall milieu of confusion and disorientation. The Church and her members, after all, may not be "of" the world, but they surely live "in" the world and cannot help but be affected (and infected) with the sin of the world.

In this issue of *Lay Witness* dedicated to the sacred priesthood, I have been asked to reflect on priestly defections. Sad but necessary. However, let's situate our concern in a slightly broader context.

In the ancient world, slaves were branded; they were literally "marked men." The brand, of course, was simultaneously cause for shame and resentment. In the Bible, we are told that Cain was "marked" after he murdered his brother; this "sign of Cain" was somewhat ambivalent, in that it set him off from the rest of humanity for his crime but likewise served as a divine protection of him. Far more appealing to think about is the *sphragis* of soldiers in antiquity; this "sign" or "seal" told all that a soldier belonged to a particular military unit and thus was a symbol of great pride and belonging. Now, this could also get a soldier into difficulty if, for example, he got captured by the enemy, for there was no way for him to deny his identity! Like most symbols, then, it cut in both directions.

The immemorial theological tradition of the Church speaks of three sacraments (Baptism, Confirmation, Holy Order) as conferring a seal, character or indelible mark. These sacraments set a person into a relationship with Almighty God which is irrevocable. And this should come as no surprise, for St. Paul teaches us that God's gifts and His call are "irrevocable" (Rom 11:29). Hence, God has marked us as His own in a most dramatic way, so that we could say that this identification is a kind of divine or spiritual genetic code which is impressed on our souls when we receive one of these three sacraments, highlighting both our origin in God and our destiny with Him.

Baptism inserts one into the Lord's paschal mystery; Confirmation seals that process; Holy Order configures a man to Christ as priest, prophet, and king. And so, it is quite correct to say, "Once a Catholic, always a Catholic." No one can ever "revoke" someone's baptismal certificate! The Church can excommunicate a person for various reasons, but that does not alter his absolute and permanent relationship with the Lord which occurred through the power of God's call, grace, and word. In the same way, once a man has been ordained a priest, he can never again really be a layman. We believe that he has been "ontologically" changed, that is, changed at the very core of his being, just as in Baptism and Confirmation. The priest, therefore, is not simply a "marked man" because he wears a Roman collar; he is "marked" in a profoundly spiritual way within the depths of his person. To be sure, the Church can remove a man's priestly faculties for the good of the Church, so that he is inhibited from serving in the name of Christ and His Church; or, a man can ask the Church to release him from his priestly obligations either for his own welfare or for that of the Church. However, "once a priest, always a priest," which is why such a man can always fulfill priestly tasks if the salvation of souls demands it.

As we concentrate specifically on the priesthood, one might be tempted to ask, "What's the big deal here, anyway? Why is it so important that a man say 'yes' and stick by it? Why shouldn't the Church just be grateful for the time a man has given or is willing to give to the service of God's People and then let him go on his merry way when he wishes?" These are not inane questions; nor are they being asked for the first time in history. Over the centuries, the Church has come to her absolute position on the matter for three basic reasons: Because of Christ; because of the needs of the Church; because of the good of the man himself.

The example of Christ comes first. The Epistle to the Hebrews repeatedly makes the point that Jesus is a priest as no other man is or ever will be. One of the unique dimensions of His priesthood is that it is "forever" (e.g., 5:6; 6:20; 7:3). Jesus' priesthood links

Him definitively in His mediatorial role both to the Father and to the Church. His work of intercession is eternal, which is why His priesthood must be the same. Not with exaggeration does St. Paul remind us that Christ was never alternately "yes" and "no" to His heavenly Father; he asserts unequivocally that He was never anything but "yes" (2 Cor 1:18f). It is good to note that Paul does not even suggest that the Lord always "*said* yes" to the Father—no, He always "*was* yes." In other words, His entire Person constituted a unified response of His being to the Will of His Father.

Second, the needs of the Church. Christ's priesthood in which a man shares through sacramental ordination is not a job or a function or a personal "hobby horse" for one's own self-aggrandizement or amusement; it is a gift given by the Lord of the Church for the good of the Church. And because it is a gift, as Pope John Paul II never seems to tire of saying, it should not and cannot be returned to the Giver without disastrous consequences ensuing for all concerned. The Church can never cease to be the Bride of Christ, nor He her Bridegroom. Similarly, her ministers who stand *in persona Christi* must be as faithful as the One they represent. Otherwise, the mission and effectiveness of the Church are compromised at her foundation. God's People need and deserve to have unfailing, consistent witnesses to the truth and to the transforming power of God's grace to effect within us what appears (and truly is) humanly impossible for us to commit to and achieve on our own "steam." But therein lies the beauty of the priesthood: No man on his own can generate souls for the Father; no man on his own can change bread and wine into the Lord's Body and Blood; no man on his own can forgive another's sins. And yes, no man on his own can say and be a perpetual "yes" to the Lord. This is all the work of grace, bringing to mind day in and day out—for the priest and the whole community of Christ's faithful—that "without Me, you can do nothing" (Jn 15:5); that "when I am weak, then I am strong" (2 Cor 12:10); that "I can do all things in Him Who strengthens me" (Ph 4:13). The total and unswerving commitment of the priest as *alter Christus* gives to the lay faithful the powerful example of saying and meaning "yes" but also of how to rely on God's grace to do the seemingly impossible. In this way, young people learn how to say "no" to fornication; married couples learn how to say "yes" to their vows and to life; the elderly learn how to say "yes" to loneliness and misunderstanding. And all will do this for the sake of Christ and through the unflagging impetus of His grace and, due in no small measure, to the "yes" of their priests.

Third, the priest himself "needs" to make a definitive commitment. God has made us in His own image. Among other things, that means that we reveal ourselves through our work and even through our attitudes. If we are to be true mirror images of the God Who is Fidelity Itself—faithful to us even when we are unfaithful to Him—then we need to reflect His never-failing and constant standing by our side. We humans must come to see that actions have consequences, and that some actions even have eternal consequences—like Christ's love for His Church and certain decisions we make under the impulse of His grace and for the good of His holy Church. Remaining faithful to commitments, then, is not just a matter of grit and determination; it is inextricably bound up with our human dignity. To be really and fully human demands the willingness and the ability to say "yes" forever; anything less falls far short of who we are and who God wants us to be as persons made in His image and likeness.

But what about our fathers in God who do give up on their ordination commitment? What can we say about them? What have we learned about them over the past three decades? Perhaps the first and most important thing to say is that very few men left the priesthood "in order to marry," contrary to the conventional wisdom. Anecdotal and hard-core data tell us that most priests left the active ministry for various other reasons; once *having* left, a not illogical choice was to marry.

What are the most commonly cited reasons for priestly departures? The first and what should be the most obvious is that all too many never had genuine priestly vocations. In "the old days," a frequent joke made its way around the clerical world: "Mrs. Smith had the vocation, but her son became the priest!" Beneath the biting sarcasm of the quip lay an unfortunate fact of life for many former priests, who felt pressured into the priesthood by good and holy but misguided persons. Other priests have indicated certain "lacks" within themselves or within the Catholic community which contributed to their decision to seek other venues to work out their salvation. Not a few say they experienced a lack of priestly identity due to changes in expectations radically different from those to which they committed themselves on the day of their ordination, in the wake of post-conciliar confusion. Some bewail the lack of priestly fraternity, while yet others contend that they experienced a lack of support for their vocation from either their bishop or people and, all too often, felt as though they were caught in a vise between those two. While no one can gainsay a man's perceived rationale for a move like this, my own experience with such men leads me to conclude that most of them departed due to problems related to faith and/or personality. This dimension of the matter may help explain the inordinately high divorce rate for men who marry after leaving the active ministry as they often learn—painfully—that the difficulty was neither the Church nor the priesthood but something deep within themselves. This should also help us understand the equally high percentage of such men who have sought to be re-admitted to priestly ministry, sometimes after years and at times decades of absence.

And so, the Church's insistence on a permanent commitment to priesthood is not simply yet another example of what some may deem the unrealistic or even inhuman demands of an over-bearing mother. No, the law exists for the good of the community and the priest at one and the same time. Fidelity does not come easily to anyone, even the Son of God. The Scriptures inform us that Jesus was fiercely tempted at least twice during His earthly sojourn: At the outset of His public ministry in the desert and at its end during His agony in the Garden. If the High Priest Himself was so tempted, those who share in His priesthood should not presume exemption from the same fate. However, if the community of the Church expects a resounding "forever" from her priests—and rightly so—then the Church also has an obligation toward her priests: To make them know they are loved and needed, and to support them with daily prayer. In this way, we behold shepherd and flock committed to one another for the sake of Christ, supporting and loving each other to ensure that shepherd and flock alike arrive at the harbor of salvation.

Review

William E. Phipps, *Clerical Celibacy: The Heritage*
New York: Continuum, 2004. 272 pp., $27.95
(*Antiphon*, volume 9, no. 2, 2005)

In case you're in a hurry and don't have time to read an extended review, let me give you a short-hand reaction: This is a 272-page screed, devoid of scholarship, riddled with horrific sentence structure, and abounding in typographical errors and purple prose.

With that said, where does one really begin with a work like this?

First of all, why should a liturgical journal be interested in a book on celibacy, except for generic theological reasons? I would submit that, scratching below the surface of attacks on priestly celibacy, one usually finds them a rejection of the sacramentality of the priesthood and traditional Christian morality—both intimately associated with notions of mediation and a theology of the body, ultimately underlying Christian reflection on signs and symbols and their incorporation into the life of the Church.

Second, this work is an ecumenical set-back. The author proudly proclaims his Protestant commitment and asserts that this ideally suits him to "bring a distinctive and moderate view to our understandings of the heritage of clerical celibacy." Jesus probably had sex. He may have been married to Mary Magdalene. He also may have been bi-sexual. This will remind astute readers of much of the Gnostic literature from the early Christian centuries, as well as its reincarnation in *The Da Vinci Code*. Priestly celibacy has been the battering ram to reinforce the Church's misogyny. Celibacy is used by the Church simply to exert total and absolute control over the lives of her priests. At certain points, one has the eery feeling of being transported back to the lurid tales of Maria Monk in the Know-Nothing era; amazingly, Phipps even quotes that genre unabashedly. This is distinctive? Moderate? An ecumenical contribution?

Now, I must say I am indeed interested in an ecumenical conversation on celibacy, so interested that I edited a book on the topic (*Priestly Celibacy: Its Scriptural, Historical, Spiritual, and Psychological Roots,* Newman House Press, 2002), choosing six (of eight) contributors from Protestantism or converts therefrom. One of our writers was actually a minister's wife (hardly anyone ever seems concerned about the perspective of the wives!). To a person, each would dispute Phipps' presentation of the scriptural, historical, spiritual, and psychological data. Even with the old canard about fixing the vocations shortage by expanding the pool to the married (by the way, Phipps thinks we should be ordaining women, too), resort to ecumenical statistics puts the lie to that, as well, for Anglicans, Eastern Orthodox, and just about every mainstream denomination is experiencing serious clergy personnel problems.

Third, Phipps relies on bad sources. His index reads like a who's who of ex-priests, left-wing theologians, and professional anti-Catholics—sometimes all rolled up into one: Jason Berry, Eugene Bianchi, Joseph Blenkinsopp, John Boswell, Peter Brown, John Calvin, James Carroll, John Cornwell, Donald Cozzens, Dominic Crossan, Charles Davis, Peter DeRosa, Paul Dinter, Richard Ginter, Peter Hebblethwaite, Ignatius Hunt, Eugene Kennedy, Alfred Kinsey, Hans Kung, Martin Luther, Richard McBrien, John Meier, Friedrich Nietzsche, Anthony Padovano. And the beat goes on through the rest of the alphabet. Nary a voice from the alternative point of view is heard, except to be pilloried. Phipps' sociological guru is Dean Hoge from The Catholic University of America, noted for pushing for a desacralized priesthood and a democratized Church. For some strange reason, he doesn't cite Andrew Greeley very much, perhaps because Greeley's rather objective research on the topic doesn't generally bolster Phipps' case.

Two of his pet *periti* are the former Jesuit Terrance Sweeney and the former Benedictine Richard Sipe, both of whom I had occasion to debate on *The Larry King Show* some years ago. Sweeney is an ideologue, pure and simple, while Sipe has no hesitation about proving true the adage that there are "lies, damned lies, and statistics," in addition to re-hashing material from work to work, *ad nauseam*.

Fourth, the author's grasp of history is pitiable. Either he is a naif or malicious. A cursory glance at his "timeline for tracing celibacy in Christianity" offers a bird's eye view of the problem. We are informed that in 400 B.C., the "Hebrew Scriptures affirm [the] sanctity of marriage." What is that supposed to mean, and which Scriptures? In 100 B.C., "Greco-Roman sexual asceticism [became] influential for centuries to come." Although I have a bachelor's degree in Classical Languages, this latter piece of information really added an element to my education that had been quite lacking, having been treated as a high school boy and college seminarian to excerpts from the poetry of Catullus and to the exploits of Nero, Caligula, and the rest of the gang. Phipps refers to Gospel accounts of Mary's virginity as "stories" and holds that the Pastoral Epistles "stipulate" that Christian ministers be married, which must have presented quite a problem for St. Paul. We learn that the Council of Elvira in 310 "imposed" celibacy on the Spanish clergy, apparently not taking the decree at its word, namely, that this was merely a reflection of what had been received from the apostles. Similarly, the Council of Trullo in 692 is touted as finally opening up priesthood to the married, which it did, albeit by falsifying decrees of earlier councils!

Looking at more recent history with Phipps, we are told that 1965 was the "beginning of [the] precipitous decline in priests worldwide." Worldwide? Asia, Africa, and Latin America would consider that an interesting revelation. In 1969, we are told, Pope Paul VI "begins accepting priests who are converted Protestant clergy." In point of fact, Pope Pius XII had been doing that a quarter of a century earlier. And, finally, in 2003 "Pope John Paul II declares [the] celibacy rule non-negotiable." As though every Pope and synod of the twentieth century (including Vatican II) had not done the same. At another point in the book, he actually admits that the Fathers of Vatican II did support clerical celibacy, with these words: "More than 99 percent of the 2,254 sheep-like council bishops followed their papal shepherd and voted for the status quo on celibacy." How's that for objective reporting?

Fifth, errors and inconsistencies dot the landscape of the text. On page 189, he informs us that John Paul II displays "his belief in the inherent evil of sexual desire." The same John Paul who has given the world a "theology of the body"? Phipps can't seem to make up his mind whether or not he likes homosexuals in the priesthood: Celibacy, obviously, attracts them; the Church persecutes them. Sloppy research results, for example, in his mistaking the Code of Canon Law for the *Catechism of the Catholic Church* at footnote 60 of the concluding chapter (there is no canon 2384!). Interestingly, Phipps says that he has "provided voluminous notes so that scholars and the public can judge for themselves the truth of what is presented." Indeed.

The Church can always benefit from an intelligent and honest discussion of the charism of celibacy. For instance, is there anything in the priesthood of the New Covenant that makes celibacy particularly apt? Is there a connection between the sacrifice of the altar and the sacrifice in the personal life of the human instrument? What is the inter-relationship between the Priesthood of Jesus Christ and a man's configuration to Him in the Sacrament of Order? Does the sign of celibacy interface with the signs and symbols of the Eucharist, especially the marital imagery? Does perpetual celibacy have anything to say about the once-for-all and eternal nature of the Eucharistic Sacrifice? These are important and worthwhile questions, which are worth raising perennially, for each age—building on the insights of those who have gone before us—can make its own contribution to the ever-deepening pool of theological reflection.

Sometimes one hears that an author "has generated more heat than light." Not even that can be said about Dr. Phipps' work. I've been reading negative literature on clerical celibacy since I entered the seminary in 1968; I found everything recycled here. Maybe that's the distinctive contribution: Read this, and you won't have to read anything else that has gone before, that is, a compendium of negativity, poor scholarship, and caricature.

HOMILIES

The priest is not a priest for himself; he does not give himself absolution; he does not administer the sacraments to himself. He is not for himself; he is for you. After God, the priest is everything. Leave a parish twenty years without priests, they will worship beasts. . . .

When people wish to destroy religion, they begin by attacking the priest, because where there is no longer any priest there is no sacrifice, and where there is no longer any sacrifice there is no religion.

— St. John Vianney

Mass of Thanksgiving

Solemnity of the Most Holy Trinity
St. Joseph's Church, Toms River, New Jersey, June 5, 1977

All the great mysteries of the Christian Faith exist to tell us about God but also about ourselves. Today we celebrate the Solemnity of the Most Holy Trinity. You know from your catechism days that the Trinity expresses our belief that our God exists as three Persons, equal and one. We believe that three distinct Persons (Father, Son, and Holy Spirit) are so totally one that a Community is formed. However, in spite of this strong unity, individual Persons are still able to be recognized; one Person does not overpower the Others, because each Person is bound to the Others by bonds of love.

If this is the case, the Trinity should be the model for all human relations, especially for people trying to live in a Christian community, which is the parish for us. Following the example of the Trinity, no one person should dominate, but all should give of themselves completely and without reserve, in love. The question to ask today is: What is my particular gift? How have I given it over for the spread of the Gospel and the good of the Christian community? Better yet, have I given it over at all?

Let's get down to the specific situation of St. Joseph's, Toms River. Is this a Christian community, or is it just a "Mass factory"? Let me respond from personal experience. I worked here my first three years in the seminary, from 1968 to 1971. I was seventeen years old when I started out, and I was amazed at the bigness. In my time, we had twenty-one weekend Masses at five locations, over one thousand children in the grade school and about seven hundred and fifty in the high school, twenty-two Sisters and four full-time priests, plus weekend help. When I quote those statistics in Boise, Idaho, they get nervous. At first, so did I.

But as time went on, I discovered that bigness need not be a stumbling block to forming community; it may be harder at times, but it is not impossible and it even has some advantages. What do you have here at St. Joseph's that could help you grow into a model parish community?

First of all, you have two excellent parish schools. I am a product of St. Joe's High School, and I know that much of what I am today is a direct result of the education I received there. Some people say that the Catholic school is a thing of the past; my opinion is that the Catholic school was never more needed. Some people say a parish school is a drain on parish finances—nothing could be further from the truth; it is the best investment a parish could make, because it is an investment in our future as a strong religious community. Capitalize on those two assets: Support them financially whether or not you have children, and support them by enrolling any children you do have.

Second, you have a broad cross-section of clergy in terms of background, training, age, and theological orientation; there should be a priest on the staff to appeal to nearly every type of parishioner. You have the choice of a priest which you would never have in a small parish.

Third, you have a wide variety of parish organizations, in fact, just about every Catholic organization possible—from the spiritual to the athletic to the social. Become involved in one that interests you and, through it, give yourself and your particular talents to the parish community.

My years at St. Joseph's as a high school student and as a minister count among the very happiest in my life, because I saw people of great faith, energy, and love working toward the goal of making the Kingdom of God a reality in this corner of the world. The biggest trap a parish like St. Joe's holds out to anyone is the temptation not to get involved, because I assume that so many others could do the job and do it better than I; never give into that temptation: Act as though you were the only one who can do the job, because you might very well be! Never get discouraged, regardless of the obstacles you encounter. Never be mastered by pessimism or negativity; they are unworthy sentiments for a Christian. Realize that you are working for a noble purpose—not for an impersonal institution, not for an individual priest, not for a building, not for your own glory; no, you are working to show others that you love after the example of Jesus Himself and want to share that love with them.

On this Trinity Sunday 1977, then, the Community of Persons of Father, Son, and Holy Spirit is inviting you to share your life and your love with the parish community of St Joseph's. The mystery of the Trinity tells us that love given is not love lost but love multiplied three-fold.

May you give of yourselves so generously that you may receive just such a reward.

Fifth Anniversary of Ordination

Friday of the Seventh Week of Easter
Church of St. Michael, Cranford, New Jersey, 1982

Believe it or not, the readings you just heard were not specially chosen for this occasion; they are the regular readings assigned to this day of the year. The Gospel is so especially apropos because it talks about my patron saint, that I thought I should mention that. This is also a Gospel passage used for the feast of a pope; maybe God is saying something!

Seriously, though, this is one of the most touching passages in all of Sacred Scripture, as it shows the tenderness and love of both Jesus and Peter. In this scene after the Resurrection, our Lord put to Peter His famous triple question about his love. To an uncritical listener, it must simply appear to be a charming exchange between good friends, but Peter knew better. That is why the Evangelist tells us that Peter was hurt by the question; it was a painful reminder of how he had handled a three-fold question just days earlier. Peter remembered, as we all remember, that he had denied even knowing our Lord three times.

It seems to me that it was not only the historical event that had hurt him but something else, as well. We are told that the Gospel of John went through many editings; it is not at all unlikely that some version of it may well have been completed before Peter's death and may well have been read at liturgies presided over by Peter. Imagine the hurt and the embarrassment in those circumstances. Peter paid dearly for his denials of Christ, as we all do. However, Jesus does not just dredge up the past; He gives everyone the opportunity to undo those denials by affirmations of love. And that is the beauty of this reading, as we see divine love in action, offering a weak sinner another chance. The result is impressive from any angle; not only does Peter make a beautiful profession of faith and love at the moment, he follows it up with a life lived for the Lord at every moment—even to the moment of death.

The Risen Christ poses the same question to Peter's successors, the bishops of Rome; to this servant of his who happily celebrates his fifth anniversary in the service of Christ's Church; in fact, to all believers in varying degrees. "Do you love me?" If we give Peter's answer, we then receive the same commission as he: Feed my lambs. Feed my sheep. Follow me." We follow Him by making the Gospel the root and foundation of our lives. We feed His sheep by first being fed ourselves by the Good Shepherd Himself through His Eucharistic Sacrifice, and then by sharing the Word of Life received by us through the Church.

The New Testament tells us that many times when people were confused or in doubt Peter stepped forward to allay their fears and to confirm their faith. The best guarantee that we have in the Church today that we are indeed heeding the Lord's invitation to follow Him completely and unreservedly is by our willingness to listen to Peter's successor, John Paul II. His messages, like that of Christ Himself, will not always be easy; it may require many sacrifices, many little deaths to self for the sake of Christ. All these little deaths, however, will be a perfect preparation for a final death which will, like Peter's, glorify God and lead not to a final death at all, but to eternal life.

May the Lord who has begun this good work in you and in me bring it to completion. Amen.

Mass of Christian Burial of My Father

Church of Our Lady of Sorrows, Kearny, New Jersey, August 13, 1983

Easter of 1979 saw me chaperoning ten high school students to Rome. It was an exciting week for all of us. I had had the privilege of serving as a Communion-priest for John Paul II's first Easter Vigil Mass as Pope. The students had had the opportunity to speak to the Holy Father personally and to have their pictures taken with him. We had all been taken up by the beauty of the Eternal City and its significance for Catholic life. In the midst of it all, one of the students said, "You know, Father, it's so easy to believe when you're here!" Yes, that is true.

Sometimes it's extremely easy to believe, as at the birth or baptism of an infant or at a child's First Holy Communion or Confirmation. It's easy to believe when one witnesses a religious make profession of vows or when a young man is ordained to the priesthood. When a couple give themselves to one another in the bond of Christian marriage, one finds it equally easy to believe. Death is another story.

It is not easy to believe in a God of life and love in the face of death, but it is essential. You just heard that touching dialogue between Martha and our Lord. He offered her hope for the resurrection of Lazarus by proclaiming Himself to be the Resurrection and the Life. Martha, who had already come to accept Jesus as the Messiah, was now led by Him to take the next step—belief in Him as the Lord of Life, which puts a whole new face on death.

The death of any person, even that of a stranger, is an invitation to consider what we believe about death, because we share the same human nature as that person did. America is a nation terrified of death. That is why we do everything possible to delay the inevitable; that is why we disguise the deceased with cosmetics in a coffin made to look like a bed; that is why so many people delight in long, drawn-out funerals, which are designed to postpone the moment of final parting; that is why our talk of death abounds with euphemisms which speak of "passing away" or "departing," but never "dying." All these situations say that we do not really accept Christ's promise of Himself as our Resurrection and Life. Grief at the death of a loved one is normal, natural, human; however, a Christian can never become consumed with grief, wallowing in grief "like those who have no hope." No, a Christian must face the death of others, as well his own, with a calmness and confidence which show him to be a true believer.

The death of any person is an invitation to consider our own preparedness to face Christ in judgment. Fear is not needed or desired; what is required is preparedness. God gives us our whole life long to prepare for that final meeting with Him which will last for eternity. If you had been called on Wednesday, would you have been ready? We worship a God of mercy, but He is also a God of justice Who will not be mocked. Life on high with Christ for all eternity depends on a life lived with Him right here on earth.

The death of any person is an invitation to consider how Christ did indeed live in that person and how that person made a home for God in his life. We are told that God is glorious in His saints. My father was not a living saint, and he would be the first to admit it. Eulogies are not permitted in the funeral liturgy, and he would be the first to scoff at the idea of being eulogized. He was a sinner like you and me. His sins we need not rehearse, for they are known to God, before Whose divine tribunal we all plead for mercy. Perhaps one of his most glaring faults or sins, though, was an unquenchable pride in his son the priest. His virtues were simple, manly, and quite a propos for Catholics today. Let me mention a few.

—My father had an undying love for the Church. He was proud to be a Catholic and could not conceive of life in Christ apart from the Church.

—He was a voracious reader, especially in the area of theology. It was he who introduced me to Chesterton and Newman. So many people today have doctorates in physics or math while retaining a second-grade understanding of their Faith. My father never completed college, but he knew Catholic theology intimately and could explain it clearly and with conviction.

—My father had a tremendous respect for clergy and religious. He had what some might consider to be that rather quaint habit of tipping his hat to them whenever he saw them on the street. However, he was never naïve enough to think them perfect, just special. Nor did he have a mere theoretical appreciation for the priesthood; it was genuine. In a time when parents actively discourage their sons from committing themselves to the priesthood, it is good to know that there have been parents who have been supportive. Since I first made my announcement about becoming a priest at the age of five, never did I receive anything but positive reinforcement from both my mother and father. And it was he who bought me my first biretta, when I was in the third grade!

—Finally, I must say that in all my years, I never heard him curse or swear or use foul language. He was what we used to refer to as a "Christian gentleman."

The death of any person is an invitation to thank God for all the good things God gave that person during his earthly life. I thank God, first of all, that he had such good, strong patrons: St. Peter, the Prince of the Apostles, and St. Michael the Archangel. You know, he may have gotten a new patron on the day of his death. As some of you may know, he was born in Lawrence, Massachusetts. Well, he died—or, better: he was born to eternal life—on the feast of St. Lawrence the Martyr. Thanks be to God for a life that was reasonably comfortable and fulfilling, with few serious health problems, except at the end. Thanks be to God for a quick and relatively painless death and one for which he could be prepared.

Like Martha, we believe in Jesus as our Lord and Messiah, which means we believe that "the souls of the just are in the hand of God." It also means we must be able to see beyond our present sorrow and say, with St. Paul, "Thanks be to God who has given us the victory through our Lord Jesus Christ."

Each day of his life, my father prayed as every good Catholic does: "Holy Mary, Mother of God, pray for us sinners now and at the hour of our death." Our prayer—the prayer of the Church—is that our Lady was indeed praying for him at the hour of his death and that she was at his side, ready to lead him to her divine Son—to be welcomed into His heavenly Kingdom. And that hope does indeed make it easier to believe.

Silver Jubilee of the Reverend Perry W. Dodds

St. Edward's Church, Twin Falls, Idaho, September 25, 1983

"Iam non dico vos servos—vos autem dixi amicos" (Jn 15:15)

A young man stood in the presence of his bishop to hear those words solemnly chanted from the Holy Gospel according to St. John: "I no longer call you slaves. . . . I have called you friends." As God in Christ thus disclosed his identity to that deacon, a relationship of intimacy was established. Within minutes, that deacon lay prostrate, publicly affirming his human vulnerability and absolute dependence on Almighty God as the source of his life and strength. He approached for the ancient gesture of the laying on of hands. The man knelt before the bishop and rose—still a man but also Christ's priest and so, a new man, a different man, one who could never again be the old man or a private individual for now, through God's grace and the Church's ministry, he had a unique relationship with Christ and, therefore, with Christ's Church.

Reflection on the priesthood is as old as the Church herself. Sometimes these meditations are unrealistic and maudlin; sometimes they are highly theological but leave us cold because they lack the poetry and beauty which belong to human reflection on the divine. Permit me to share with you some thoughts which come close to doing the job.

Cardinal Suhard of Paris asserted: "The priesthood is not something. It is someone: Christ." St. Francis of Assisi, himself never a priest, said: "If I saw an angel and a priest, I would bend my knee first to the priest and then to the angel." St. John Vianney, patron of parish priests, declared from experience: "After God, the priest is everything. Leave a parish twenty years without priests; they will worship beasts." He went on to say: "The priest will not understand the greatness of his office till he is in Heaven. If he understood it on earth, he would die, not of fear, but of love." Following up on that same notion, the French spiritual writer Père Gatry said something we really need to ponder today: "If people could realize what the priesthood is, there would be too many priests." Where does the priesthood find its great dignity? In this simple but awesome realization put forth by St. Vincent Ferrer: "The Blessed Virgin opened Heaven only once; the priest does so at every Mass."

The reverence and respect of the Catholic people for their clergy is directed, then, not toward the man himself—who always remains a man, always weak, always sinful, and sometimes too much so. Rather, Catholics love their priests because they are ordained to do for the faithful what, in the mysterious plan of Providence, the faithful cannot do for themselves: Priests are a touchstone with divinity.

Even the regularly assigned Scripture readings for this Sunday have something to say about what we celebrate today. No, I am not talking about the line in the Gospel which says, "Once there was a rich man who dressed in purple and linen and feasted splendidly every day. . . ." While our jubilarian may look as though he feasts splendidly every day, until one of his friends in Rome does something about it, I don't think we'll find him dressed in purple. Instead, I am referring to the Second Reading; that sets the stage: "Man of God that you are, seek after integrity, piety, faith, love, steadfastness, and a gentle spirit. Fight the good fight of faith. Take firm hold on the everlasting life to which you were called when, in the presence of many witnesses, you made your noble profession of faith" (1 Tim. 6:11–12).

Twenty-five years ago, this man did indeed make a "noble profession of faith." Once again, today, in the presence of many witnesses, he renews that noble profession; in fact, he does it every time he celebrates Christ's redemptive sacrifice as he renews his intention day after day to be an *alter Christus*, to stand *in persona Christi* for the community of the redeemed. An anniversary is a time to recommit oneself to the ideals of the event commemorated. An anniversary of priestly ordination is an opportunity for both priest and people to reaffirm their love for the priesthood and their gratitude to our Lord for the gift of the priesthood.

To my brother priest and very dear friend, whom I am so privileged to honor in your name, I wish to present a challenge. Last Christmas, a Sister sent me a card with a poem enclosed; I would like to share it with you:

> FATHER, BE A PRIEST
> Father, please be a Priest,
> Don't try to be "just one of us."
> God has asked you to be different,
> So that we may get a glimpse of Him
> Through you.
> God has chosen you,
> And given you divine powers to consecrate at Mass,

So as to put divine value into our offerings.
We need you there as a Priest.
We need you in the confessional,
To direct us, as well as to absolve us.
We need you to do these things for us,
That we cannot do for ourselves.
We need you especially to be a man of prayer,
To be an example to us, and our daily intercessor before God.
So, Father, please be—and remain—a Priest of God.

That letter is signed "Your People." The Sister added in her own hand: "You are! Continue to be, with God's grace." I say the same to you. As St. Paul says elsewhere in the Pastoral Epistles, "stir into flame the gift of God bestowed when my hands were laid on you" (2 Tim 1:6).

At the age of nineteen, you became convinced that God was calling you to union with Him through His Son's Church; three years later, you answered God's call once more to follow His Son unreservedly in the priesthood. As you responded to that call then and ever since, may God give you the grace to respond every day of your life. May the God Who gave joy to your youth, now renew your youth and give you the enthusiasm and sense of mission "to preach the word, to stay with this task whether convenient or inconvenient—correcting, reproving, appealing—constantly teaching and never losing heart" (2 Tim 4:2). Especially, never lose heart.

And to you, his people, I offer this challenge: Love your priests; pray for your priests, for they can lead you to God. You have come here because you do respect and love this particular priest, and that is good. But you should extend this attitude to all priests: to faithful, fervent priests and also to unfaithful, tepid priests; to lonely or desolate priests; to young and old priests; to sick and dying priests; to priests with a deep faith, a firm hope, and a burning love, but also to priests whose faith is weak, whose hope is faltering, and whose love is flickering. Pray that the Eternal High Priest would keep them all close to His Sacred and Priestly Heart and that He would bless them abundantly in time and eternity. I am not suggesting that you make excuses for lazy or unfaithful priests; on the contrary, call them to be zealous, but do it with love. And that kind of attitude will bear fruit. I think that is what Josef Sellmair meant when he said: "A people that does not desert its priests is not deserted by God."

To the many young men and boys present, a further challenge: I offer the invitation of Jesus Christ Himself: "Come, follow me."

Thirty-three years, ago our jubilarian took God at His word; fifteen years ago this month, I did the same. And I can tell you for myself and for him, we would do it all over again. We have no regrets. Every day of my life, I pray Lacordaire's *Prayer of a Priest*, and that last line still brings a lump to my throat: "What a life, and it is yours, O Priest of Jesus Christ!" That life can also be yours— Come, follow us. Follow Christ. If you are interested in what kind of a present to give our jubilarian, my young friends, consider giving him yourselves as his sons in the priesthood. Nothing could make him happier.

In the priesthood, one finds a commonality, a fraternity, an unspoken bond—and rightly so, because in reality there is only one Priest and one Priesthood. Jesus Christ is the Eternal High Priest, and those of us called to the Church's ministry share in His unique Priesthood. Therefore, the unity of all priests. But there is also diversity, and that comes from the special and unique gifts God has given to each man for the building up of the Body of Christ, which is His Church. And I say, *vive la différence*, especially with this priest! To say that he is a complex man is to succumb to understatement: A lover of books and politics; a connoisseur of fine food and wine; a patron of the arts; a Russophile and an observer of Orthodox relations; a Renaissance man and a Christian gentleman; a convert and a devoted pastor; one who never darkened the door of a Catholic school as a child but would want nothing more than to re-open the parish school; a veteran Vatican-watcher who proved his skill by predicting the election of Cardinal Albino Luciani (Pope John Paul I). And how could we ever omit his spirit of joy—from the jolly laugh to the knowing twinkle of his eye? He has used his gifts well and wisely for the good of the Church as a parish priest, a diocesan editor, a Newman chaplain.

All these charisms, joined with the experience of life, make for true growth in priestly life and in Christian life generally. The priesthood, you know, is like marriage in many ways: On one's silver jubilee, one should be more in love than he was twenty-five years before. They say the story of St. Pius X—and I would add: of John Paul II—is the story of a fascinating romance: the romance of a priest madly in love with the priesthood. I submit that is also true of our jubilarian, and thanks be to God for that!

We are told that of all the titles the great English convert Cardinal Newman held, the one which had the most meaning for him was that of "Father." "*Non servum. . . autem amicum.*" "Not a slave, but a friend," a companion of Christ, an intimate collaborator with

Him for the salvation of the world. And on that very account, "Father" to us. In giving this honor to our priests, we remind them of what the Lord wants them to be: our fathers in God, in the family of the Church.

May Mary—Mother of Christ, Mother of the Church and Mother of the Clergy—watch over and protect this priest and all priests. For the gift of this priest's life and for the gift of Christ's priesthood in the Church, we echo the words of St. Paul and praise the God Who "is the blest and only ruler, the King of kings and Lord of lords who alone has immortality and who dwells in inapproachable light, whom no human being has ever seen or can see. To him be honor and everlasting rule! Amen" (1 Tim 6:15–16).

First Solemn Mass of the Reverend J. H. Scott Newman

Fifteenth Sunday throughout the Year
Stella Maris Church, Diocese of Charleston, July 11, 1993

To the praise and honor of the Triune God: Father, Son, and Holy Spirit.

Dearest friends, after struggling with a direction for this homily for quite some time, I jumped up from my bed in the midst of a deep sleep one night with an idea, proving true the Scripture which says that the Lord gives to his beloved in sleep. I am one of the Lord's beloved, not by right but by God's inscrutable choice. And by the wily choice of our celebrant, I find myself the homilist today. I say "wily" because, with the dignity and decorum of the liturgy imposed on me, I cannot tell you so many of the tales I would have loved to recount and which you would have been delighted to hear. I hope the dinner's toastmaster can fittingly regale you, but if he is short on material, I would be pleased to supply some for his consideration and your entertainment. Seriously, though, I am honored to assume this role for this happy occasion for which we have all waited so eagerly.

The First Mass of this new priest occurs on the day when the Church traditionally honors the memory of St. Benedict. I was tempted to say that this is an especially happy coincidence, but there are no coincidences for Christians; rather, this is a most appropriate and providential occurrence since so much of the life of today's principal celebrant has been touched by persons and institutions with a Benedictine connection. The young convert tried his vocation for a time at St. Anselm's Abbey in Washington; he completed his bachelor's degree at Belmont Abbey College; he spent so many happy months working among the people of St. Benedict's Parish in Greensboro under the loving and dedicated tutelage of Father Conrad Kimbrough. And so, the Father of Western Monasticism speaks to this would-be son of his; down the corridors of history echo the opening lines and wise counsel of the Rule of St. Benedict: *"Obsculta, O fili, praecepta magistri tui"* (Listen, O son, to the precepts of your master). As you must realize, knowing someone so long and so well makes preaching incredibly difficult. Which biretta does one wear for the event? Priest, friend, confidant, big brother, father? Taking my cue from the great Cardinal Newman's motto, let us proceed with *"Cor ad cor loquitur"* (Heart speaks to heart). Speaking of mottos, I believe it is a good idea for a newly-ordained to choose one, to set a course for his priestly life and ministry. When I was ordained, I chose a line from the Liturgy of the Hours: *"Pro mundi salute"* (For the salvation of the world). And so, when conflicts arise and a decision must be made, I seek to gauge the value of a particular action by whether or not it is faithful to my motto. May I suggest to our new priest that he do the same? I am even going to be bold enough to propose a tentative motto, which comes from the liturgy of Ash Wednesday: *"Memento, homo, quia pulvis es et in pulverem reverteris"* (Remember, man, that thou art dust and unto dust thou shalt return). Actually, the first two words are the most important, and that would leave you room for other items in your coat-of-arms. Why have I alighted on that line? Because I believe that the primary task of a priest is to remember and to cause others to remember. Where does such an idea find its grounding? In the Upper Room on Holy Thursday night as our Blessed Lord constituted His chosen band of apostles to be priests of the new and everlasting covenant, Jesus bade them to remember Him and to cause Him to be remembered by offering the Eucharistic Sacrifice.

Memory, then, is the key to the Christian life, and the priest is, by divine vocation, the man who brings the entire community of believers to remember our great High Priest in the most profound and significant way. The priest, you see, does not need to be incredibly ingenious or innovative; in fact, a desire to be such could actually prove detrimental to the fulfillment of his God-given role. The priest does, however, have to be possessed of the memory of an elephant. His mind and heart are truly the storehouse of his personal memories, as well as those of the entire Church. The priest who suffers from amnesia, either personal or collective, is of no use to the Church, in my judgment. Hence, dear son and now a brother in the priesthood, permit me to lead you on a necessarily abbreviated trip down Memory Lane, and be kind enough to allow all our friends to eavesdrop.

Memento, homo; remember, man: The teenager who first wore a Roman collar as an act of sneering mockery of divine realities. The luncheon arranged by friends who loved so much that they wanted to share with you not only their friendship but their faith. That first fearful visit to an inner-city rectory as you summoned up the humility to be instructed in the "mysteries of the Kingdom." Remember this priest's question that very first meeting: "How long have you been thinking about the priesthood?"

Memento, homo: The long walks at the Princeton Think Tank as Jesus, Emmaus-like, was the unseen Partner to those journeys and conversations. The discussions at Jersey beaches as the Lord, reminiscent of Easter morning, "splashed water in the face of unbelief." November 5, 1982, when you finally swam the Tiber, never knowing that one day you would live on her shores. And the Poor Clare nuns who chanted your reception Mass so beautifully, while you wistfully dared to hope you could one day return the favor for them. Remember, man: Father Romanus, Bob Royal, Joe Sobran, Father Rutler, and Monsignor Shenrook; John Barres and Keeney Jones, both now priests; Jack Hawkins and Simina Farcasiu, now united in Holy Matrimony; and, of course, Bishop Sean—all a part of what Father Dimock has so aptly dubbed the web of grace, by which Almighty God sets us down in particular places causing us to encounter particular people who will lead us more deeply into Him.

Memento, homo, likewise, the mistakes and the detours, and, yes, even the sins, thanking God because all these things helped reveal the power of God's grace to love and save. Remember, too, the kid brother given you not by nature but by grace—who wants to be here but cannot and who even more longs to join his elder brother at God's altar in three years. And yes, *memento, homo*, this poor sinner who has attempted to love you into the priesthood.

My dear people, contrary to appearances, this has not been a personal nostalgia trip, for appearances can be deceiving as we must always remind ourselves whenever we look at the Sacred Species of the Eucharist. No, this trip down Memory Lane is not to serve as the yellow brick road to Oz; rather, it opens onto a broad and high way leading to that more universal and cosmic memory of eternal consequence. And what is that? Let me challenge you, O priest of Jesus Christ, to remember some great, beautiful, and powerful truths which are clearer to you today than they were yesterday and then to consider their implications.

Memento: Yesterday Jesus gave you access to the mysteries of the Kingdom—knowledge not given to all or even most of the human race or even most in the Church. This is not said to puff you up; it is noted to bring you ever more closely into the heart of those mysteries and thus enable you to lead others there, too. Knowledge is a dangerous thing; ignorance can truly be bliss, because once a person knows the truth, he is compelled to act on it and to share it. You cannot claim the bliss of ignorance, because the Lord has told you the whole truth about Himself and His Church; you have no choice but to share the knowledge of that truth with everyone you meet, and for this you are forever a marked man. St. Paul knew the seriousness of all this when he cried, "Woe to me it I do not preach the gospel" (1 Cor 9:16). The knowledge imparted must be shared, or else it will stand as a mark against you on the Day of Judgment. No fear of unpopularity nor concern for human respect should make you more fearful than to fail to give to the Church and the world "the truth, the whole truth, and nothing but the truth," so help you God.

Memento: Yesterday Jesus the High Priest shared His Sacred Priesthood with you and commanded (yes, commanded) that you offer the Eucharistic Sacrifice for the living and the dead in His memory. That unique call and relationship is summed up in the Orate Fratres of the Mass as we priests ask the assembly of the faithful to pray that "*ac meum ac vestrum sacrificium*" (my sacrifice and yours) may be acceptable. Why "my sacrifice and yours"? Because your relationship to the Sacred Mysteries changed yesterday as you became configured to Christ the Priest in a totally marvelous and nearly unfathomable manner. On Friday, you had the dignity of being a member of the Body of Christ through Baptism; on Saturday, in God's mysterious plan, you were made an *alter Christus* as you now stand *in persona Christi*. Through the power of God's Holy Spirit, you now are what you were not a mere forty hours ago; by the power of God's Holy Spirit, you now can do what you could not do but a day-and-a-half earlier. This is not your doing; it is God working in and through you. Thus you bear a dignity beyond your own, beyond that which you possessed as a human being or even as a Christian; live up to that dignity. Never be ashamed of it, and never bring shame to it.

Memento: Yesterday as you stood at the altar and participated in the one and eternal offering of Calvary for the first time in an entirely new manner, Jesus gave you the same special gift He gave to the virgin disciple and priest, St. John—He gave you His holy Mother. See in that action the Lord's desire to unite you ever more closely to Him and to every other priest. His Mother is now yours in a unique way and, having her in common with Him and with every other man who shares His priesthood, brings you into intimacy with the Mother of the Church who has a special place in her heart and maternal care for her Son's brothers in the Holy Priesthood. Therefore, the wonderful mother God gave you by nature has her motherly desires for you fulfilled in ways that only a good mother could fondly hope and trust; her prayers are now entrusted to the powerful intercession of the Mother who heard her dying Son say: "Woman, behold your son. Behold, your mother."

Memento: Yesterday amid the glory and splendor of the liturgy, you were inserted more deeply into the Lord's paschal mystery—an indispensable component of which is the Passion. In the ancient papal coronation rite, a Capuchin friar was always deputed to remind the new pope of this fact by pushing his way to the fore as he cast a cord of blazing hemp at the feet of the Sovereign Pontiff, with the somber and sobering words, *"Sic transit gloria mundi"* (Thus passes the glory of the world). Many latter-day forms of spirituality so stress Easter joy that they by-pass the wisdom of the ages: *Post crucem, lucem*; only after enduring the agony of the Cross can one expect the glory of the Resurrection. Therefore, when moments of trial come; when celibacy is more an onus than a joy; when obedience hardly seems rational; when being a constant faithful, visible witness gets tiresome—in those times, look to the Crucified One and remember. For Jesus never forgets His Sacred Passion; indeed, He is perpetually reminded of it as He looks at His holy wounds which He bears even in His risen life. And as He beholds those wounds and recalls His bloody Passion, He renews His love for the sinners He thus redeemed. By remembering, have Christ remember to enfold you in His saving embrace and to lift you up in prayer as He raises His priestly hands to make intercession to His Heavenly Father for you and for the whole world.

Memento: Yesterday the Lord made you a sower of the seed of His Word. Be scrupulously faithful to that trust, preaching the truth of God, "both when convenient and inconvenient" (2 Tim 4:2). "Blessed are your eyes because they see and blessed are your ears because they hear. I assure you, many a prophet and many a saint longed to see what you see but did not see it, to hear what you hear but did not hear it." By your joyful proclamation of the Gospel, let all men know that you do consider yourself blest, and that you wish to share that blessedness with them by offering to them "the word of life" (Phil 2:16). As one of the Mass formularies of the Roman Missal puts it, strive to be an "ardent but gentle servant of the Gospel." Don't develop a "Messiah complex," either; never forget that it is God's Word, and He is quite capable of seeing to it that His Word shall not return to [Him] void, but shall do [His] will, achieving the end for which [He] sent it." Just be sure you are doing His will, and He will take care of the rest. One more note in this regard: Don't be too hard on yourself if people reject God's message when you have truly done your best. While Father Stravinskas is an academic taskmaster expecting at least a 70-percent success-rate in a final examination, God—being God—is more understanding: The parable of the sower reminds us that Almighty God is delighted with a 25-percent success-rate. So, choose your words wisely and know your audience, and then wait for the hundredfold return with patience and confidence.

Memento: Yesterday the Lord God made you a father in the family of His Son's Church. When your namesake became a cardinal, the Fathers of the Oratory asked him how he would now like to be addressed. The great convert-theologian replied that of all the titles and honorifics which had been bestowed upon him during his long and productive life, the one which meant the most was "Father." Being a father in the natural order is a burden, but also an inestimable joy; it is no different in the supernatural order. Never let me hear that you have been dragged into the company of men who belong to the cult of the slob and say, "Just call me Scott." Nor into the society of the self-important who suggest, "You may call me Dr. Newman." Cherish the title of father, because it comes with the love and devotion of your spiritual family and because it serves as a constant challenge for you to act like a priest, to look like a priest, to be the priest who is *semper et pro semper* a father.

And now, for a bit of reality therapy: Someday, Father Newman, you are going to die—as will all of us. That's the second half of "*memento, homo,*" isn't it? In fact, of course, the only reason for the Church or the priesthood is that we are all terminal cases, who need the grace of Christ to make this journey through earthly life to eternal life as safely and surely as possible. As one of the "*dispensatores mysteriorum Dei*" (dispensers of the mysteries of God), it will be your obligation and privilege to lead your flock, your family, on that journey. In the Byzantine liturgy, as the Creed is chanted, the priest stands at the head of his people—all facing the Rising Sun together; throughout the profession of faith, he waves the chalice veil continuously between himself and the tabernacle as a reminder that the propositions of faith being proclaimed are not the full reality, for they but point us toward the complete and final revelation which comes at the hour of our death. As the Byzantine priest lies in his coffin fully vested to join in the Liturgy of Heaven, the chalice veil is placed over his face to symbolize the awesome fact that now in death he stands on the other side of the veil, beholding face-to-face the Mystery which he proclaimed and celebrated merely in sign. So, remember your beginning and remember your final end, dearest son and brother, and cause your people to remember them, too, as we all "eagerly await the revelation of the Sons of God." Be, then, the voice of memory in the community of the Church; be also her sign of memory until the memory is subsumed into the mystery, and "God will be all in all" (1 Cor 15:28).

Amen.

First Solemn Mass of the Reverend Joel M. Kovanis

Pentecost Sunday
Church of Our Lady of Lourdes in Dunedin, Florida, May 22, 1994

Wind, fire, thunder and lightning. The Sacred Scriptures are replete with instances of divine revelation accompanied by these awe-inspiring phenomena in nature. The Book of Genesis tells us that "a mighty wind swept over the waters" (1:2) at the dawn of time; in the Book of Exodus, we learn how God gave the Law to Moses on Mount Sinai with thunder and lightning as the communicators of His Will and Word (see Ex 19). But less fearsome signs have also been used by the Almighty, as we recall how the gentle breath of God brought Adam to life (see Gen 2:7) and how the breath of Jesus on the apostles gave them the ability to bring to life again men spiritually dead through sin (see Jn 20:22). All of these events are connected to God's self-manifestation or, even better, His self-communication to the human race and, most especially, to the Chosen People.

The Pentecost being observed by the apostolic community was a major feast of covenant renewal, harking back to that primal giving of the Law to Moses, that act of God which essentially formed the people of Israel and made them His own special portion. Each time the Church gathers to celebrate the Eucharistic Sacrifice, she engages in a similar ceremony of covenant renewal, and the same Spirit which hovered over the waters of the abyss bringing creation from chaos, the same Spirit which hovered over the Blessed Virgin Mary making her the Mother of the Messiah—that self-same Spirit hovers over the elements of bread and wine, transforming them into the Lord's Body and Blood which saved the world two thousand years ago and makes present that invitation to salvation day in and day out, until He "comes in glory." Hence, it is possible to say that every time the Sacrifice of Calvary is sacramentally renewed, a little Pentecost occurs. How appropriate, then, for a priest to offer that Sacrifice for the first time *in persona Christi* on this solemn day. (It is a grace which, coincidentally, I share with our newly ordained.)

As we endeavor to plumb the depths of the mystery of the presence of God's Holy Spirit in the Church's sacramental life, Holy

Mother Church offers us a rather full plate of food for thought; in reality, we are beset by an embarrassment of riches. What shall we make of it all? How can I ever hope to do justice to the high honor given me to lead you in this reflection on the holy priesthood which is the principal instrument by which the Lord has willed to continue the sanctifying work of His Holy Spirit?

On the first Christian Pentecost, a terrified band of persecuted believers huddled together for safety and mutual support. And then, in nothing less than a miracle, God's Holy Spirit came crashing into their lives, changing them at the core of their being in such wise that they made "bold proclamation as the Spirit prompted them." I do not think it far-fetched to see in that mass of frightened souls a kind of foreshadowing of small groups of seminarians who today must endure persecution from within and scorn from without as they await the Spirit's definitive entrance into their lives at ordination. The point to ponder, however, is not so much the period of fear but the moment of liberation effected by the action of the Holy Spirit—a liberation given for the noble purpose of sharing the Gospel message in all its fullness and truth.

When the Eleven emerged from the Upper Room, what did they find? People who were "confused," says St. Luke. They were confused because they were overly impressed by the linguistic feat performed but I would suggest they were even more confused because they knew these men to be naturally weak and reticent and they could not fathom what had gotten into them, or better yet, Who had gotten into them. Something comparable happened to this man yesterday, and we have the right to expect similar results. Your task, dear Father, is to speak incessantly and courageously about the *magnalia Dei,* "the marvels God has accomplished." It must be your special and daily prayer to take the refrain of today's Responsorial Psalm as the theme of your priestly life and ministry: "Lord, send out your Spirit, and renew the face of the earth"— through *me!* It is interesting that when St. Peter gave that earth-shattering first sermon of his on the first Christian Pentecost, he chose to link up the happenings of that occasion with the fulfillment of the prophecy of the coming of the Holy Spirit delivered by the mouth of God's spokesman, Joel. In God's remarkable ways, we find today another Peter with another Joel as the elder challenges the junior to be a contemporary prophet of the Holy Spirit. How significant this charge is becomes apparent when we read that wonderful new document from the Congregation of the Clergy on the life and ministry of priests, as it underscores this fact: "It is . . . the

Holy Spirit Who by ordination confers on the priest the prophetic task of announcing and explaining, with authority, the Word of God. . . . Therefore, the priest with the help of the Holy Spirit and the study of the Word of God in the Scriptures, with the light of Tradition and of the Magisterium, discovers the richness of the Word to be proclaimed to the ecclesial community entrusted to him" (no. 9). Where do we find the program of action for this task? Let us continue our reflection by returning to the food placed before us by the Church in the Liturgy of the Word.

Father Joel, this work assigned to you by Christ's holy Church cannot be done, "except in the Holy Spirit," as St. Paul taught the Corinthians. And if you are foolish enough to think that you can pull it off otherwise, you will soon learn differently and the hard way. The priestly ministry cannot be effective without reliance on the Holy Spirit for the simple reason that the priesthood is the chosen channel for the Holy Spirit. Just consider the beautiful "Golden Sequence" of today's liturgy. So many of the titles we accorded to the Spirit and the things for which we prayed are applicable to the priest and his ministry in the Church and in the world. We priests, by the mysterious workings of grace, are called to "shed a ray of light divine." It is our particular privilege to be "the Father of the poor," not merely to those economically disadvantaged but even more to those who are spiritually malnourished and who cry out for the food of the truth of Christ. By standing at the altar and saying the awesome words of Christ at the Last Supper, we give the Lord's People access to "sweet refreshment here below," which is a foretaste of the "rest most sweet; grateful coolness in the heat; solace in the midst of woe," all of which anticipates the glory of the Liturgy of Heaven. It is our responsibility to teach all who would listen that where God's Holy Spirit is not present, "man hath naught, nothing good in deed or thought, nothing free from taint of ill."

By God's design, it is ours to heal wounds, renew strength, and "wash the stains of guilt away." That almost incredible power was given to the apostles and their successors on Easter night, when our Blessed Lord linked for all time the possession of genuine peace to the forgiveness of sins. Nevertheless we live in such a world that the psychiatrist Karl Menninger could entitle his book *Whatever Became of Sin?* Modern man has lost his sense of sin which, of course, explains why he has also lost the key to full and lasting peace. We priests must remind the world that sin exists, not in the fashion of a dreary and depressing Cassandra, but with an attitude of joy and enthusiasm. In this context, Father Kovanis, permit me to bring your former roommate Father Newman among us—at least spiritually—as I cite his namesake, that great convert and cardinal, John Henry Newman. In admirable humility and with love for sinners, the priest of the poem says to the fallen: "Look not to me—no grace is mine; But I can lift the Mercy-sign. This wouldst thou? Let it be! Kneel down, and take the word divine, *Absolvo te*." In the confessional, the priest seeks to "bend the stubborn heart and will; melt the frozen, warm the chill; guide the steps that go astray."

Yes, the work of absolution is central to the priesthood as those words are uttered in Baptism, Penance, and the Anointing of the Sick, paving the way for any other sacramental encounters which increase the divine life within. Once the roadblock of sin is removed, then the process of divinization can begin—and only then. From the Garden of Eden until the present, man has wanted to be like God—and that is not bad in itself; in truth, it is a holy desire implanted within us by the Creator as a way of bringing us into union with Him. And so, we shall pray at the commingling of the water and wine: "May we come to share in the divinity of Christ Who humbled Himself to share in our humanity." A bold prayer, to be sure, but a good one, so long as we go about it all in God's way, rather than our own. And that is why our Divine Savior gave us priests—to provide for the divinization of the human race, so that Christ's faithful can attain to "virtue's sure reward. . . [and the] joys that never end."

An image which looms large over the landscape of today's celebration is that of fire, which can warm or destroy, enlighten or consume. From the smoke and fire of Mount Sinai to the fiery flames of the Cenacle, this symbol bespeaks the power and majesty of God. Even in ancient, pagan Rome this was so, as it fell to the Vestal Virgins to keep the flame alive before the altar of the goddess. Those superstitious Romans believed that if the fire went out, so would the glory of Rome. And so, the Vestal Virgin who would fail in her duty would have her life snuffed out. Christ's priest as an instrument of the Holy Spirit is, in a preeminent manner, the keeper and the bearer of the flame of God. Notice that I do not say only "the keeper," for it is not enough for the priest to possess that flame for himself or to preserve it as a museum piece; he is required to impart that flame to all. In what does that flame consist? Exactly what is he called to share?

The priest is the keeper and the bearer of the flame of truth. In all too many ways, Pontius Pilate can be seen as the true ancestor of western civilization since the so-called Enlightenment. His cynical question, "What is truth?" has echoed down the corridors of time to our own day which not only questions the existence of absolute truth and objective reality; it has made it the one and only acceptable dogma of modernity that we must hold all truth to be relative, with every opinion claiming equal authority. How particularly silly for an age which demands such rigid standards of scientific evidence for almost every other aspect of life. The priest must stride into such a world with all the confidence and assurance of the author of *Veritatis Splendor*, asserting that the true dignity of the human person needs nothing less than "the splendor of the truth," which comes from the Holy Spirit, Whose special mission it is to lead us "to all truth" (Jn 16:13). In this way, the priest helps "renew the face of the earth."

The priest is the bearer and keeper of the flame of the sacred. I said earlier that we must restore a sense of sin, but we must also restore the sense of the sacred; I am fully convinced that the two tasks go hand-in-glove. In all the great theophanies of both Testaments, the human person is graciously granted a glimpse of the divine but immediately becomes conscious of the tremendous gap which exists between himself and the Almighty and responds accordingly, which is with awe and wonder. The priest must recapture that attitude for his people by prodding them into reverence and devotion through the tried and true practices of the Catholic Tradition: bowing one's head at the holy name of Jesus; genuflection before the Blessed Sacrament; fitting attire for worship; a holy silence in the house of God; liturgy which truly raises the mind and heart to the Blessed Trinity. When the sacred and the profane merge, contrary to some theories, only unfortunate results ensue: Not only is God dethroned, but man is progressively debased. On the other hand, when the precincts of the sacred are honored, man is progressively elevated. When the priest reminds his flock that the ground on which they stand is holy, he is helping to "renew the face of the earth."

The priest is the keeper and the bearer of the flame of unity. St. Paul understood this all so well, which is why he urges his readers to appreciate God's manifold gifts and ministries as being "given for the common good," in order to build up the "one body," which is Christ's Church. All too often in recent years, clergy, religious, and laity alike have seen personal projects as means of self-aggrandizement or, even worse, as providing access to what they tritely term "empowerment." Service in the Church can never be perceived in that manner, and to do so is a blasphemy and sin against the Holy Spirit for it is destructive of that unity for which the Lord Jesus prayed on the night before He died. Ecclesial unity or communion is not just a pleasant concept or a sociological nicety which makes for the smoother running of the ship; it is an absolute necessity, as Jesus Himself saw it: "That they may all be one." But why? He goes on: "That the world may believe that you sent me" (Jn 17:22–23). The miracle of Pentecost occurred due precisely to the unity of the apostolic college in and under Peter, and the formula is the very same today: The guarantee of Catholic unity and apostolic fruitfulness comes from intimate, loving communion with Peter's successor, our Holy Father, the Bishop of Rome. In the lovely preface for this solemnity, the Church asks for the gift of having "one voice to profess one faith." When the priest strengthens the bonds of ecclesial communion, he builds up the Church in love and thus helps "renew the face of the earth."

The priest is the keeper and the bearer of the flame of fidelity and commitment. When the Risen Christ appeared to His apostles on Easter night, the first thing He did was to "show them His hands and His side." How strange, you say? Not really, for He was offering them the evidence of His saving love, which love is everlasting. The love of Christ, which was a love unto death, is epitomized in those wounds of His which He retains even in His risen life of glory. And those tokens of sacrificial love beckon His sons in the priesthood to be as faithful in their sacrifices as He. Fidelity seems so hard—even so impossible—to the vast majority of our people. Fidelity to promises, to contracts, to friendships, to marriage is so seldom seen anymore. But we all know, in our heart of hearts, that life without commitment is hardly a life worth living at all. That is why our present Holy Father said it so well when, in Philadelphia in 1979, he recalled to our minds and hearts that "priesthood is forever—*tu es sacerdos in aeternum*—we do not return the gift once given. It cannot be that God Who gave the impulse to say 'yes' now wishes to hear 'no.'" And so it is that onto the scene of massive infidelity, the priest comes with his promise of faithful and lasting service. In this way, he becomes an example worthy of emulation, as well as a beacon of hope, and yes, this is how he helps "renew the face of the earth."

The priest is the keeper and the bearer of the flame of chastity. Ours, my dear friends, is a sex-saturated culture, which has made an idol of sexual gratification—an idol more pernicious than the golden calf of the Hebrews of old, more dangerous because it is so all-consuming. I can scarcely make a trip on public transportation and not find myself approached by someone who has a question or comment about some aspect of human sexuality. The adage has it that the Victorians tried to fall into love without falling into sex, while we moderns try to fall into sex without falling into love. Yet once again, the Church sends out her contemporary apostles as signs of contradiction, challenging the prevailing wisdom, by asking them to be chaste and celibate for the Kingdom, reminding all that there is indeed more to life than sex and that once one has truly encountered God, every other human attraction—even things good and holy in themselves—must be judged as but temporary and transient. As Cardinal Newman put it: "Unveil, O Lord, and on us shine In glory and in grace; This gaudy world grows pale before the beauty of Thy face. And thus, when we renounce for Thee Its restless aims and fears, The tender memories of the past, The hopes of coming years, Poor is our sacrifice, whose eyes are lighted from above; We offer what we cannot keep, What we have ceased to love."

Interestingly enough, even the rabbinic scholars teach that after Moses encountered the Almighty on Mount Sinai, so powerful and moving was that event, that he never again had relations with his wife. This does not say that conjugal love is bad or ugly, by no means; it does say that the eternal puts it all into perspective. And the celibate priest is in a unique position to assist married couples who struggle to live Catholic marital morality by his own joyful witness of celibate love. He likewise shines forth as a model for the unmarried and even the unhappily married or, more tragically, the separated or divorced. The priest living celibately in this world points the way to eternity where, our greatest celibate Lover told us, men "neither marry nor are given in marriage" (Mk 12:25). And thus, the priest helps "renew the face of the earth."

So, Father Kovanis, you have been given a tall order, some might think, but our faith informs us that "I can do all things in Him Who strengthens me" (Phil 4:13), so "do not be afraid" (Acts 18:9). You have become a new man. The recent *Directory for the Life and Ministry of Priests* stresses this: "In priestly ordination, the priest has received the seal of the Holy Spirit which has marked him by the sacramental character in order always to be the minister of Christ and the Church. Assured of the promise that the Consoler will abide 'with him forever,' the priest knows that he will never lose the presence and the effective power of the Holy Spirit in order to exercise his ministry and live with charity his pastoral office as a total gift of self for the salvation of his own brothers" (no. 8).

Yes, you are a "marked man," interiorly but also externally. That same document repeats the traditional and wise discipline of the

Church in this regard as it notes the importance of being clearly identifiable at all times and under all circumstances as a priest of the Church. It states: "[A cleric's] attire, when it is not the cassock, must be different from the manner in which the laity dress, and conform to the dignity and sacredness of his ministry." And yet more strongly, it warns that "a cleric's failure to use this proper ecclesiastical attire could manifest a weak sense of his identity as one consecrated to God" (no. 66). Therefore, never be a clericalist but always feel honored to be a priest and see in even the externals the Lord's way of making you a constant and consistent instrument of the Holy Spirit.

As we prepare ourselves to move into the Liturgy of the Eucharist, we must remember that the word means "thanksgiving" and so it is our bounden duty to give thanks for this new priest and to those who have brought him *ad altare Dei*. First of all, his family. What a great privilege it is to have a priest in one's family and, unfortunately, how few Catholic families seem to believe that any longer. The mother of a priest is always special in this sense, and the present case is no exception. Mrs. Kovanis, in the name of the Church, I thank you for giving this son of yours to the service of Christ and His People. May he always make you as justifiably proud of him as you are today, but may I ask that you not be quite so proud as my own mother who, after telling a stranger her name feels compelled to say that her only child is a priest! And then our thoughts go to Mr. Kovanis, who was always so supportive of his son, Joel. God has given him the joy of participating in this liturgy "from another shore and in a greater light." Last but not least, the Sisters of Notre Dame whose exemplary religious witness certainly fostered the new priest's vocation, if it did not actually stir up the first flames. How good they should feel as they behold one of "their boys" now configured to Christ the High Priest.

Oh, yes, one more person must be mentioned, and it is "Notre Dame" herself, our Lady. *The Directory for Priests* highlights the necessary relationship between every priest and the Mother of our great High Priest: "Like John at the foot of the cross, every priest has been entrusted, in a special way, with Mary as Mother. Priests, who are among the favored disciples of Jesus, crucified and risen, should welcome Mary as their Mother in their own life, bestowing her with constant attention and prayer. The Blessed Virgin then becomes the Mother who leads them to Christ, who makes them sincerely love the Church, who intercedes for them, and who guides them toward the Kingdom of Heaven" (no. 68).

Now Mary once more stands at the foot of the cross and invites to the altar of this church dedicated to her this newest brother of her Son the Priest. She who is the Spouse of the Spirit readies the heart of this priest to beg that same Spirit to enter our midst and overtake the bread and wine which we shall soon present, bringing the life of Heaven to mortals here on earth. In the most profound way possible, then, God will have sent forth His Spirit to "renew the face of the earth."

First Solemn Mass of the Reverend Nicholas L. Gregoris

Solemnity of the Sacred Heart
Church of the Holy Innocents, New York City, June 6, 1997

As my namesake exclaimed, "Lord, how good it is for us to be here!" (Mt 17:4). Just a bit more than two months ago, we gathered to witness our celebrant's diaconal ordination, and now the priesthood with his First Solemn Mass of Thanksgiving. I should note at the outset, however, that I don't think it advisable for any of you to anticipate his episcopal consecration two months from now! Seriously, though, this is the day toward which we have all looked with eager longing for so many years, the day which at times seemed all too remote, but the day for which this man was born. And when God decides to act—in His own good time and according to His own good pleasure—He acts with dispatch.

Will you indulge a spiritual father's pride today and permit me to begin in a somewhat biographical vein? Ten years ago this coming September, a young boy of fifteen came into my life—and neither of us has been the same since. Not by accident, indeed by Providence, that first encounter occurred at a Mass at the Church of Our Lady of Vilna downtown.

What impressed me about this youngster, both instantaneously and with the passage of time? Several things. First, he reminded me of the title of a book I had read when I was about ten years old—*Boy in a Hurry*—a biography of St. Gabriel Possenti, who was so much "in a hurry" to become a Passionist priest and a saint. His holy anxiety earned him entry into the Passionist Order and sanctity, even though he died before ordination. The young Nicholas was possessed of that same "holy anxiety."

Second, he exhibited an extraordinary openness and willingness to conform his will to God's. He made no pretensions to have the corner on the market in terms of knowledge or truth or holiness. Like the blind beggar Bartimaeus, the line that could sum up his state of mind was the simple but profound request: "Lord, I want to see"(Mk 10:51).

Third, this city boy was a diamond in the rough; what you saw was what you got. St. Bartholomew would be pleased to share Jesus' evaluation of him with our friend as the Lord said he was a man "without guile" (Jn 1:47).

Fourth, he effused a spirit of gladness; he was playful and a source of cheer for others. Already St. Philip Neri, the apostle of joy, was preparing him to be one of his sons. Already the words of Psalm 42 had sunk deep into his consciousness: "*Introibo ad altare Dei, ad Deum qui laetificat iuventutem meam*" (I will go unto the altar of God, to God Who gives joy to my youth).

Fifth, being a son of Adam, as well as a son of God, he didn't always succeed in achieving perfect sanctity the first time around, but even in the midst of moments of understandable and youthful rebellion, he placed himself in the camp of the young man in the parable who may have said "no" to his father but ultimately always did "yes" (see Mt 21:28–31).

That means that our new priest manifested all the "human qualities" which Pope John Paul II describes in *Pastores Dabo Vobis* as so essential to become the building blocks for a priestly vocation. Grace builds on nature, and God had already done a mighty work of grace in fashioning the mind and the heart of this young man to share in the priesthood of His divine Son. And this is why, literally from the first day we met, I felt like the old priest Zechariah who looked down at his newborn son, John the Baptist, and saw in him not the present reality of a helpless infant but the future glory of a mighty precursor for the Messiah and Lord. Zechariah's prophecy took on particular significance for me: "*Et tu puer, propheta Altissimi vocaberis; praeibis enim ante faciem Domini parare vias eius*" (And you, child, will be called the prophet of the Most High; for you will go before the Lord to prepare his ways; Lk 1:76). All priests need to be able to look into the face of young men and see the promise of hope and fulfillment, and I want to thank you, dear one, for giving me such an opportunity.

I should observe that Nicholas got himself a nickname out of this, as well: Because he was invariably the youngest member of any religious community in which he has lived, he became known as "*Puer*," Latin for "child" or "boy." Even at The Oratory, he remains the youngest although now a priest! But that's what happens when someone hears the voice of God and responds, and Almighty God gives him a very special gift in return for such responsiveness. The great Oratorian, John Henry Cardinal Newman, spoke about it eloquently and passionately: "Blessed are they who give the flower of their days and their strength of soul and body to Thee. Blessed are they who in their youth turn to Thee Who didst give Thy life for them, and wouldst fain give it to them and implant it in them, that they may live forever."[1]

And that leads us to the present moment in which we find ourselves. What a splendid day on which to celebrate one's first Solemn Mass as the Church pays homage to the Sacred Heart of Jesus. And once more we find the Hand of Providence active. As many of you know, Father Nicholas received his elementary education from the Apostles of the Sacred Heart. This wonderful community of Sisters taught him by word and example the depths of God's love and inspired in him a priestly vocation; for this formation in faith, he is and needs to be eternally grateful. Just a few days before his ordination, I spoke with Sister Mary Matthew and Sister Cora; I'm sure I don't have to tell you how delighted they were to learn that one of "their boys" in whom they had long ago perceived a priestly calling had indeed made it to God's altar.

There is another connection between our celebrant and the Sacred Heart, about which not many folks are aware. When Nicholas was a teenager, he was very much taken by the life story of Archbishop George Matulaitis, who was beatified by Pope John Paul II in 1987. One of the things that struck the youthful Nicholas was that the young George had likewise been convinced very early on of his vocation and had adopted a motto, much as bishops do, to set a direction to his life and to keep him on course. Nick said he would like to do the same. Having looked at the circumstances of his life, he noted that every time things looked bleak, God showed His love and compassion, renewing in him hope and courage to face the future. Perhaps he had learned this lesson from the Gospel according to Peanuts. In one scenario, Lucy is playing Cassandra, as usual, regaling Charlie Brown with her laundry list of negativity: "Floods, fire and famine!" she intones, as Father Nicholas' beloved Snoopy dances. "Doom, defeat and despair," she rages, as the Beagle dances on, finally forcing her to declare: "I guess it's no use. . . . Nothing seems to disturb him!" Snoopy, Charles Schultz tells us, understands God's prevailing and conquering love. Nicholas, too, intuited a link between God's love for us and our love for God, resulting in his selection of *"diligentibus Deum,"* the first words of the verse from St. Paul's Epistle to the Romans, which asserts that "God works for good for those who love him" (Rom 8:28).

And then there are yet other convergences between Father Nicholas and the Sacred Heart. Our holy Founder, St. Philip Neri,

---

[1] Daniel M. O'Connell, S.J., ed., *A Cardinal Newman Prayerbook: Kindly Light* (Denville, N.J.: Dimension Books, n.d.), p. 23.

was completely overtaken by divine love, so much so that his own heart literally broke through his rib cage on one occasion when he became overwhelmed by the realization of the depths of Christ's love. Beyond that, Cardinal Newman, whose name graces our Oratory, took for his own motto, "*Cor ad cor loquitur*" ("Heart speaks to heart"), which points to the intimate conversation which takes place when God begins to speak to man at the core of his being.

In point of fact, under normal conditions Father Gregoris should have celebrated his First Solemn Mass last weekend, but my schedule with a two-year-old commitment to conduct a diaconal retreat in Denver made that impossible. And so, I think it fair to say that our Blessed Lord clearly wanted this newest priest-son of His to offer this Mass of Thanksgiving on the day when the hearts of the whole Church are turned in a special way to the Heart of His Divine Son. Indeed, as one spiritual writer has expressed it so beautifully, "the Heart of Jesus is a son's heart," [2] and this new priest's heart beats in a new way since his priestly ordination ten days ago on the feast of St. Philip, the saint and apostle of love. Indeed, he is a son to the Father in an entirely new manner, precisely because he has been configured to Christ the Priest through the Sacrament of Holy Orders.

As Pope Pius XII pointed out in his magnificent encyclical on the Sacred Heart, *Haurietis Aquas*, the Scriptures are replete with references to the love of God. In Hosea, often called "the prophet of divine love," we hear these words of Almighty God: "When Israel was a child, I loved him and called him out of Egypt as my son. . . . I took my people up in my arms, but they did not acknowledge that I took care of them. I drew them to me with affection and love. I picked them up and held them to my cheek; I bent down to them and fed them" (Hos 11:1–4). That tenderness and pathos of God resound in Jeremiah, as we hear: "People of Israel, I have always loved you, so I continue to show you my constant love." The prophet goes on to say that God will make a "new covenant" with His People, in which "I will put my law within them and write it on their hearts." (Jer 31:3, 33). St. Paul rhapsodized on this love in his Epistle to the Ephesians: "For this reason I bow my knees before the Father, from whom every family in Heaven and on earth is named, . . . that Christ may dwell in your hearts through faith; that you, being grounded in love, may have power to comprehend with all the Saints what is the breadth and length and height and depth, and

---

[2] Jesús Solano, S.J. *Getting to Know the Heart of Jesus: Points for Thought and Study* (Rome: C.d.C. Press, 1980), p. 161.

to know the love of Christ which surpasses knowledge, that you may be filled with all the fullness of God" (Eph 3:14-19). This love, of course, finds its consummation in the Lord Jesus' redeeming death on the cross, as His pierced Heart pours forth water and blood, which the lovely Preface for this day speaks of as "the fountain of sacramental life in the Church," symbols of Baptism and the Eucharist. In a most particular and unique manner, Christ's saving action is brought to memory and renewed in every offering of the Eucharistic Sacrifice. The Heart of Christ is laid bare for all the faithful, and it is the task of the priest to perform that sacred action.

The priest is deputed by Christ and the Church to reveal his own union with the Sacred Heart. How does he do this? First of all, through prayer, which is our poor human attempt to continue the conversation which God first began with each of us in Holy Baptism. The priest, like Christ the great High Priest, has the obligation and the privilege to be the intercessor for the whole Church. On the day of his diaconal ordination, the future priest pledges to pray the Liturgy of the Hours each day for the Church and the world. From the day of his priestly ordination onward, the good priest will never allow a day to pass without making contact with the Eucharistic Lord through the celebration of Holy Mass.

The priest's union with the Sacred Heart is revealed in and through his celibate state. While the love of spouses within the Sacrament of Matrimony is a sign which reminds us of Christ's present love for His Bride the Church, the celibacy of the priest underscores powerfully and dramatically the love for which we are destined in Heaven—a love which is centered on God alone, a love which is undivided, a love which is eternal. Priestly celibacy sets our sights on that time and place where God "shall be all in all" (1 Cor 15:28).

The union between the Heart of Jesus and the heart of one of his priests is revealed in sacrifice, which is to say that it is a manly love. What kinds of sacrifices are demanded of a priest? The priest lives in obedience to Christ, to his bishop or religious superiors, to the teaching authority of the Church. The priest demonstrates his willingness to sacrifice by acts of compassion, which are reflections of the compassion he has experienced from Almighty God and which that same God bids us offer to our fellow man. The sacrifice of the priest is preeminently the sacrifice of the ego, so that he can freely and lovingly relinquish what passes itself off as personal fulfillment for the sake of Christ and His Church. He must make his own the declaration of St. John the Baptist when, referring to Christ, he said: "He must increase, but I must decrease" (Jn 3:30).

The union of the priestly heart with that of Christ is revealed in the witness the priest offers through his preaching the truth of the Gospel, his teaching even when results seem meager, his writing to explain and clarify, his silent but eloquent rendering present of Christ the Priest as his Roman collar introduces the sacred into the secular city on streets, in restaurants, in stores, in places of entertainment. But most of all, the priest witnesses to his own personal union with the Heart of Jesus in his daily offering of the Eucharistic Sacrifice, which he never finds tiresome or boring. Karl Rahner gave a true spirituality to this sacred, repetitive action when he said:

> For we celebrate the hour when a man, consecrated to be a priest of Jesus Christ, performs for the first time that act which in a noble, God-like monotony he is to perform every day for the rest of his life, until his life is finally consumed in that sacrifice that he daily celebrates and in whose acceptance alone all earthly reality sees itself accepted before the infinite majesty of God.[3]

Furthermore, his reverent, faithful and loving celebration of the Sacred Mysteries is a mighty testimony to how he has been touched by love. Indeed, we can say without exaggeration that the priest's action in the Eucharist is a marvelous form of love-making of which he never wearies and to which he always looks forward.

How is a priest able to do all this? Is he some kind of "Superman"? Not at all. Every priest knows, from long, painful, personal experience, that we are far from supermen, and so we do fail—far more often than our prideful human natures would prefer. But what we do well, we do because of what God has done in and for us. On the day of Father Nicholas' priestly ordination, we heard the Master say in St. John's Gospel, that His disciples would no longer be regarded by Him as servants but as friends (Jn 15:15). And so, we are capable of doing good, precisely because the Lord has deigned to make us His friends. We act out of love, not fear. And when we fail, we must bring to our mind's eye the scene of Jesus and Peter after the Resurrection. Our Lord asks Peter three times if he loves Him, giving him the opportunity to undo his three-fold denial. At each juncture, Jesus renews Peter in his role as shepherd of the flock. And He does the same with every one of His priests ever since. We say we love the Lord, but we sin; He gives us the occasion to repent and, right in the midst of receiving His forgiving love, He sends us

---

[3] Karl Rahner, *Meditations on the Sacraments* (New York: Seabury Press, 1977), p. 60.

forth once more to tend and feed His flock. That is love, the love which Christ has for all, but especially for His priests.

Having been forgiven by God for our many offenses, we must then be ready to extend that forgiveness to others. Even the old pagan Roman poet Virgil understood that when he proclaimed, "*Non ignara mali miseris succurrere disco*" (Having suffered myself, I know how to treat others in misery).[4] Dear Father, you have been given the awesome power of being an instrument of mercy and absolution; always consider this one of God's greatest gifts to you. But you must also forgive in other ways, much more human and at the same time quite divine. You must be willing to forgive those who have injured you by their envy, by their pettiness, by their vindictiveness; such injuries you have already sustained, but you will also endure them in the years which lie ahead. Be as prompt to forgive and to forget as the Lord has always been with you.

Which brings us to a sobering fact—please do not be so naïve as to assume that the sweetness and light of these days will be a permanent feature of your priestly life and ministry. If your heart has truly been configured to that of Christ, it must be "a heart capable of suffering."[5] And if you are doing what you are supposed to do as a priest and being who you are supposed to be, you will have ample opportunity to identify with the Suffering Lord.

So, *puer mi*, as we come to the end of our reflections, would you be gracious enough to allow me the prerogative of giving you some fatherly advice? I'm sure you know, it won't be the last time, either! Also, will you let our dear friends eavesdrop? It's always good to have witnesses.

First of all, may I suggest that you make a resolution today at the very outset of your public ministry? Let it be this: That you would always be a churchman. Churchmen are in as scarce supply these days as are statesmen. Unfortunately, our society is overflowing with politicians, but we have precious few statesmen. In much the same way, we must admit shamefacedly that our Church has a superabundance of ecclesiastical functionaries and careerists, but, ah! so few churchmen. You know what a churchman is; it is a priest who loves Christ and His Church with every fabric of his being—and for that reason, he is committed to preach the saving truth of the Gospel, both when convenient and inconvenient, regardless of the cost, doing so for the simple reason that this is what

---

[4] *Aeneid*, book 1, 630.
[5] Francis Larkin, SS.CC., *Enthronement of the Sacred Heart* (Boston: St. Paul Editions, 1978), p. 422.

the Church ordained him to do, doing so out of a deep-seated dedication to the Truth, doing so because he is possessed of an abiding love and devotion for God's holy people, doing so because he has a shepherd's heart—indeed, *the* Shepherd's Heart.

Second, young Father, take as my personal telegram to you the loving counsel offered by St. Paul to Timothy, his son in the priesthood: "Let no one despise your youth" (3 Tim 4:12). When you were a seminarian of sixteen and I assigned you to teach the adult education classes at Holy Trinity in Newark, you parroted the lines of Jeremiah; I gave you back God's answer to Jeremiah: "Do not say, 'I am only a youth'; for to all to whom I send you you shall go, and whatever I command you you shall speak. Be not afraid of them, for I am with you to deliver you.'"[19] For a long time to come, you will still be *"puer"* in the priesthood—a boy not only in age but also in terms of hands-on experience. But that will be a salutary thing because it will force you to rely on the only real power of which any of us priests can boast—the power of Christ and the wisdom which comes from His Holy Spirit. Capitalize on those sources of strength, and no one will ever dare "despise your youth" (Jer 1:7–8).

Third, never lose that joyful and even playful spirit. Nothing is ever so dull and so deadly to an individual or to the priesthood than the anomaly of one commissioned to be a proclaimer of good news, the gospel, who is morose. On your twenty-fifth anniversary and on your fiftieth, may you be able to say with gusto, "I have no regrets." Some years ago, Cardinal Ratzinger, at another priest's First Mass, asked Almighty God to "give us the courage to put our hand to the plough in order to become ministers of His joy in this world."[6] On yet another similar occasion, he offered the following prayer, which I would like to echo: "We want to ask that [God] will always let something of the splendor of this joy, if it is necessary, fall on our life; that He may give the radiance of this joy ever more deeply and purely to this priest who today for the first time comes before the altar of God; that He will still continually shine upon him when he does so for the last time, when he comes before the altar of eternity in which God shall be the joy of our eternal life, our never-ending youth."[7]

Fourth, closely tied to joy is zeal. Laziness and resignation to the way things are, either in our own personal lives or in the life of the

---

[6] Joseph Ratzinger, *Ministers of Your Joy: Scriptural Meditations on Priestly Spirituality* (Ann Arbor, Mich.: Servant Publications, 1989), p. 37.

[7] Ibid., p. 23.

Church, is the death-knell for a happy, fulfilled and fulfilling priesthood. I once heard someone remark about a priest: "He's a nice man; he's a good man; he's probably even a holy man, but he's got no fire in his belly." "Fire in the belly." That's a rather "down-home" expression, but it says a great deal. Fire is a symbol of the Holy Spirit, and where the Spirit is present in the life of any believer, but especially in that of priest, we find zeal, love, enthusiasm, and devotion to divine affairs. Lukewarmness is but a step removed from coldness. Keep the fire burning warmly and brightly, and you'll discover that your flame is not alone, because it will be the source for many other fires which will flare up together, to the honor of God, to bring about a new Pentecost, for the salvation of the world.

Fifth, stay close to our Lady, the Mother of our High Priest and of every other priest. Way back, in the Age of Faith, St. Bernard urged believers: "Look to the star; call upon Mary." In our era of disbelief, Pope John Paul II has reminded priests of the special bond which they should cultivate with that woman who is both Virgin and Mother, and thus a model for us called to bring forth children for the Father in the celibate state. In his 1988 Letter to Priests, the Holy Father wrote: ". . . it is necessary that our priestly choice of celibacy for the whole of our lives should also be placed within her heart. We must have recourse to this Virgin Mother when we meet difficulties along our chosen path. With her help we must seek always a more profound understanding of this path, an ever more complete affirmation of it in our hearts."[8]

Our Lady took part in her Son's first and only Mass; invite her to be part of every Mass you ever offer. Make her as much a part of your life as she was of the Beloved Disciple, who stood courageously and loyally with her at the foot of the cross for that very First Mass of salvation history. In this way, we make for a union of hearts—Jesus', Mary's, and our own.

Sixth and last of all, keep before you in clear focus what it means to be a priest, a man of mystery, a man who brings the mystery of redemption, the mystery of the eternal into the world of the passing. By God's will, weak, sinful men like us are made agents of the supernatural. The convert poet-monk Thomas Merton wrote about this in mystical terms:

> The world was created without man, but the new creation which is the true Kingdom of God is to be the work of God in

---

[8] Pope John Paul II, *Holy Thursday Letters to My Brother Priests* (Chicago: Midwest Theological Forum, 1992), p. 198.

and through man. It is to be the great, mysterious, theandric work of the Mystical Christ, the New Adam, in whom all men as "One Person" or one "Son of God" will transfigure the cosmos and offer it resplendent to the Father. Here, in this transfiguration, will take place the apocalyptic marriage between God and His creation, the final and perfect consummation of which no mortal mysticism is able to dream and which is barely fore-shadowed in the symbols and images of the last pages of the Apocalypse.[9]

When we cease being comfortable with being one of "those mysterious priests," as our friend and hero Archbishop Fulton Sheen so aptly phrased it, we have lost our one and only reason to exist; we have lost our ability to raise men's minds and hearts to God; we have lost our capacity to transform the boring into the exciting, the human into the divine, the temporal into the eternal. Don't be a puzzle to yourself or to others, but do be a mystery.

My dear people, the British composer Ralph Vaughan Williams wrote a lovely hymn entitled "At the Name of Jesus," in which he urges: "In your hearts enthrone Him, there let Him subdue, all that is not holy, all that is not true." On this day of the Sacred Heart of Jesus, make that your prayer for yourselves, for the Church, for the world. And every time your hearts are brought to His Sacred Heart in prayer, kindly remember this new priest who makes his first solemn thank-offering on this magnificent feast.

And you, dear Father, take to yourself the plea of the Song of Solomon: "Set me as a seal upon your heart." And remember, "many waters cannot quench love," for "love is strong as death" (Song 8:6–7). Indeed, "*diligentibus Deum . . .*," as you well know.

It was often common in more cultured times for an author to end his work with the line: "*Sit finis libri, non finis quaerendi*" (Let this be the end of the book, but not the end of seeking). May I suggest that the action in which we participate today, which some might consider a kind of grand finale to years of prayer, study, and preparation, is in reality but the beginning of what we have reason to hope will be a grand and glorious life of priestly service and personal fulfillment. The heart and soul of this new mode of existence is and must be the Mass. And so, allow me to close this over-long reflection with the ever-insightful and penetrating thoughts of our dear patron, Cardinal Newman:

---

[9] Thomas P. McDonnell, ed., *A Thomas Merton Reader* (Garden City, N.Y.: Image Books, 1974), p. 488.

To me, nothing is so consoling, so piercing, so thrilling, so overwhelming as the Holy Mass. . . . I could attend Masses forever, and not be tired. It is not a mere form of words—it is a great action, the greatest action that can be on earth. It is, not the invocation merely, but if I dare use the word, the evocation of the Eternal. He becomes present on the altar in flesh and blood, before Whom angels bow and devils tremble. This is that awful event which is the scope, and the interpretation, of every part of the solemnity. Words are necessary, but as means, not as ends; they are not mere addresses to the throne of grace, they are instruments of what is far higher. . . of consecration, of sacrifice. They hurry on, as if impatient to fulfill their mission.

Thou dwellest on our altars, Thou the Most Holy, the Most High, in light inaccessible, and the angels fall down before Thee there; and out of visible substances and forms Thou choosest what is choicest to represent and hold Thee. The finest wheat-flour and the purest wine are taken as Thy outward symbols; the most sacred and majestic words minister to the sacrificial rite; altar and sanctuary are adorned decently or splendidly, as our means allow; and Thy priests perform their office in befitting vestments, lifting up chaste hearts and holy hands.[10]

Father Gregoris, please—now and for as long as the Good God gives you life and breath—lift up for us and all God's Holy Church a chaste heart and holy hands. *Ad multos gloriosque annos!*

---

[10] John Henry Newman, *Loss and Gain: The Story of a Convert* (London: Longmans, Green, 1911), pp. 327–328.

First Solemn Mass of Thanksgiving of the Reverend Thomas Kocik

Church of Our Lady of Mount Carmel
Seekonk, Massachusetts, June 15, 1997

To the praise and honor of the Triune God: Father, Son, and Holy Spirit.

Well, Father Tom, you've made it! And all of us here today thank God for the fact. As I was reflecting on our new priest's long and winding road to God's altar, I was reminded of the parable of the sower (see Mt 13:3–8), and I thought of how that story can be applied to his vocational journey. We all recall the details of how some seeds fell along the path, so that the birds of the air came and ate them up. Still others landed on rocky ground, such that some young plants sprouted but were eventually burnt by the scorching sun, for lack of depth. Yet other seeds fell among thorn bushes and were choked, while some had the good fortune of falling on good soil, which brought about a bountiful harvest. Bad formation directors, along with petty and jealous ecclesiastical bureaucrats, provided the thorns and rocky ground but, because God never tests us beyond our endurance, this vocation also had the benefit of good Catholic parents, a Catholic education from the wonderful Felician Sisters, and the incomparable value of Mount St. Mary's Seminary in Emmitsburg.

The truth of the matter, of course, is that the difficulties Father Kocik faced in his priestly preparation are not unique to him; sad to say, his experience is all too common. At the very same time and quite ironically, however, some try to convince us that we are on the precipice of a massive shortage in vocations when the reality is quite different: I believe that we have a crisis in sowers and cultivators of priestly vocations, which is to say, that all too often we have allowed the foxes into the henhouse. However, we need not belabor that point on so joyous an occasion—even if honesty compels us to note this important fact of life in today's Church.

As I observed at the outset, we are here to engage in an act of thanksgiving. But why? The pagan Roman orator Cicero maintained that gratitude was the mother of all virtues and man's supreme duty. This concept was not unknown in Judaism, either. A charming Hasidic tale relates that when God had finished the work of creation, He asked the angels their opinion of it all. One of them supposedly replied that the world was so immense and perfect that nothing was lacking—except for a voice to offer God that which is His due—an expression of gratitude. For six thousand years, we who stand in the tradition of the covenant begun with Abraham, have made our own the sentiments voiced by the Psalmist who sang: "What shall I render to the Lord for all His bounty to me? I will lift up the cup of salvation and call on the name of the Lord" (Ps 116:12–13). Beyond that, our faith informs us that the finest and purest expression of gratitude was uttered in the Word-Become-Flesh, especially as that Word resounds throughout history in the Eucharist, the Church's wondrous sacrifice of praise and thanksgiving. So, we thank Almighty God today, not according to our own fashioning, but in the way which He ordained. Therefore, we have the assurance that our thank-offering will be acceptable.

Nevertheless, we are compelled to ask ourselves: "For what do we give thanks?" To be sure, we are delighted that our friend has achieved what the Lord placed within his heart when he but existed in the mind of God, but there are even more fundamental things for which we must be grateful. We must thank the good Lord, first of all, for the triumph of grace, as well as for the glory of the priesthood. Let us direct our attention to each for a bit.

Just what is grace? In our recent past many of us conceived of grace as a quantifiable object, so that one spoke of gaining "more grace." Without stooping to caricature, it would not be unfair to say that some Catholics have regarded the Church and the sacraments as some kind of spiritual "filling station." A far better view of grace is one which sees it as a relationship between the individual believer and Christ. Grace (which comes from the Latin word for "gift") is nothing other than the very life of God Himself, that gift which restores us to divine friendship and life. It is appropriately termed "sanctifying grace," that is, that gift of God which makes us holy. When first conferred on us in Baptism, it imparts to us divine filiation, so that we become "sons in the Son." We become by grace what Jesus is by nature; hence, we must stress the reality of this new life, a shocking reality, if you think about it, so beautifully and poetically encapsulated in the prayer recited at the commingling of the water and wine: "May we come to share in the divinity of Christ, Who humbled Himself to share in our humanity."

How is grace obtained? Through a process of divine–human

encounter and divine–human cooperation. An analogy with the Incarnation might be helpful. When God sought a home within the human family, He approached the Blessed Virgin with His plan (the encounter). As Mother Teresa says, our Lady "gave God permission" (cooperation). Catholic theology has always explained the operation of grace in the sacraments in exactly the same way. In every sacramental encounter, God takes the initiative by making His offer of grace (*ex opere operato*); the believer accepts the offer and opens himself up to the intervention of the divine (*ex opere operantis*). This process was repeated in St. Mary's Cathedral yesterday. To hold both aspects in a healthy tension is necessary to avoid both a "magical" view of the sacraments, as well as one which places the human response above the divine call.

The experience of the past three decades, however, requires us to admit that if one element of sacramental theology has been sidelined of late, it is grace—and yet it is absolutely central. The story is told of how an interviewer asked Malcolm Muggeridge after writing *Something Beautiful for God* why, given his tremendous admiration for Mother Teresa and Pope John Paul II alike, he had not followed them into the Church. His response? "No grace!" Some years later, both he and his wife did in fact become Catholics. The question was then posed, "Why now?" "Grace," came the reply. Everything, my dear people, is grace: Grace initiates, accompanies, and completes our journey to the heavenly Kingdom.

Grace not only makes us holy; it keeps us holy and even returns us to holiness, if need be. Living a Gospel life is not easy, as the Savior Himself acknowledged when He declared, "for man it is impossible." Yet He went on, "but not for God." "With God all things are possible" (Mt 19:26). Because of the Father's great love for us, He has given us His Son to be not only our model of perfect obedience, as you heard in the Second Reading, but also to be the very power within us to do His Will. Christ gives us His grace, to begin with, in Baptism, making us exactly what St. Paul said we are, "a new creation" (2 Cor 5:17). God's grace is not simply a higher octane of our normal human steam or energy; it is a totally different mode of existence, which enables us human beings—with all our faults and failings—to live a new life. In other words, Jesus does not come and merely stand by our side as some kind of holy cheerleader; He enters into the very fabric of our lives and becomes the operative principle for our response of faith to the demands of the Gospel. Jesus, the God-Man, identifies with us and makes possible our "yes" to His Heavenly Father and, simultaneously, makes possible our possession of eternal life. That grace of Christ comes to us in prayer, in the reading of Sacred Scripture, and in the celebration of the Church's sacraments, most especially in and through the Eucharistic Sacrifice.

Yesterday, my friends, God's grace overtook this man in so powerful a manner that he will never again be the same. By God's free and omnipotent Will, this man can act in God's Name, so that the words he speaks are God's words and the actions he performs are God's actions. Of course, we must also confess that divine grace does not annihilate our human nature; it perfects it, so that our humanity in its frailty remains as a potent witness to one and all. And so, do not expect to see an entirely new "Tom Kocik" henceforth: We will still encounter a friend who is witty and sensitive and, yes, he will still exhibit some of the qualities of a ditzy, absent-minded egghead. After all, God would never dream of obliterating some of our more endearing characteristics!

Our second goal of thanksgiving this afternoon is for the Sacred Priesthood. Reflection on the priesthood is as old as the Church herself. Sometimes these meditations are unrealistic and maudlin; sometimes they are highly theological but leave us cold because they lack the poetry and beauty which belong to the human contemplation of the divine.

Permit me to share with you a sampling of texts which come close to doing the job. Cardinal Suhard of Paris once asserted: "The priesthood is not . . . something. It is someone: Christ." St. Francis of Assisi (never a priest but a permanent deacon, remember) said: "If I saw an angel and a priest, I would bend my knee first to the priest and then to the angel." St. John Vianney, patron of parish priests, declared from experience: "After God, the priest is everything. Leave a parish twenty years without priests; they will worship beasts." He went on to say: "The priest will not understand the greatness of his office till he is in Heaven. If he understood it on earth, he would die, not of fear, but of love." Following up on that same notion, the French spiritual writer Père Gatry said something we really need to ponder in our time: "If people could realize what the priesthood is, there would be too many priests." Where does the priesthood find its great dignity? In the simple but awesome recognition of St. Vincent Ferrer: "The Blessed Virgin opened Heaven only once; the priest does so at every Mass."

The reverence and respect of the Catholic faithful for their clergy is directed, then, not toward the man himself but toward Christ Who is the Priest of the new eternal covenant and toward the priesthood any man derives from Him and shares with Him. An anecdote from history may demonstrate our very reasonable approach to all this. One day, during Pope Pius VII's imprisonment by Napoleon, the Pope and Emperor were again drawn into what had become a daily round of confrontations. The Pope said something which made the little dictator more angry than usual, causing him to rise to his full five feet, point his finger in the Holy Father's face, and scream, "If you don't behave yourself, I will destroy both you and your Church!" Which caused the Pope simply to smile, condescendingly, and say: "Silly little man, my clergy and I haven't destroyed this Church for nineteen centuries, and you think you can do it single-handedly?" Realism. And even the Modernist heretic Alfred Loisy understood something of this when he sarcastically mused: "They tell me that every Sunday in Paris more than ten thousand sermons are preached. And the people still believe!" Realism again, even if jaundiced.

Why can such assessments be made? Indeed, why must they be made? Because of a fundamental theological truth. Vatican II's *Sacrosanctum Concilium* emphasized a point frequently neglected or forgotten in regard to the celebration of the sacraments, namely, that it is Christ Who is active in the administration and reception of each sacrament, which is an action of Christ and an extension of His paschal mystery offered to the believer in the here and now. It is not the priest, not the individual, and not even the Church which is the focus of our attention but Jesus Himself. Priest, individual, and Church draw their meaning from Christ and are instruments and beneficiaries of His redemptive sacrifice—an important reminder in this era of personality cults.

As St. Luke recounts the proceedings at the Last Supper, just verses after the passage that was proclaimed today, we hear of some very unpleasant things that took place. First, Jesus feels compelled to announce that one of His own would betray Him. Second, we learn that a dispute erupted among that Chosen Band. Over what? Over questions of power, prestige and authority. So clerical envy is nothing new, except that now we also have heavy doses of anti-clericalism, to boot. So, some folks will argue that events like a Solemn First Mass are but a regrettable leftover of an excessively clericalistic and triumphalistic age in the Church, but as formidable and insightful a theologian as Father Karl Rahner would disagree mightily. "Why do we celebrate such a day?" he asks. "Does the Church invite her faithful to make a kind of first installment of the laurels to a young man who has not yet done anything else but offer

God his heart and his life, when actually it is only the completed sacrifice that ought to be celebrated?" He answers thus:

> No, we are not honoring any man. We are honoring only the priesthood of Jesus Christ. We are honoring the Church, the entire Church of all those redeemed, made holy, and called to eternal life. We are honoring her to whom we all belong, whether we are priests or "merely" believers and sanctified. For we are all knit so closely into one body that the grace, dignity, or power that comes to one man graces and lifts all the others, and in one man's being called to service we glimpse the holy dignity of all.[1]

What the German theologian was seeking to advance was a notion of the Church as the communion of saints, wherein we would never find resentment, hostility, jealousy, or power-plays. By venerating the ministerial priesthood, we pay homage to God's grace and to His Son's redeeming love, which are made accessible to us through His priests. In other words, we are celebrating the gift of that salvation we begin to know here on earth, as we look toward its consummation in the life to come.

Surrounded by joy as we are this day, we must nevertheless keep our balance. Yesterday, dear Father, amid the glory and splendor of the Sacred Liturgy, you were inserted more deeply into the Lord's paschal mystery—an indispensable component of which is the Passion. In the ancient papal coronation rite, a Capuchin friar (a distant relative perhaps of your Bishop!) was always deputed to remind the new pope of this fact by pushing his way to the fore as he cast a cord of blazing hemp at the feet of the Sovereign Pontiff, with the somber and sobering words: *Sic transit gloria mundi* (Thus passes the glory of the world). Many latter-day forms of spirituality so stress Easter joy or a life which is more connected to clerical privilege than priestly identification with the great High Priest, that they bypass the wisdom of the ages: *Post crucem, lucem*; only after enduring the agony of the cross can one expect the glory of the resurrection. Therefore, when moments of trial come; when celibacy is more an onus than a freedom; when obedience hardly seems rational; when wearing your collar as a permanent fixture (like the priesthood itself) gets tiresome—in those times, look to the Crucified One and remember. For Jesus never forgets His sacred Passion; indeed, He is perpetually reminded of it as He looks at His holy wounds, which He bears even in His risen life. And as He

---

[1] Karl Rahner, *Meditations on the Sacraments* (New York: Seabury Press, 1977), 61.

beholds those wounds and recalls His bloody passion, He renews His love for the sinners He thus redeemed. By remembering, have Christ remember to enfold you in His saving embrace and to lift you up in prayer as He raises His priestly hands to make intercession to His Heavenly Father for you and for the whole world.

Today secular society celebrates what the Church celebrates every day: Fathers' Day. But this is a special one for us gathered together for this event because yesterday the Lord God made this son of His by Baptism a father in the family of His divine Son's Church. When John Henry Newman became a cardinal, the Fathers of the Oratory asked him how he would now like to be addressed. The great convert-theologian replied that of all the titles and honorifics which had been bestowed upon him during his long and productive life, the one which meant the most was "Father." Being a father in the natural order is a burden, but also an inestimable joy; it is no different in the supernatural order. Father Tom, never let me hear that you have been dragged into the company of men who belong to the cult of the slob and say, "Just call me Tom." Nor if you are sent for graduate studies some day, that you end up joining the ranks of the self-important, causing you to suggest, "You may call me Dr. Kocik." Cherish the title of father, because it comes with the love and devotion of your spiritual family and because it serves as a constant challenge for you to act like a priest, to look like a priest, to be the priest who is *semper et pro semper* a father.

Just last week I came upon a new poem written as a tribute to priests on Fathers' Day. Allow me to share some excerpts with you. As I read it, may I ask all of you to renew your own personal esteem not only for this new priest, not only for priests you like and respect naturally, but for all who share in Christ's one priesthood, the only reason being that they have been configured to Christ to do for men what leads us to God. Barbara Fader writes with manifest love and tenderness:

> Who are you, man of Mystery, our Father?
> By what arrogance do you approach the Holy
> —offering your manliness to mate with Sacred Spouse,
> and vowing with such singular abandonment
> to wed yourself to Holy Mother Church
> and sow with her, in promiscuity divine, the seeds of life?

> Or can it be that, led by ceaseless calling,
> summoned by the Matchmaker Who serves the cause
>   of Love,
> pursued by the Relentless One, you have
>   succumbed—
> and so it is submission which, to unholy eyes, appears
>   presumption?
> How is it that, child-free, you are our Father?
> Is it that you daily bear God's children?
> Is it that, with human voice, you speak a Father's
>   Word?
> Is it that you, fasting and breaking fasts, call us to
>   supper
> and gather us at table . . . ?
> Or that you celebrate our rites of passage,
> advising, chastising, baptizing us with water and with
>   fire?
> Is it that you lift us in your prayer, holding,
> embracing and blessing as only a Father might?
> Or that you hear our calling in the dark
> and come to take our hand and light a light—
> Or, in your priestly parenting,
> you come anointing, pointing the way past death to
>   life?
> Who are you, man of Mystery, our Father?
> You've wed yourself to Holy Mother Church and,
>   everywhere,
> you sow with her, in promiscuity divine, the seeds of
>   Life.
> You bear and speak and feed, you shape and renew
> and heal and bless as only a Father can do.
> And so we, on this Fathers' Day, your untold children,
>   grateful, pray,
> "May life and Holy Spouse and God bless you." [2]

In lovely language, the poet says what a theologian like Josef Sellmair put more starkly years ago: "A people that does not desert its priests is not deserted by God."

And now, for a bit of reality therapy. Someday, Father Kocik, you are going to die—as will all of us. In fact, of course, the only

---

[2] Barbara M. Fader, "Poem to a Priest on Father's Day," *The Priest* (June 1997), p. 5.

reason for the Church or the priesthood is that we are all terminal cases, who need the grace of Christ to make this journey through earthly life to eternal life as safely and surely as possible. As one of the *dispensatores mysteriorum Dei* (dispensers of the mysteries of God), it will be your obligation and your privilege to lead your flock, your family, on that pilgrimage. In the Byzantine liturgy (which you so admire), as the Creed is chanted, the priest stands at the head of his people—all facing the Rising Sun together; throughout the profession of faith, he waves the chalice veil continuously between himself and the tabernacle as a reminder that the propositions of faith being proclaimed are not the full reality, for they but point us toward the complete and final revelation which comes at the hour of our death. As the Byzantine priest lies in his coffin fully vested to join in the Liturgy of Heaven, the chalice veil is placed over his face to symbolize the awesome fact that now in death he stands on the other side of the veil, gazing face-to-face on the Mystery which he heralded and celebrated merely in sign.

But between that final day of your life and now, you will be celebrating the Eucharistic Sacrifice; always do so in the conscious awareness that what we do here on earth is done in union with the whole court of Heaven, particularly with our Lady. As the *Catechism* puts it so lovingly (no. 1370): "In the Eucharist the Church is as it were at the foot of the cross with Mary, united with the offering and intercession of Christ." Just as the Blessed Mother was instrumental in leading her Son into His first sign at Cana, that transformation of water into wine which foreshadowed the yet greater transformation of bread and wine into His sacred Body and Blood, now she beckons you, her Son's newest brother in the priesthood and hence her newest son, to the Calvary of this church. For the first time at this altar, say for us the words and do for us the actions which bring us light and life, joy and peace.

This request is an ancient one—no more and no less than that of the five scouts we meet in the Book of Judges, those men who then represented the desire of the entire People of God: ". . . Come with us, and be to us a father and a priest." And the response of that priest of old, dear Father, we hope will be yours today and every day until the good Lord brings you to concelebrate the Liturgy of Heaven. We read: "And the priest's heart was glad . . . and [he] went in the midst of the people" (Judg 18:19–20). The Saints in Heaven, the souls in Purgatory and we still struggling here on Earth—the whole Church—await your glad response.

Tenth Anniversary of the Priestly Ordination of the Reverend Michael Lankford

Good Shepherd Sunday
Church of St. Jerome, West Long Branch, New Jersey, April 21, 2002

Well, you've made it! And we—your family, friends, and parishioners—are delighted that you have. However, I should note that in the grand scheme of things, you're still a baby—in fact, just working on your permanent teeth! As someone celebrating his twenty-fifth anniversary, I know what it's like to move beyond that stage into getting false teeth!

I have known Father Lankford for most of his ten years in the priesthood and have known about him even before that. As I was going to dinner in Manhattan the other night, I recalled that he and I had been to the same restaurant about eight years ago. After a wonderful evening of good food, good wine, and good company, we walked out onto First Avenue to find my car gone; the saga found us at two in the morning in the Brooklyn impounding center of New York City. Although we both had studied the parking signs, to this day he maintains the whole debacle was my fault and that he was merely an innocent bystander. In addition to his complete innocence, whether guilty or not, we who know him and love him anyway, cannot help but thinking of things English when he comes to mind; in truth, I'm amazed he's not still in mourning for the "Queen Mum." Exquisite taste is, of course, synonymous with the name of Father Lankford, which a cursory overview of his suite would confirm. On occasions like this, people often want to be regaled with tons of stories like these. Well, I'm not Marc Antony and I have come neither to bury Caesar nor to praise him. I will, however, relate other Lankfordesque anecdotes, if pressed to do so at the reception. Seriously, though, what the Church wants me to do and what Father Michael wants me to do because he is a loyal son of the Church—a genuine churchman—is to reflect on the mystery of the priesthood in his life and in the life of the Church.

More than a century and a half ago, a bright Anglican at the University of Oxford studied his way into the Catholic Church, especially under the influence of the Fathers and the witness of history. Our celebrant today followed the path of the great Cardinal

Newman, led by the kindly light of the truth. Even before his entrance into full communion with the Catholic Church, the scholarly and devout young Michael was already possessed of a profound sense of the sacred, a filial devotion to the Mother of God, a love for the Sacred Liturgy, and an awareness of the centrality of the Eucharist in the Christian life. Like Cardinal Newman and so many other "converts," Michael's decision to "swim the Tiber" was just the logical conclusion to the syllogism of his studies and prayer. That doesn't mean it was easy; it was not because, like the long procession of Anglicans who have "poped" in the past hundred and more years, becoming a Catholic in fact and not only in mind or heart involved emotional and cultural upheaval and, most especially, what Newman referred to as "the parting of friends." But when the Holy Spirit convicts a person of the truth, when someone is "cut to the heart" by the Spirit of Truth, one must echo the audience of Peter's Pentecost homily: "What are we to do, my brothers?" The first pope presented them with a plan of action and, we are told, three thousand responded that day. Michael did the same.

The decision to follow Christ in His holy Catholic Church, however, is not a one-shot deal and certainly does not mean that the struggle is over. On the contrary, in many ways, it is all just beginning. The sacred author of our Second Reading today knew that, and thus he counseled his readers: "Beloved: If you are patient when you suffer for doing what is good, this is a grace before God. For to this you have been called, because Christ also suffered for you, leaving you an example that you should follow in his footsteps." And Michael's *sequela Christi* took him beyond a juridical relationship with the Church of Christ; he heard the voice of the Good Shepherd calling him in a way that few others in Christ's flock are called. Once again, he responded, embarking on a program of priestly formation which resulted in his insertion into the priesthood of Jesus Christ through the ancient and apostolic gesture of the laying on of hands on May 16, 1992. Because sacramental ordination configures a man to Christ in a manner so real and so intimate, Father Michael's life has never been the same; nor has the Church's, thank God.

The priesthood, however, is not Father Michael's personal possession or hobbyhorse, nor that of any other individual priest. It is Christ's priesthood, which He graciously and lovingly shares with His Church and for His Church. Therefore, it would be well if we broadened our horizons for a bit.

For thirty-two years now, the Church Universal has used this

Sunday to "pray the Lord of the harvest to send forth laborers into His harvest." But prayer for priestly and religious vocations takes place in a context—both social and ecclesial—as does the response to such calls. What is the contemporary context in which we are asking the Lord to open the hearts and minds of our youth to hear His summons? What can or ought we do to enable His voice to be better heard?

Some time ago, one observer wrote about what he called "the utter contempt into which Catholicism has fallen" in this land. Believe it or not, that analysis actually came from the pen of Cardinal Newman, as well, on the very brink of the Oxford Movement's major successes. I cite him to provide some type of historical framework for our own analysis and also by way of recalling that, not infrequently, the adage is correct: It is always darkest before the dawn. But hope should not be confused with presumption, nor should a Christian optimist lapse into the role of a Pollyanna. So, let us survey the landscape, using the style of a Caravaggio—*chiaroscuro*, looking at the total picture with its lights and shadows.

What is the image of priesthood and religious life to those outside the Church? The average American knows of priests who are pedophiles, women religious who are radical feminists, theologians who are chafing under Roman oppression and struggling to free the Catholic faithful from medieval patterns of existence. We know that the Church of "60 Minutes" is not the real Church, or at least not the whole story of the real Church. We know that the priesthood represented by a film like *Priest* does not reflect the real priesthood, or at least not the whole story of the real priesthood. We know that *The New York Times*' version of American Catholic theology and practice is not the real story of our theology and practice, or at least not the whole story of our theology and practice. So, what should we do?

I would suggest a two-pronged approach. First, let us be honest enough to acknowledge that—unfortunately—there is truth in what the media say about us: We do have pedophiles, adulterers, radicals, and dissenters within our bosom; indeed, in all too many places they hold positions of power and authority and exert strong influence on the formation of our national and diocesan priorities, as well as in their execution. It seems to me that if we wish to attack the media elite for their unfair handling of Catholic affairs (and we should), we also need to clean up our own house. That will involve both devoted prayer and serious work. We must pray Almighty God to move the embarrassing sheep within our sheepfold to an experience of genuine conversion, so that their lives are brought into accord with the commitments they freely and, presumably, honestly made many years ago. At the same time, we must never tire of prevailing upon the bishops—our fathers in God and the chief shepherds of the local churches—to take seriously their responsibility to deal effectively with those who mar the image of the spotless Bride of Christ by their infidelity and counter-witness.

Then we can take on the media with a measure of conviction and integrity. And that is critical to do because not only is vocation recruitment adversely affected by the negative images of the Church abroad in society, but the Church's overall work of evangelization. Inaccurate images perpetuate stereotypes which form popular perceptions, and perceptions create reality, whether we like it or not. The persecution against the apostolic Church alluded to in today's Second Reading could not be stemmed by those early believers; it was completely beyond their control. That is not the case with the present onslaught against the Church and her mission to teach and preach the truth of Christ; we are full-fledged citizens of a democratic republic, with rights and responsibilities to add our voices to the chorus of a pluralistic and free nation. A refusal to do so is to fail both our homeland and our God. It is to sell short a society which has been intrigued and even captivated to some extent by the teachings of *Veritatis Splendor* and *Evangelium Vitae*. No, the picture is not without bright spots.

Now, what do we see within the Church? Or better yet, what do our young people see when they seek out images of priesthood and religious life? The Church-at-large has been fed a line which argues that the vocational well has dried up, that no young people are willing to "buy into" the traditional notions of priesthood and religious life. When we assert, without fear of contradiction, that such a contention is patently false and an exercise in wishful thinking, we have been most charitable in our evaluation. The young themselves are often put through the paces by ecclesiastical bureaucrats who intend to screen out those who have the mind of the Church and in this way to obviate the true renewal of the Church envisioned by the Second Vatican Council and, at the same time, to create such a dearth of vocations that their own aspirations for Catholic life will become the operative terms of the discussion, by dint of circumstances. Bishops also play into the hands of such people—not infrequently in an unwitting manner—by committing themselves and their dioceses to pastoral plans which take defeat and disaster as "givens" with programs like the appointment of non-ordained parochial administrators and the encouragement of so-called priestless Eucharists. Good religious abet the further deterioration of religious life by adopting the herd instinct of "going along to get along" and maintaining silence in the face of wrong-headed schemes. Priests who are not normally identifiable as priests in the day-to-day affairs of the secular city make the priesthood even more invisible and eccentric; beyond that, deputing lay people to perform their sacramental responsibilities simply reinforces notions of a priesthood in which there is very little to recommend a lifelong, celibate, and sacrificial response.

Once more, though, we must realize that this is by no means the total story. For there are dioceses and religious congregations in which we find such a glut of youthful vocations as almost to stretch our credibility and imagination. What image do they project? One sees young clergy and religious on fire with love for Christ, His Gospel, and His Church. One sees confident disciples who know the truth and desire to spend their lives communicating it. One sees clerics and consecrated women and men who are proud of their vocations, want the world to know that, and intend to encourage countless others to follow them in responding to the invitation of the Master. And the result of all this? Dioceses and communities like that will not know what to do with all their candidates and will eventually be sending them out as missionaries to other ecclesial settings which are in danger of extinction because of prior decisions to embark on programs of action which have been suicidal. In point of fact, that is already happening in many places.

The Book of Revelation speaks about those "who have survived the great period of trial." I submit that you and I are among that number. When Cardinal Newman took a realistic look at the situation in which he found himself, he ultimately concluded that "it is the coming of a Second Spring; it is a restoration." We can have a similar confidence, not because of our own genius, creativity, ingenuity, or gimmickry but because this is the Church of the Good Shepherd, and it is He Who will shepherd us. He has promised it, and His Word never fails.

In 1992, the year of our celebrant's ordination, Pope John Paul II issued an apostolic exhortation on priestly formation. He entitled it, *Pastores Dabo Vobis*, harking back to the prophecy of Jeremiah as God assured His people: "I will give you shepherds after my own heart." The "will" of that verb is not a simple future; it conveys a determination on God's part to give us the shepherds that we need. Therefore, even when society tries to dirty our faces, God "walks ahead" of us and says, *"Pastores dabo vobis."* Even when Church officials sit on their hands in the face of crises, God "walks ahead"of us and says, *"Pastores dabo vobis."* Even when the vessels of election show themselves to be vessels of clay, indeed "thieves and robbers," God "walks ahead" of us and says, *"Pastores dabo vobis."* And they are to be shepherds of a most special kind—shepherds after the heart of none other than the Good Shepherd Himself.

The Holy Father reflects on the divine pledge thus:

> Today, this promise of God is still living and at work in the Church. At all times, she knows she is the fortunate receiver of these prophetic words. She sees them put into practice daily in so many parts of the world, or rather, in so many human hearts, young hearts in particular. On the threshold of the third millennium, and in the face of the serious and urgent needs which confront the Church and the world, she yearns to see this promise fulfilled in a new and richer way, more intensely and effectively; she hopes for an extraordinary outpouring of the Spirit of Pentecost (no. 82).

Our current crisis, my dear people, is not the first time that shepherds have failed their flocks in the history of the Church. We are scandalized today to hear that one or two percent of our priests have come "only to steal and slaughter and destroy," and rightly so. However, do you realize that, before the Council of Trent in the sixteenth century, one could point to no more than 1 or 2 percent of the clergy who were living upright lives? So deplorable was it all that Pope Hadrian VI in 1522 felt compelled to say: "We are well aware that for some years now many abominable things have taken place at this Holy See: abuses in matters spiritual, transgressions of the commandments; indeed that all has turned for the worse. So it is not surprising that the sickness has spread from the head to the members, from the pope to the prelates. All of us, prelates and clergy, have departed from the right way."[1] While even one wayward shepherd is one too many, we need to thank the Lord for the outstanding shepherd He has given us in the person of Pope John Paul II, and in the thousands upon thousands of faithful priests, including the man we honor today.

Which brings me to one more thought, which I would like to address to all you members of Christ's lay faithful. When was the last time you acknowledged a priest's good homily or reverent celebration of Holy Mass? When was the last time you prayed for the priest who baptized you or witnessed your marriage? When was the last

---

[1] Cited in Hans Kung's *Short History of the Catholic Church*.

time you thought lovingly about the wonderful women religious who gave you a Catholic education? When was the last time you thanked a Sister for looking like one? The Liturgy of the Hours during the first week of Lent puts a petition on our lips for Wednesday Vespers: "Holy Father, Who gave Christ to be the Shepherd of our souls, be present to the shepherds and the people entrusted to their care, lest the shepherd's care be lacking to the flock—or the obedience of the flock be lacking to the shepherd." I think that prayer is saying two things. First, pastors have obligations to their people—and people have obligations to their pastors, among which is obedience. Obedience comes from the Latin word which means "to listen intently." When your priests echo the voice of Christ and His Vicar, you must listen intently; otherwise, you run the risk of not recognizing the Good Shepherd's voice when He calls you to enter the gate of the sheepfold for all eternity. If you have been listening to the voice of strangers, purveyors of falsehoods about the nature of God and man alike, whether in the media or the entertainment industry or hostile academia, your hearing needs to be fine-tuned to the voice of Jesus Christ and putting a filter on would also be a good idea. Secondly, that prayer is also a reminder that those in the priesthood and consecrated life are human, with human needs and expectations. If it is true that you want to be able to count on our affirmation and support, then recall that we should be able to count on the same in return.

My dear friends, may our poor prayers and efforts always seek to be worthy of God's holy determination to provide His flock with the shepherds it needs, shepherds of appropriate quality and quantity, shepherds after the Lord's own heart.

Ah, one more matter. I would be grossly remiss if I did not seize upon this opportunity to invite young men present to consider carefully if the Good Shepherd is not whispering an invitation into their ears to share in His ministry. From the time I entered the seminary as a seventeen-year-old collegian at Seton Hall and to the present, I am happy to say that I have had not a single regret and, yes, I would do it all over again. I know that Father Lankford would say the same. Therefore, as our Holy Father never tires of saying, *"Noli timere. Duc in altum"*—Do not be afraid. Put out into the deep. You will not be alone, for Christ will be walking ahead of you and His holy people will be there to support you. And to young ladies present, do not be afraid to commit yourselves to communities of women religious who are faithful to Christ and His Church; in this parish, you are fortunate to have the wonderful example of the Religious Teachers

Filippini. Join that throng of intelligent and holy women who helped make the Church in our nation the great Church it has been because of their commitment to our schools and social services. Young people, do not become discouraged because those responding to the Shepherd's voice are fewer in number than in other times; see in this an exciting challenge to make a difference--one with eternal consequences for yourselves and for the people you will serve.

And so, Father Michael, I am sure I speak for this entire body of Christ's faithful when I thank you for having heard Christ's call to His holy Church and priesthood many years ago and for having responded promptly and generously, and likewise for your constant witness to the good, the true, and the beautiful, which give us even on earth a foretaste of the good, the true, and the beautiful we all hope to experience for all eternity. With Cardinal Newman, dear Father, we applaud your priestly dedication and say: "Blessed are they who give the flower of their days and their strength of soul and body to Thee, [O Lord]. Blessed are they who in their youth turn to Thee Who didst give Thy life for them, and wouldst fain give it to them and implant it in them, that they may live forever."

Finally, as your elder brother whom you have honored with this task of preaching God's holy Word on this glorious day, permit me to suggest that you make your own today and for as long as the good God gives you life and breath the words of Cardinal Newman as he reflected on his priestly vocation: ". . . let me dwell often upon those, His manifold mercies to me and to my brethren, which are the consequence of His coming upon earth; His adorable counsels, as manifested in my personal vocation; how it is that I am called and others not; the wonders of His grace towards me, from my infancy until now; the gifts He has given me; the aid He has vouchsafed; the answers He has accorded to my prayers."

Ad multos gloriosque annos!

On the Occasion of My Mother's Death

Committal Service, Hoban Chapel of Cathedral Cemetery
Scranton, Pennsylvania, April 10, 2004

Permit me to begin my reflections this morning with several words of thanks. First of all, to the wonderful staff of St. Mary's Villa Nursing Home and the Sisters of Jesus Crucified, who own and operate the facility. After my mother broke her hip in September of 2000, it became clear she could no longer live on her own. Given her tremendous independence, even at the age of 84, I knew that the inevitable transfer to a more protected environment would not be easy for her and, therefore, not for me, either! I contacted the Sisters, who said there would be "room in the inn." She arrived at the Villa's assisted living building just at the hour of First Vespers for the Solemnity of the Immaculate Conception. At that moment, I entrusted her to the care of our Lady and, as St. Bernard put it in his Memorare, we were not "left unaided." As time went on and Mother had to move "to the other side" as they say, she had confidence in my judgment and in that of the staff because of all the love and consideration she had been given to that point. Every day of her stay at the Villa—no matter where I was in the world—I called her; whenever I could, I visited her. And with every contact with the staff, I found them uniformly interested, helpful, competent, and loving. I cannot tell you how much that meant to this only son, whose work caused him to be so far away so often. I must single out for special mention Sister Carmelita who, particularly in the last days, was ever-present to my mother—praying with her and for her. Also a most inadequate but most heartfelt word of gratitude to Kathleen and Frank Flynn, whom Mother came to love so dearly and to regard as family and whose frequent visits she so treasured. Finally, thanks to all of you who have come—some from a great distance—on such short notice and at such an inconvenient time, to pray for my mother and to honor me by your most welcome presence.

The death of any person. but especially one we know and love, is an opportunity to consider that all-too-often ignored fact of life we call death. What lessons might my mother's death hold out to each of us?

Blessed John XXIII was 78 years old when he was elected pope.

At an early press conference, a reporter rather indelicately asked him how long he thought he might be around. With his characteristic jovial approach to life and good, old peasant humor, the Pontiff replied: "Any day is a good day to be born, and any day is a good day to die. My bags are packed, and I'm ready to go."

As some of you know, my mother was born on April 8 and, yes, she died on April 8. Now, those of you with a classical background will recall that the ancients put much stock in such a coincidence. Indeed, they believed that the truly great people of history always died on their birthdays. Furthermore, the day of my mother's birth was Good Friday that year; she died on Holy Thursday, thus completing the full liturgical cycle. Furthermore, how appropriate that a priest's mother die on Holy Thursday. And one more angle on the date of death: She was always perturbed if her birthday fell during Holy Week because it meant her priest-son couldn't be with her to celebrate. I can't help but think that she put in a "plug" with the Lord to get me there for her birthday this year. As usual, she got her way. Thus, even though Good Pope John was right about the non-consequential nature of the date of one's birth or death, Mother's dates are vested with a unique meaning.

Let us turn our thoughts next to the Pope's other concern—preparedness for death. At funerals, I always ask the congregation if they would have been ready to face Christ as Judge, had they been called three days ago. This is not intended as a scare tactic but as a wake-up call. As I said for my father's funeral homily twenty years ago, I say again about my mother: She was no saint, as she would readily admit. Due to more than her fair share of hard knocks in her youth, she could be very suspicious of persons and their motivations; she was extremely determined; she had a fiery disposition; she could be, shall we say, very earthy! And how could I fail to note some of the skirmishes between her and me, not atypical I'm told for only children and their mothers? Well, let's be frank: Back in Newark we would say that she was "a tough old broad."

All of us have traits that our better side would prefer to deny or wish away, but neither is a solution. God has a more effective plan. He wants us to take our personality flaws—potential and real—and to submit them to the action of His grace over the long haul of our lives. When Mother was admitted to the Villa and I was so apprehensive, Cardinal Stafford (also an only child) assured me that this would be for the best. He said I would see my mother grow in ways I had never imagined and that our own relationship would develop in an equally unimaginable manner. He was right on both scores.

Surrounded by love and cared for totally, what could have been major personality weaknesses were slowly but surely either eliminated or turned to great assets. When added to her natural strengths of generosity, fairness, selflessness, humor, and desire for perfection, what emerged was one of the most beloved residents of the Villa—a point made to me repeatedly by the staff and witnessed by me in a profound way on the day of her death. And Almighty God is willing and able to do that for each of us, if we but submit ourselves to the gentle action of His grace, being as patient with ourselves as He is with us, knowing that human cooperation in conjunction with divine grace is an unbeatable combination.

When I arrived on Thursday, Kathleen Flynn said, "What a privilege for the mother of a priest to die on Holy Thursday!" Truth be told, I hadn't really seen a connection initially but, by Holy Thursday night, I was reminded of a story that Father Nicholas and I heard about last year during our trip to Poland. It seems that the week before a young man's ordination, his mother approached him with a bag, which she declared to be his ordination gift from her. Upon opening it, he found it filled with grains of wheat. Seeing his puzzled look, his mother explained: "Since you were five or six years old and first told me you wanted to be a priest, I have prayed and sacrificed even day to make that dream of yours come true. And every time I made a sacrifice for that intention over the past years, I placed a grain of wheat in this bag as a symbol. Take this sack, get the grains crushed, made into flour, and then bread; use it for your First Mass."

Mother had a fierce loyalty for the Church, but especially for the priesthood. It would have been a tragic mistake on your part to attack the priesthood in general or any individual priest in her presence, for that fiery nature of hers would come into full play. She was not naïve about priests; in fact, she had an almost-infallible capacity to estimate them. From my first year in the seminary, I remember bringing classmates or priests home for dinner or vacations (living at the Jersey Shore seemed to increase my popularity for some reason!). Within a half-hour of their being with us, my mother would yank me out into the kitchen and give her evaluation: "He'll make a fine priest." Or, "He'll never last." No, she knew too many priests too well to be blind to our human foibles, but she couldn't abide negativity toward men that she thought had a unique place within the Heart of Christ and who, at least at some moment in their lives, had zeal and fervor, even if now lost or hidden.

In this context, I feel compelled to say how fortunate I have always felt to have had both parents so supportive of my priestly vocation. Today it is regrettably common to find Catholic parents of even large families unwilling to offer their children to the priesthood or religious life. Both my parents eagerly and lovingly offered their only son to the Lord and the service of His Church, and they deemed my ordination their proudest accomplishment; I suspect the good Lord would agree. The dress my mother is wearing in the coffin and into eternity is the gown she wore for my priestly ordination; she never wanted to wear it for anything else and often expressed the hope that I would remember to have her clothed in it in death. Some of you might remember that in the "old days," the manutergium or cloth that bound the newly-ordained priest's hands after anointing was given to his mother, precisely for inclusion in her casket; that practice was stopped with the revised rites of ordination. Of all the post-conciliar changes, that one annoyed my mother in a most personal way. Well, Mother, here's second-best.

I would be most remiss if I did not speak about my mother's bond with Sisters, for whom she felt a special affection. Interestingly, she had a close bond with them throughout my years in grammar school and high school, working for them and with them day after day and year after year. Although she never said it, I suppose she credited them with her return to the practice of the Faith. When she put me into Catholic school both she and my father were "fallen-aways." Being around the Sisters and seeing their loving devotion brought her and my father home. That's why she was so disappointed as religious life began to unravel in the sixties and seventies. That pushed her into an amusing apostolate from that time forward: Whenever she saw a nun on the street or in a supermarket, she would make a point of going up to her and saying, "Thank you, Sister, for wearing your habit." By the eighties. she also would stuff a dollar bill into the Sister's hand! Perhaps you can see now why I wanted my mother to live out her last days in an institution overseen by women religious. And neither Mother nor I was disappointed.

Today, my dear friends, is the "deadest" day of the liturgical year, but that does not mean that Christ was not busy on that first Holy Saturday. Indeed, St. Peter tells us that the Lord spent His time evangelizing the souls of the patriarchs, prophets, and all the other just men and women who had preceded His coming but looked toward it with eager longing. An ancient homily by an unknown author is assigned to the Liturgy of the Hours for today. In that work, the preacher imaginatively depicts Jesus as going down to

Sheol and grasping old Adam by the hand and bringing him up as the first to share in His risen life. May our Lord be similarly occupied at this moment on behalf of my dear mother.

The Venerable John Henry Cardinal Newman composed hundreds of prayers, but one of my favorites graces the holy card printed as a memorial for my mother's death. It is the Cardinal's prayer for a happy death. Now, in our neo-pagan culture, to speak of a "happy" death sounds like an absurdity or at least an oxymoron, but people with the gift of faith know that deaths can indeed be happy. Cardinal Newman believed it at the very core of his being, thus prompting him to pen these lovely lines:

> Oh, my Lord and Saviour, support me in that hour in the strong arms of Thy Sacraments, and by the fresh fragrance of Thy consolations. Let the absolving words be said over me, and the holy oil sign and seal me, and Thy own Body be my food, and Thy Blood my sprinkling; and let my sweet Mother Mary breathe on me, and my Angel whisper peace to me, and my glorious Saints . . . smile upon me; that in them all, and through them all, I may receive the gift of perseverance, and die, as I desire to live, in Thy faith, in Thy Church, in Thy service, and in Thy love. Amen.

That prayer was fulfilled in my mother; may it be so for each of us, as well.

LECTURES AND PAPERS

When you see a priest, you should say, "There is he who made me a child of God, and opened Heaven to me by holy Baptism; he who purified me after I had sinned; who gives nourishment to my soul."

At the sight of a church tower, you may say, "What is there in that place?" "The Body of our Lord." "Why is He there?" "Because a priest has been there, and has said Holy Mass."

. . . The priesthood is the love of the Heart of Jesus. When you see the priest, think of our Lord Jesus Christ.

— St. John Vianney

Recruiting Candidates for What?

An address to the Downtown Chicago Serra Club, February 6, 1992

Permit me to begin with an autobiographical touch. From the first day of kindergarten in 1955, I knew what I wanted to be "when I grew up," and that was: a priest—a decision from which I never wavered, even during the turmoil of those normally confusing high school years, let alone during a period when clergy and religious were abandoning their commitments in numbers unknown since the time of the Protestant Reformation. In the parish high school I attended, out of four priests, two left and got married, while seven of the eleven Sisters followed suit. I don't know what, besides the grace of God, kept me fixed on my goal.

At any rate, in spring of 1968, the Sister-Principal announced that the senior class would have to make a "closed retreat," with the girls going off to the Dominicans and the boys to the Jesuits. Needless to say, in that rebellious and anti-institutional time, mandatory events were not popular, causing several students to declare that they had no intention of making any retreat. The principal, however, stood her ground and asserted: "No retreat, no graduation." And no one challenged her to determine whether or not she was bluffing. When we boys got to the retreat house, a few of the fellows decided to make the retreat master's time a miserable experience; little did they know that this big, strapping, seasoned Jesuit had handled far worse than they! In the opening talk, he put all the cards on the table, informing them that they and he really did have some common ground on which to build: They didn't want to be there, and he didn't want them there. Beyond that, he suggested that they should really regard him as a friend, because, if they failed to cooperate and he sent them home early, they wouldn't be getting a diploma in June. That put a finer face on the issue for many of the would-be agnostics or atheists.

At the end of the first very fine conference (which even the skeptics admitted), Father Clancy greeted each student at the door of the chapel. As he and I exchanged a few words, he said abruptly, "Meet me in my room in ten minutes." I was panic-stricken. Did he think I had been fooling around during his talk? Had I exhibited negative body language? What was the problem?

I was waiting outside Father Clancy's room when he arrived. He ushered me in, motioned for me to sit, and then asked: "So, what do you intend to do after graduation?" "I'm entering the seminary, Father," I replied. "I figured as much. You've got 'priest' written all over you." Noticing my embarrassment, he quipped: "Oh, don't worry, it's not a disease. And if it were, I wish it were contagious." "Well, where are you going?" "I've applied to the diocese, Father, and have just been accepted to study at Seton Hall." "Very good," he cooed. Then I added very quickly and sincerely, "But I'm also interested in the Society, Father," meaning the Society of Jesus (or Jesuits). I thought that that additional piece of information would make him happy, and went on to mention that I had been enamored of the Jesuits since late grammar school. To my amazement, a scowl came over his rather serene face: "Young man," he said as he stood up to his full six-foot-four, "you put that thought right out of your head. If you come to us, you'll lose not only your vocation but also your faith!"

Needless to say, I was stunned, especially since the image of the Jesuits in our neck of the woods was still rather positive through the late sixties. Father Clancy went on to explain that trouble had been brewing for some time and was about to explode. Very kindly and compassionately, he said that anyone who fostered vocations to the priesthood or religious life performed a most noble task, but one with grave obligations, as well. Therefore, he said, he could not simply function like a used car salesman, hoping that no problems would surface until after the warranty was up. No, a vocations promoter was establishing a perduring relationship with a potential candidate, with implications of eternal consequence. It sounded a great deal like something I had just read in French class from Antoine de Saint-Exupéry's *Little Prince*, where we learn that we must take responsibility for the plants or animals we tame, but also for the people whose lives we touch and form. I should add by way of footnote that I found Father Clancy to be my American History professor at Seton Hall the following term, ended up working weekends with him a decade and a half later, and had the privilege of concelebrating his Funeral Mass just two years ago.

Well, what does all this have to do with you good folks? Your special apostolate is fostering vocations by prayer, by consciousness-raising in the Catholic community, by making the priesthood appear as a normal and worthwhile vocational choice, and by providing assistance to seminarians in a variety of ways. All of these are good and important, but I would urge you to be careful—very careful—in your recruitment work. It is not enough to surface potential candidates; one must be concerned about the next several steps, as well. Into which dioceses are you directing them? Or which religious congregations? Which seminaries? You must know the answers to those questions before you can honestly and legitimately and—yes, let me say it—morally, send young men off to an uncertain future or, worse yet, to certain disaster.

Last May, I wrote an article for the *National Catholic Register*, in which I indicated that my experience with priesthood candidates leads me to conclude that the biggest problem we face is not a dearth of vocations, but the wrong people involved as vocations directors in hundreds of dioceses and religious communities. Never has one article of mine elicited such a response: Hundreds of lay people expressed shock at the allegations; an almost equal number of seminarians or would-be seminarians confirmed every statement of mine with their own tales of woe; vocations directors wrote in to accuse me of being negative, neanderthal, and, worst of all, "preconciliar." Allow me to share the main points of that piece with you this afternoon and then move on to the phase after the diocesan vocations office hurdles are cleared.

Many of today's potential candidates and seminarians have several things in common: They are bright and orthodox; they have a deep devotion to the Sacred Liturgy as it should be celebrated; they love the Holy Father and our Lady. And they have one additional common element—they are all too often the victims of institutional harassment, either from "vocations directors" or from seminary professors.

Until we decide what to do with this unpleasant fact (and the evidence is incontrovertible), there is little reason to weep about difficulties in vocations recruitment. The right candidates are out there, but in too many instances they are deliberately steered away from the pipeline or weeded out once in. As result, bishops need to have a very clear picture of the type of priests they want and what qualities they should embody—before looking for future priests and certainly before appointing a vocations director or team of such directors. Once a proper image is in place, only then will we all know what our seminarians should be and do.

Typically, today's average Joe who has gone to a Catholic high school and thought about the priesthood since grammar school will be referred to the diocesan director of vocations. If Joe belongs to a typical diocese, the priest he meets will be in his late thirties or early forties; he will have had little or no parochial or teaching experience; he will have been theologically confused and cowed by various lobby groups within the diocesan bureaucracy, often including domineering, feminist nuns; and, he has probably had just enough schooling in psychology to be dangerous.

If the director is wearing clerical clothes at all, the collar may be open to give an air of studied informality. He may encourage the boy to "just call me Tom." His mannerisms may come off as weak and his voice as indecisive; he will repeatedly stress how little will be required of the candidate, except that he be "open," particularly if the young man seems to know exactly what the priesthood is about and what he senses he should be doing next. If the fellow has been exposed to good, solid citizens in the priesthood in his parish or high school, he will of course wonder what's going on, unless he has been warned in advance what to expect and how he should behave—that is, with an appropriate degree of hesitancy and politically correct jargon.

When he is quizzed by "Tom" about liturgy, priesthood, celibacy, the pope, and priestesses, the uninitiated youth may well give the "wrong" answers, meaning the Catholic responses. This will cause his application to be dropped or result in his being entered into a year's worth of group activity for "growth," which generally means being force-fed massive doses of discredited seventies' notions of ecclesiology and priestly life and ministry.

Now, some bishops actively seek out a vocations director like the one just described; most, however, do not have the slightest clue of what goes on behind the scenes in the candidate-discernment process. But if a bishop really wants candidates impressive in both quality and quantity, he needs the right public relations man. That individual should be fiercely loyal to Christ and His Church, unabashedly orthodox, given over to prayer, hard-working and zealous (as evidenced by his attitudes and actions), manly (not necessarily the reincarnation of John Wayne or a former high school quarterback, but clearly a man), and sensitive but not emasculated. This sort of vocations director will ensure that future priests will be attracted and then be given appropriate formation all along the road to the altar.

Switching gears for a bit, what should we look for in a seminary candidate? Ideally, a young man, not much past his college years and preferably right out of high school (while not ruling out older men, we must realize that no "corporation" builds its future on second-career people, and neither should the Church). He should have no axe to grind, simply knowing and appreciating the meaning of *sentire cum ecclesia*. Hence, he doesn't run after Tridentine Masses or enroll in liturgical dance seminars. The young man should not be any more Catholic than the Pope—but no less Catholic, either. He should be a cultured gentleman, or at least willing to become one. We should be on the look-out for one who is theologically clear-headed and well-adjusted, both socially and sexually.

This ideal "catch" should also have an intense desire to be a priest—even a holy anxiety; which is why seminaries or dioceses which discourage their students from looking and acting like priests are so curiously off-base. He also needs the psychic energy to endure the "head games" which he will often encounter as he goes through the system. He has a right to feel needed, wanted, and accepted in a seminary, in the parish where he works (and not simply as one of a thousand other lay workers), as well as part of the priestly fraternity of his diocese or religious congregation.

If you can see your way through the process thus far and you think the vocations director passes this test, strain your vision just a bit more to look at the seminary he will attend. What criteria should be decisive? The institution should be faithful to the Magisterium; there should be no liturgical nonsense, and a balanced use of psychology by truly qualified professionals and not priests and nuns who merely use "psycho-babble" to browbeat papal loyalists. Attendance at daily Mass and the Liturgy of the Hours should be required, as should clerical garb. A manly spirituality must be formed, along with a tender devotion to the Blessed Mother. I would caution against an excessive presence of women—not for fear of temptations but because young men have to develop a male identity and a leadership sense, precisely as men, indeed as fathers in the community of the Church. Wholesome education in celibacy and chaste living should occur, with no tolerance for dating, let alone any kind of sexual activity.

Suppose now that you can safely see the young recruit past the vocations director and seminary. What kind of diocese and presbyterate or religious congregation would he be entering? Some characteristics come to mind immediately. There should be: love for the Pope; obedience to liturgical norms; respect for the Magisterium and total acceptance of its positions; a strong bishop or superior; a clear vision of the Church, faithful to the real Vatican II—the one found in the pages of the sixteen documents emanating from that synod and not the figment of someone's fertile imagination. We should also find in this community a genuine hunger for new vocations and no confusion between the complementary but different roles of clergy and laity.

Anticipating your next question, let me offer the names of a few places where the criteria laid out here would be realized. Please understand that this list cannot be anything but some suggestions of communities I know to exemplify what I have outlined. The three best seminaries in the country, in my judgment, are: Mount St. Mary's, Emmitsburg, Maryland; St. Charles Borromeo in Philadelphia; St. Joseph's, Dunwoodie, New York. I regret to say I would be hard-pressed to add any others from the dozens I know. Dioceses in which a healthy priestly image is conveyed and lived include: Peoria, Bridgeport, Arlington, Charleston, Lincoln, Fall River. When we try to come up with religious communities, the roster is quite spare; I could recommend only a handful, like the Dominicans of the eastern province or the Oblates of the Virgin Mary in Boston—which is why I generally encourage fellows to get ordained as secular clergy first and then, if they still feel the call to religious life, to pursue that after ordination.

The long and the short of my comments today is rather simple. First, I want to exhort you to continue your outstanding work of vocations promotion—and to applaud you for it. Secondly, though, I want you to take a bit more responsibility for the men you surface, being as honest with them as Father Clancy was with me twenty-four years ago. Be sure that you send them in directions where they will lose neither their faith nor their vocation.

Holy Orders

Originally printed in A Tour of the Catholic Catechism
(Libertyville, Ill.: Marytown Press, 1996)

The treatment of the Sacrament of Order in the *Catechism of the Catholic Church* begins with the reminder that this is "the sacrament of the apostolic ministry," conferred in three degrees: episcopate, presbyterate, diaconate; the first two orders are a "ministerial participation in the priesthood of Christ," while the last "is intended to assist and serve" the first two (no. 1550). The word "presbyterate" is used here, as well as in the ordination rite, to distinguish the priesthood of the presbyter from that of the bishop; when the ministry they hold in common is intended (e.g., offering the Eucharistic Sacrifice), "priesthood" is used.

Why is this sacrament called by the name it has? The word "Order," in Roman antiquity, designated a body of people constituted to fulfill a particular purpose, especially governance; "ordination" signifies incorporation into an "order." From the earliest days (within the New Testament period itself), the Church has utilized that structure for divine objectives.

A brief overview of the history of the sacrament in the economy of salvation is given, starting with the tribe of Levi among the Chosen People. Very quickly, we are brought up to the "unique priesthood of Christ" (no. 1544), which serves as the model and pattern for all Christian priesthood. Some Fundamentalists, for example, express concern or even shock over talk about Christian priests other than Jesus Christ. This is to misunderstand the nature of Christ's communication of His power and authority to the apostles and their successors. At the same time, with St. Thomas Aquinas, we realize that, in the strictest sense, "Christ is the sole true priest, others being only His ministers" (no. 1545).

In point of fact, all Christians share in the priesthood of the Lord through Baptism, so that the entire People of God is a priestly people; there are, however, certain men taken from among the body of the faithful to participate in Christ's priesthood in a special manner. Thus it is that the Church speaks of the ordained priest as one who "acts *in persona Christi Capitis*" (in the person of Christ the Head). By the ordained ministry, especially that of bishops and priests, the presence of Christ as Head of the Church, is rendered visible in the midst of the community of believers" (nos. 1548–49).

As lofty as all this is, the *Catechism* also realistically notes that the grace of the Holy Spirit "does not guarantee in the same way all the actions of ministers." In fact, the sinfulness of the ordained can have the effect of diminishing "the apostolic fruitfulness of the Church" (no. 1550). The text goes on to stress that "the priesthood is *ministerial*," that is, it is "a true *service*." Furthermore, "it depends entirely on Christ and His unique priesthood. The Sacrament of Order communicates a 'sacred power,' which is nothing other than that of Christ" (no. 1551).

The priest represents Christ to the Church and equally the Church to God. That should not be misunderstood to mean, however, that "priests are the delegates of the community," for they are always and everywhere first of all the representatives of Christ: "It is because the ministerial priesthood represents Christ that it can represent the Church" (no. 1553).

The episcopate is given full consideration, relying heavily on Vatican II, which did so much to put as fine a face on this ministry as Vatican I did with the papacy. Hence, we read that "bishops, in an eminent and visible fashion, hold the place of Christ Himself, Teacher, Shepherd and High Priest" (no. 1558). The point is made that "for the legitimate ordination of a bishop, a special intervention of the Bishop of Rome is required today, due to his nature as supreme visible bond of the communion of the particular churches in the one Church and of their liberty" (no. 1559). At the same time, this theology of *communio* demands that bishops be concerned for the good of the entire Church, and not simply the local church over which they preside; the bishop embodies ecclesial unity in a singular way, which comes across particularly when he celebrates the Eucharist; in that moment, it "has an entirely unique significance, as an expression of the Church united around the altar under the presidency of the one who visibly represents Christ, the Good Shepherd and Head of His Church" (no. 1561).

The second rank of ordained ministers is that of presbyters, "co-operators of the episcopal order in the accomplishment of the apostolic mission confided by Christ." With the bishops, presbyters "build, sanctify and govern" Christ's Body, His Church. In this work, priests "depend completely on the bishops," with whom they share "the priestly dignity." Priests "are consecrated to preach the Gospel, to be pastors of the faithful, and to celebrate divine worship as true priests of the New Testament" (nos. 1562–64). They are never more priests than in the celebration of the Eucharist; beyond that, "from this unique sacrifice, all their priestly ministry draws its power" (no. 1566).

Great emphasis is laid on the unity of bishops and priests, who together form "a sole *presbyterium* with diverse functions." The promise of obedience to the bishop made at ordination and the bishop's kiss of peace have important and on-going implications, for in the latter is signified that "the bishop considers [the priests] as his collaborators, sons, brothers and friends, and that in return they owe him love and obedience." The unity of the priesthood is also highlighted when all priests attending an ordination join the bishop in imposing hands on the ordinands (nos. 1567–68).

Deacons are ordained, with only the bishop imposing hands to denote their special attachment to him "in the tasks of his *diakonia* [service]." The functions of a deacon are outlined, and mention is made of the re-institution of this ministry as a permanent order in the Latin Rite (the East had always kept it so) at the Second Vatican Council (nos. 1569–71).

Moving on to the liturgical celebration of the sacrament, the *Catechism* observes that, whenever possible, it should be administered on a Sunday, in the cathedral church, with solemnity, in the midst of the Eucharist. "The essential rite of the Sacrament of Order is established, for the three degrees, with the imposition of hands by the bishop on the head of the one to be ordained, along with the specific consecratory prayer which asks of God the pouring forth of the Holy Spirit and His gifts appropriate to the ministry for which the candidate is ordained" (no. 1573). For the ordination of priests and bishops, the anointing with chrism signifies the work of the Holy Spirit, Who will make fruitful the ordinand's ministry. A good explanation is given for the items conferred on the bishop during his ordination: ring, miter, crosier.

A bishop is the only possible minister of this sacrament. Regarding the recipient of the sacrament, we are told that "only a baptized male validly receives sacred ordination." The *Catechism* says this is so because "the Church considers herself bound by the choice of the Lord Himself. That is why the ordination of women is not possible." It continues to argue that "no one has a *right* to receive the Sacrament of Order" (emphasis in original), asserting that "no one arrogates this duty to himself." On the contrary, one who perceives the call of God "must humbly submit his desire to the authority of the Church, to which belongs the responsibility and the right to call a man to Orders." And most importantly, "like every grace, this sacrament can only be received as an unmerited gift" (no. 1578). Some discussion is offered on the charism of celibacy required for priesthood in the West, as well as the esteem in which it is held in the East, and on its necessity for all episcopal candidates in East and West alike (nos. 1579–80).

A sacramental, indelible character is conferred in Holy Orders, just as it is in Baptism and Confirmation. Answering those who press for a "temporary" commitment to priesthood, the *Catechism* reminds us that this character can neither be repeated "nor conferred for a time." Granted, a man can be discharged from ministerial functions or can be enjoined from exercising them for a just cause, "but he can no longer return to lay status in the strict sense" because "the vocation and mission received on the day of his ordination mark him in a permanent manner" (no. 1583).

The section concludes with two salutary reminders in this day of a priestly "identity crisis." St. John Vianney muses that "if one well understood the priest on earth, one would die not from fright but from love" (no. 1589). Finally, St. Ignatius of Antioch taught eighteen centuries ago that so irreplaceable is the hierarchical constitution of the Church that "without the bishop, the priests, and the deacons, one cannot speak of the Church" (no. 1593).

The Holy Spirit in the Sacraments and His Gifts

An address delivered at the eighteenth annual Seminar for Seminarians, sponsored by Opus Dei
Arnold Hall in Pembroke, Massachusetts, April 16, 1998

This coming September will mark the thirtieth anniversary of my entrance into preparations for the priesthood as a freshman in college at Seton Hall University. Believe it or not, that was less than one month after the promulgation of *Humanae Vitae*, with all the confusion and dissent which that implies. In many ways, you men cannot begin to imagine how disconcerting those eight years of would-be formation were, with liturgical aberrations galore, doctrinal disorientation, and moral fuzziness. Yet, having said that, I feel compelled to say that I have no regrets whatsoever. Why? Because this May will mark twenty-one years in the priesthood of Jesus Christ and, yes, Gentlemen, I would do it all over again—because all the pain and suffering are now as nothing, compared to the incomparable joy of being Christ's priest for over two decades. And so, I would like to begin by applauding your decision to follow Christ in His holy priesthood and to encourage you to move forward in that commitment, no matter what, because the goal is more than worth the sufferings and trials.

My topic, as you know, is "The Holy Spirit in the Sacraments and His Gifts." Undoubtedly, many speakers this week have lamented how ignored the Holy Spirit has been in the Western tradition. However, as a son of St. Philip Neri and a devotee of the great Anglican convert John Henry Newman, I must help "balance the budget," at least a bit.

As some of you know, one of the hats I wear is that of a professor of education. We learn in Education 101 that a good teacher tells a class what he intends to do, he does it, and then reminds them of what he said. In that spirit, let me alert you to the direction in which we shall be heading. I would like to survey the work traditionally assigned to the Holy Spirit, especially as that is revealed in and through the Church's sacraments, in general. Then, we shall consider each of the sacraments—ever so briefly—to discover how the Spirit is operative in them. Finally, it would be worthwhile to see how the Holy Spirit is active in the sacrament to which all of you aspire, namely, Holy Orders. As our particular guides through this process, I wish to enlist the Fathers of the Church, Cardinal Newman, and Pope John Paul II.

The Holy Spirit and the Sacraments in General

One of the questions I receive at *The Catholic Answer* with amazing frequency is this: If the sacraments were indeed instituted by Christ, why don't the creeds of the Church ever mention them? Now, having no doubt that all of you have studied the *Catechism of the Catholic Church* in great detail, I am sure it will come as no surprise when I remind you that immediately following the article of the Apostles' Creed dealing with the Holy Spirit, we meet the Church and, not long thereafter, mention of the *communio sanctorum*. The point of all this, of course, is that the Holy Spirit gives us the Church and she, in turn, gives us the sacraments. St. Augustine taught us, "what the soul is to man's body, the Holy Spirit is to the Body of Christ, which is the Church. The Holy Spirit does in the whole Church what the soul does in the members of the one body." [1] This realization led Cardinal Newman to declare that "Holy Church in her sacraments . . . will remain, even to the end of the world, after all but a symbol of those heavenly facts which fill eternity." [2] And what do these sacraments accomplish? Nothing less than the divine indwelling, which Newman describes thus: "our Lord, by becoming man, has found a way whereby to sanctify that nature, of which His own manhood is the pattern specimen. He inhabits us personally, and this inhabitation is effected by the channel of the sacraments." [3] How does this all come about? Through the imposition of hands, which Tertullian refers to, in a most felicitous phrase, as "inviting and welcoming the Holy Spirit." [4] As Pope Leo XIII remarked in his *Divinum illud Munus*, this awesome reality—although certainly a work "of the whole Blessed Trinity—'We will come to Him and make our abode with Him' [Jn 14:23]—nevertheless is attributed to the Holy Ghost" (no. 9). To be sure, you and I have access to the Triune God in ways far greater than the apostles and disciples who walked and talked with Our Blessed Lord for three years. As St.

---

[1] *Sermo*, no. 267.
[2] *Apologia pro Vita Sua*, ed. Martin J. Svaglic (Oxford: Clarendon Press, 1967), 36–37.
[3] *Select Treatises of St. Athanasius*, II, 194.
[4] *On Baptism*, no. 8.

Augustine put it, for "that giving or sending forth of the Holy Ghost after Christ's glorification was to be such as had never been before; not that there had been none before, but it had not been of the same kind."[5] This point led Pope Leo to assert: "... that which now takes place in the Church is the most perfect possible, and will last until that day when the Church herself, having passed through her militant career, shall be taken up into the joy of the saints triumphing in Heaven" (no. 6). This idea was not a novelty of either Newman or Leo XIII; we find Hilary of Poitiers—already in the fourth century—referring to the Spirit as the "*donum in omnibus*"[6]; furthermore, He is the "*munus*" given for the "*usus*" of God and for eternal life.[7] Newman does, however, say ever so graciously: "The Spirit came to finish in us, what Christ had finished in Himself, but left unfinished as regards us. To [the Spirit] it is committed to apply to us severally all that Christ had done for us. As a light placed in a room pours out its rays on all sides, so the presence of the Holy Ghost imbues us with life, strength, holiness, love, acceptableness, righteousness."[8] And yet again, he says that Christ shines through His sacraments, "as through transparent bodies, without impediment, ... effluences of His grace developing themselves in external forms.... Once for all He hung upon the cross, and blood and water issued from His pierced side, but by the Spirit's ministration, the blood and water are ever flowing."[9]

Wind, fire, thunder, and lightning. The Sacred Scriptures are replete with instances of divine revelation accompanied by these awe-inspiring phenomena in nature. The Book of Genesis tells us that "a mighty wind swept over the waters" (1:2) at the dawn of time; in the Book of Exodus, we learn how God gave the Law to Moses on Mount Sinai with thunder and lightning as the communicators of His Will and Word (cf. chapter 19). But less fearsome signs have also been used by the Almighty as we recall how the gentle breath of God brought Adam to life (cf. Gen 2:7) and how the breath of Jesus on the apostles gave them the ability to bring to life again men spiritually dead through sin (cf. Jn 20:22). All of these events are connected to God's self-manifestation or, even better, His self-communication to the human race and, most especially, to the Chosen People.

[5] *De Trinitate*, 1, 4, 20.
[6] *De Trinitate*, 2, 1.
[7] Ibid., 1, 36.
[8] *Parochial and Plain Sermons,* V, Sermon 10.
[9] *Parochial and Plain Sermons,* III, Sermon 19.

The Sacraments Individually

Let's take a quick look at each of the sacraments individually.

Pope John Paul II establishes the connection between the Holy Spirit and Baptism by asserting: "In the light of Pentecost we can also understand better the significance of Baptism as a first sacrament, insofar as it is a work of the Holy Spirit." He goes on: "This baptismal walk in newness of life began on Pentecost day at Jerusalem."[10] Cardinal Newman recalls that "not only [is] the Holy Ghost . . . in the Church, and that Baptism admits into it, but that the Holy Ghost admits by means of Baptism, that the Holy Ghost baptizes."[11] And what about the effects of Baptism? The great apologist notes that "we but slowly enter into the privileges of our Baptism; we but gradually gain it."[12] In fact, he says, "nothing shows, for some time, that the Spirit of God is come into, and dwells in" the soul of the baptized.[13] Novatian puts it all in a nice, neat package when he writes: "It is [the Holy Spirit] that effects with water a second birth. He is a kind of seed of divine generation and the consecrator of heavenly birth, the pledge of a promised inheritance, and, as it were, a kind of surety bond of eternal salvation. It is He that can make of us a temple of God, and can complete us as His house; He that can accost the divine ears for us with unutterable groaning, fulfilling the duties of advocate and performing the functions of defense; He, that is an inhabitant given to our bodies, and a worker of holiness."[14]

Like patristic theologians and modern ones, too, Newman held that "Confirmation seals in their fullness, winds up and consigns, completes the entire round of those sanctifying gifts which are begun, which are given inchoately in Baptism."[15] The Holy Father spells out the "Spirit-dimension" of it thus: "Confirmation, the sacrament connected to Baptism, is presented in the Acts of the Apostles in the form of an imposition of hands through which the apostles communicated the gift of the Holy Spirit."[16]

The Pope teaches that "in the Sacrament of Reconciliation (or Penance), the connection with the Holy Spirit is established through

[10] General Audience, September 6, 1989.
[11] *Parochial and Plain Sermons,* III, Sermon 19.
[12] *Parochial and Plain Sermons,* VI, Sermon 8.
[13] *Parochial and Plain Sermons,* VIII, Sermon 4.
[14] *Trinity.*
[15] *The Letters and Diaries of John Henry Newman,* ed. Charles Stephen Dessain et al. (Oxford: Clarendon Press, 1984), 6:80.
[16] General Audience, January 30, 1991.

the power of the word of Christ after His Resurrection." He likewise observes that these same post-resurrectional words "can also refer to the Sacrament of the Anointing of the Sick." [17]

Regarding Holy Matrimony, Pope John Paul observes: "This sacrament is the human participation in that divine love which has been 'poured out into our hearts through the Holy Spirit' (Rom 5:5). According to St. Augustine, the Third Person of the Blessed Trinity in God is the 'consubstantial communion' (*communio consubstantialis*) of the Father and the Son. Through the Sacrament of Matrimony, the Spirit forms the human 'communion of persons' between a man and woman." [18]

The Pentecost observed by the apostolic community was a major feast of covenant renewal, harking back to that primal giving of the Law to Moses, that act of God which essentially formed the people of Israel and made them His own special portion. Each time the Church gathers to celebrate the Eucharistic Sacrifice, she engages in a similar ceremony of covenant renewal, and the same Spirit which hovered over the waters of the abyss bringing creation from chaos, the same Spirit which hovered over the Blessed Virgin Mary making her the Mother of the Messiah—that self-same Spirit hovers over the elements of bread and wine, transforming them into the Lord's Body and Blood which saved the world two thousand years ago and makes present that invitation to salvation day in and day out, until He "comes in glory." Hence, it is possible to say that every time the Sacrifice of Calvary is sacramentally renewed, a little Pentecost occurs. How fortunate I always regard myself that I had the great grace of being able to celebrate my First Mass on Pentecost!

Not surprisingly, we hear Pope John Paul explicitate what St. John Damascene enunciated thirteen centuries ago in *De Fide Orthodoxa*, and so many other Fathers and Doctors. Hence, the Pontiff notes: "Christian Tradition is aware of this bond between the Eucharist and the Holy Spirit which was expressed, and still is today, during the Mass when, in the *epiklesis* the Church requests the sanctification of the gifts offered upon the altar. . . . The Church emphasizes the mysterious power of the Holy Spirit for the completion of the Eucharistic consecration, for the sacramental transformation of bread and wine into the Body and Blood of Christ, and for the communication of grace to those who participate in it and to the entire Christian community." [19] In *Dominum et Vivificantem*, we

[17] Ibid.
[18] Ibid.
[19] Ibid.

read: "Guided by the Holy Spirit, the Church from the beginning expressed and confirmed her identity through the Eucharist.... Through the Eucharist, individuals and communities, by the action of the Paraclete-Counselor, learn to discover the divine sense of human life" (no. 62). By the plan of Providence, it is the priest who imparts, through Word and Sacrament, this "divine sense of human life."

The Holy Spirit and Holy Orders

Therefore, as we continue our effort to plumb the depths of the mystery of the presence of God's Holy Spirit in the Church's sacramental life and as we reflect in particular on the holy priesthood, which is the principal instrument by which the Lord has willed to continue the sanctifying work of His Holy Spirit, let us return in mind and heart to that fiftieth day after the Lord's saving Resurrection, there discovering not only the identity of those apostles but also there to learn the effects upon the world from the gifts they had received. In that way, we shall have some objective criteria by which to judge our own effectiveness.

On the first Christian Pentecost, a terrified band of persecuted believers huddled together for safety and mutual support. And then, in nothing less than a miracle, God's Holy Spirit came crashing into their lives, changing them at the core of their being in such wise that they made "bold proclamation as the Spirit prompted them" (Acts 2:4). I do not think it farfetched to see in that mass of frightened souls a kind of foreshadowing of small groups of seminarians who today in many places must endure persecution from within and scorn from without as they await the Spirit's definitive entrance into their lives at ordination. The point to ponder, however, is not so much the period of fear but the moment of liberation effected by the action of the Holy Spirit—a liberation given for the noble purpose of sharing the Gospel message in all its fullness and truth.

When the Eleven emerged from the Upper Room, what did they find? People who were "confused," says St. Luke (Acts 2:6). These folks were confused because they were overly impressed by the linguistic feat performed but I would suggest they were even more confused because they knew these men to be naturally weak and reticent and they could not fathom what had gotten into them—or better yet, Who had gotten into them. Something comparable happens to every man who is ordained, and we have the right to expect similar results. Our task is to speak incessantly and courageously about the *"magnalia Dei,"* "the marvels God has accomplished" (Acts 2:11).

It must be our special and daily prayer to take the line from Psalm 104 as the theme of our priestly life and ministry: "Lord, send out your Spirit, and renew the face of the earth"—through *me*! It is interesting that when St. Peter gave that earth-shattering first Pentecost sermon of his, he chose to link up the happenings of that occasion with the fulfillment of the prophecy of the coming of the Holy Spirit delivered by the mouth of God's spokesman, Joel. We, too, must be prophets of the Holy Spirit. How significant this charge is becomes apparent when we read that wonderful document from the Congregation of the Clergy on the life and ministry of priests, as it underscores this fact: "It is . . . the Holy Spirit Who by ordination confers on the priest the prophetic task of announcing and explaining, with authority, the Word of God. . . . Therefore, the priest with the help of the Holy Spirit and the study of the Word of God in the Scriptures, with the light of Tradition and of the Magisterium, discovers the richness of the Word to be proclaimed to the ecclesial community entrusted to him" (no. 9). Where do we find the program of action for this task? Let us move forward with our reflection by returning to the food placed before us by the Church in God's holy Word.

This work assigned to us by Christ's holy Church cannot be done, "except in the Holy Spirit," as St. Paul taught the Corinthians (1 Cor 12:3). And if anyone is foolish enough to think that he can pull it off otherwise, he will soon learn differently and the hard way. The priestly ministry cannot be effective without reliance on the Holy Spirit for the simple reason that the priesthood is the chosen channel for the Holy Spirit. Just consider the beautiful *"Veni, Sancte Spiritus"* of the Pentecost liturgy. As an aside, I should mention that I had decided on this particular approach several weeks ago; you can imagine my surprise—and my delight—to see that the Holy Father in his Holy Thursday letter to priests this year had a similar notion, except that he used the *"Veni, Creator Spiritus."* So many of the titles we accord to the Spirit and the things for which we pray in that "Golden Sequence" are applicable to the priest and his ministry in the Church and in the world. We priests, by the mysterious workings of grace, are called to "shed a ray of light divine." It is our particular privilege to be "the Father of the poor," not merely to those economically disadvantaged but even more to those who are spiritually malnourished and who cry out for the food of the truth of Christ. By standing at the altar and saying the awesome words of

Christ at the Last Supper, we give the Lord's People access to "sweet refreshment here below," which is a foretaste of the "rest most sweet; grateful coolness in the heat; solace in the midst of woe," all of which anticipates the glory of the liturgy of Heaven. It is our responsibility to teach all who would listen that where God's Holy Spirit is not present, "man hath naught, nothing good in deed or thought, nothing free from taint of ill."

By God's design, it is ours to heal wounds, renew strength, and "wash the stains of guilt away." That almost incredible power was given to the apostles and their successors on Easter night, when our Blessed Lord linked for all time the possession of genuine peace to the forgiveness of sins. Nevertheless we live in such a world that the psychiatrist Karl Menninger could entitle his book *Whatever Became of Sin?* Modern man has lost his sense of sin which, of course, explains why he has also lost the key to full and lasting peace. We priests must remind the world that sin exists, not in the fashion of a dreary and depressing Cassandra, but with an attitude of joy and enthusiasm. Cardinal Newman, in his poem "Absolution," introduces us to a priest who, in admirable humility and with love for sinners, says to the fallen: "Look not to me—no grace is mine; But I can lift the Mercy-sign. This wouldst thou? Let it be! Kneel down, and take the word divine, *Absolvo te*."[20] In the confessional, the priest seeks to "bend the stubborn heart and will; melt the frozen, warm the chill; guide the steps that go astray."

Yes, the work of absolution is central to the priesthood as those words are uttered in Baptism, Penance, and the Anointing of the Sick, paving the way for any other sacramental encounters which increase the divine life within. Once the roadblock of sin is removed, then the process of divinization can begin—and only then. From the Garden of Eden until the present, man has wanted to be like God—and that is not bad in itself; in truth, it is a holy desire implanted within us by the Creator as a way of bringing us into union with Him. And so, we pray at the commingling of the water and wine: "May we come to share in the divinity of Christ Who humbled Himself to share in our humanity." A bold prayer, to be sure, but a good one, so long as we go about it all in God's way, rather than our own. And that is why our Divine Savior gave us priests—to provide for the divinization of the human race, so that Christ's faithful can attain to "virtue's sure reward. . . [and the] joys that never end."

---

[20] *Prayers, Verses, and Devotions* (San Francisco: Ignatius Press, 1989), 516.

An image which looms large over the Pentecost landscape is that of fire, which can warm or destroy, enlighten or consume. From the smoke and fire of Mount Sinai to the fiery flames of the Cenacle, this symbol bespeaks the power and majesty of God. Even in ancient, pagan Rome this was so as it fell to the Vestal Virgins to keep the flame alive before the altar of the goddess. Those superstitious Romans believed that if the fire went out, so would the glory of Rome. And so, the Vestal Virgin who would fail in her duty would have her life snuffed out. Christ's priest as an instrument of the Holy Spirit is, in a preeminent manner, the keeper and the bearer of the flame of God. Notice that I do not say only "the keeper," for it is not enough for the priest to possess that flame for himself or to preserve it as a museum piece; he is required to impart that flame to all. In what does that flame consist? Exactly what is he called to share?

The priest is the keeper and the bearer of the flame of truth. In all too many ways, Pontius Pilate can be seen as the true ancestor of western civilization since the so-called Enlightenment. His cynical question, "What is truth?" has echoed down the corridors of time to our own day, which not only questions the existence of absolute truth and objective reality; it has made it the one and only acceptable dogma of modernity that we must hold all truth to be relative, with every opinion claiming equal authority. How particularly silly for an age which demands such rigid standards of scientific evidence for almost every other aspect of life. The priest must stride into such a world with all the confidence and assurance of the author of "*Veritatis Splendor*," asserting that the true dignity of the human person needs nothing less than "the splendor of the truth," which comes from the Holy Spirit, Whose special mission it is to lead us "to all truth" (Jn 16:13). In this way, the priest helps "renew the face of the earth."

The priest is the bearer and keeper of the flame of the sacred. I said earlier that we must restore a sense of sin, but we must also restore the sense of the sacred; I am fully convinced that the two tasks go hand-in-glove. In all the great theophanies of both Testaments, the human person is graciously granted a glimpse of the divine but immediately becomes conscious of the tremendous gap which exists between himself and the Almighty and responds accordingly, which is with awe and wonder. The priest must recapture that attitude for his people by prodding them into reverence and devotion through the tried and true practices of the Catholic Tradition: bowing one's head at the holy name of Jesus; genuflection before the Blessed Sacrament; fitting attire for worship; a holy silence in the house of God; liturgy which truly raises the mind and heart to the Blessed Trinity. When the sacred and the profane merge, contrary to some theories, only unfortunate results ensue: Not only is God dethroned, but man is progressively debased. On the other hand, when the precincts of the sacred are honored, man is progressively elevated. When the priest reminds his flock that the ground on which they stand is holy, he is helping to "renew the face of the earth."

The priest is the keeper and the bearer of the flame of unity. St. Paul understood this all so well, which is why he urges his readers to appreciate God's manifold gifts and ministries as being "given for the common good," in order to build up the "one body," which is Christ's Church (1 Cor 12:7). All too often in recent years clergy, religious, and laity alike have seen personal projects as means of self-aggrandizement or, even worse, as providing access to what they tritely term "empowerment." Service in the Church can never be perceived in that manner and, to do so, is a blasphemy and sin against the Holy Spirit for it is destructive of that unity for which the Lord Jesus prayed on the night before He died. Ecclesial unity or communion is not just a pleasant concept or a sociological nicety which makes for the smoother running of the ship; it is an absolute necessity, as Jesus Himself saw it: "That they may all be one." But why? He goes on: "That the world may believe that you sent Me" (Jn 17:22–23). The miracle of Pentecost occurred precisely due to the unity of the apostolic college in and under Peter, and the formula is the very same today: The guarantee of Catholic unity and apostolic fruitfulness comes from intimate, loving communion with Peter's successor, our Holy Father, the Bishop of Rome. In the lovely preface for the Solemnity of Pentecost, the Church asks for the gift of having "one voice to profess one faith." When the priest strengthens the bonds of ecclesial communion, he builds up the Church in love and thus helps "renew the face of the earth."

The priest is the keeper and the bearer of the flame of fidelity and commitment. When the Risen Christ appeared to His apostles on Easter night, the first thing He did was to "show them His hands and His side." How strange, you say? Not really, for He was offering them the evidence of His saving love, which love is everlasting. The love of Christ, which was a love unto death, is epitomized in those wounds of His which He retains even in His risen life of glory. And those tokens of sacrificial love beckon His sons in the priesthood to be as faithful in their sacrifices as He. Fidelity seems so hard—even so impossible—to the vast majority of our people. Fidelity to promises, to contracts, to friendships, to marriage is so seldom seen anymore. But we all know, in our heart of hearts, that life without commitment is hardly a life worth living at all. That is why our present Holy Father said it so well when, in Philadelphia in 1979, he recalled to our minds and hearts that "priesthood is forever—'*tu es sacerdos in aeternum*'—we do not return the gift once given. It cannot be that God Who gave the impulse to say 'yes' now wishes to hear 'no.'" And so it is that onto the scene of massive infidelity, the priest comes with his promise of faithful and lasting service. In this way, he becomes an example worthy of emulation, as well as a beacon of hope, and, yes, this is how he helps "renew the face of the earth."

The priest is the keeper and the bearer of the flame of chastity. Ours, my dear friends, is a sex-saturated culture, which has made an idol of sexual gratification—an idol more pernicious than the golden calf of the Hebrews of old, more dangerous because it is so all-consuming. I can scarcely make a trip on public transportation and not find myself approached by someone who has a question or comment about some aspect of human sexuality. The adage has it that the Victorians tried to fall into love without falling into sex, while we moderns try to fall into sex without falling into love. Yet once again, the Church sends out her contemporary apostles as signs of contradiction, challenging the prevailing wisdom, by asking them to be chaste and celibate for the Kingdom, reminding all that there is indeed more to life than sex and that once one has truly encountered God, every other human attraction—even things good and holy in themselves—must be judged as but temporary and transient. As Cardinal Newman put it: "Unveil, O Lord, and on us shine In glory and in grace; This gaudy world grows pale before The beauty of Thy face.... And thus, when we renounce for Thee Its restless aims and fears, The tender memories of the past, The hopes of coming years, Poor is our sacrifice, whose eyes Are lighted from above; We offer what we cannot keep, What we have ceased to love."[21]

Interestingly enough, even the rabbinic scholars teach that after Moses encountered the Almighty on Mount Sinai, so powerful and moving was that event, that he never again had relations with his wife. This does not say that conjugal love is bad or ugly, by no means; it does say that the eternal puts it all into perspective. And

---

[21] *Prayers, Verses, and Devotions*, pp. 688–689.

the celibate priest is in a unique position to assist married couples who struggle to live Catholic marital morality by his own joyful witness of celibate love. He likewise shines forth as a model for the unmarried and even the unhappily married or, more tragically, the separated or divorced. The priest living celibately in this world points the way to eternity where, our greatest celibate Lover told us, men "neither marry nor are given in marriage" (Mk 12:25). And thus, the priest helps "renew the face of the earth."

So, we have been given a tall order, some might think, but our faith informs us that "I can do all things in Him Who strengthens me" (Phil 4:13), so "do not be afraid" (Acts 18:9). Through the Holy Spirit, every priest becomes a new man. The *Directory for the Life and Ministry of Priests* stresses this: "In priestly ordination, the priest has received the seal of the Holy Spirit which has marked him by the sacramental character in order always to be the minister of Christ and the Church. Assured of the promise that the Consoler will abide 'with him forever,' the priest knows that he will never lose the presence and the effective power of the Holy Spirit in order to exercise his ministry and live with charity his pastoral office as a total gift of self for the salvation of his own brothers" (no. 8).

Yes, the priest is a "marked man," interiorly but also externally. That same document repeats the traditional and wise discipline of the Church in this regard as it notes the importance of being clearly identifiable at all times and under all circumstances as a priest of the Church. It states: "(A cleric's) attire, when it is not the cassock, must be different from the manner in which the laity dress, and conform to the dignity and sacredness of his ministry." And yet more strongly, it warns that "a cleric's failure to use this proper ecclesiastical attire could manifest a weak sense of his identity as one consecrated to God" (no. 66). Therefore, never be a clericalist but always feel honored to be a priest and see in even the externals, the Lord's way of making you a constant and consistent instrument of the Holy Spirit.

Toward the end of this year's Holy Thursday letter, the Pope deals with our very topic under the rubric of "The Gifts of the Holy Spirit in the Life of the Priest." He says to all of us: "The Holy Spirit re-establishes in the human heart full harmony with God and assuring man of victory over the Evil One, opens him to the boundless measure of divine love. Thus the Spirit draws man from love of self to love of the Trinity, leading him into the experience of inner freedom and peace, and prompting him to make his own life a gift. And so, by means of the sevenfold gift, the Spirit guides the baptized to the point where they are wholly configured to Christ and are in complete harmony with the horizon of the Kingdom of God." He goes on: "This is the path along which the Spirit gently urges each of the baptized; but, in order that they may exercise their demanding ministry with profit, the Spirit reserves a special attention for those who have received Holy Orders" (no. 5).

Some Concluding Thoughts

Today we have sought to gain a deeper appreciation, a more profound insight into the Church's sacramental life, seeing in all these encounters the gentle but powerful presence of the Holy Spirit. Newman had it exactly right when he referred to the sacraments as "the embodied forms of the Spirit of Christ," which "persuade" by their "tenderness and mysteriousness."[22] This is why Pope John Paul can urge what he calls "a sacramental practice which is ever more consciously docile and faithful to the Holy Spirit Who, especially through the 'means of salvation instituted by Jesus Christ,' brings to fulfillment the mission entrusted to the Church to work for universal redemption."[23]

As we spend our lives receiving and administering sacraments—"the embodied forms of the Spirit of Christ"—we turn to our Lady as both model and intercessor. The Directory for Priests highlights the necessary relationship between every priest and the Mother of our great High Priest: "Like John at the foot of the cross, every priest has been entrusted, in a special way, with Mary as Mother. Priests, who are among the favored disciples of Jesus, crucified and risen, should welcome Mary as their Mother in their own life, bestowing her with constant attention and prayer. The Blessed Virgin then becomes the Mother who leads them to Christ, who makes them sincerely love the Church, who intercedes for them, and who guides them toward the Kingdom of Heaven" (no. 68).

In every liturgical action, she who is the Spouse of the Spirit readies the heart of every priest to beg that same Spirit to enter our midst. Most especially in the Eucharistic Sacrifice, she stands once more at the foot of the cross and moves our hearts to beseech the Holy Spirit to overtake the bread and wine, bringing the life of Heaven to mortals here on earth. In the most profound way possible, then, God will have sent forth His Spirit to "renew the face of the earth."

[22] *Letters and Diaries*, 5:46–47.
[23] General Audience, January 30, 1991.

In *Tertio Millennio Adveniente,* the Holy Father expresses the hope that this preparatory year dedicated to the Holy Spirit would lead to "a renewed appreciation of the presence and activity of the Spirit, Who acts within the Church both in the sacraments . . . and in the variety of charisms, roles and ministries which He inspires for the good of the Church" (no. 45). I hope we have contributed in some small way to the fulfillment of that hope today. St. Basil said it best when he wrote: "Creatures do not have any gift on their own; all good comes from the Holy Spirit." [24] Permit me to conclude, then, with the beautiful prayer of the Byzantine liturgy of Pentecost, which prayer, I believe, sums up what was the goal of this presentation:

> Heavenly King, Consoler, Spirit of Truth,
>   present in all places and filling all things,
> Treasury of Blessings and Giver of Life:
> Come and dwell in us,
>   cleanse us of all stain,
>   and save our souls, O Good One!

---

[24] *De Spiritu Sancto.*

The Understanding of Holy Orders in the Roman Catholic Church Since Vatican II

Nineteenth Annual Atlantic Theological Conference
Halifax, Nova Scotia, June 22, 1999

May I suggest that it was not pure coincidence that my presentation was scheduled for the day on which the Church honors the memory of Saints John Fisher and Thomas More? Indeed, I would like to call them to stand beside me as I endeavor to share with you the Catholic understanding of Holy Order, a concept and a reality for which I daresay they gave their lives.[1]

Permit me to be a bit autobiographical before I launch into my formal remarks. Since 1971, my life has been deeply affected by the Anglican Communion. As a teenage candidate for the priesthood during the silly sixties and the even sadder seventies, I found myself in a seminary which was largely heterodox theologically and just plain "goofy" liturgically. The second fact drove me and five other fellows (the most "conservative" of our class), ironically, into the arms of *Mater Ecclesia Anglicana!* Solemn Vespers in our seminary had been downgraded to a "Quakeresque" rite, minus the silence and reverence. And Benediction of the Blessed Sacrament was effectively banned. The combination of those facts set us to look for "alternative worship experiences," to use the jargon of that day. Which we found at St. Mary the Virgin in Manhattan, a.k.a., "Smokey Mary's." And since the good God is never outdone in either generosity or humor, not only did we find Solemn Vespers and Benediction, but they were in Latin!

That first visit and hundreds of others thereafter taught me that a vernacular liturgy can truly be transcendent and beautiful. At the same time, as I befriended many Anglican clergy, I came to appreciate much more my own ecclesial heritage as a Catholic, especially how important it is to have a body of doctrine, a mechanism to transmit that doctrine, and a means of ensuring acceptance and compliance. As the summer of 1974 hit with the attempt to ordain women in Philadelphia, many of my friends began to see that there had to be more to the "catholicity quotient" of Anglicanism than

---

[1] Fisher even wrote a tract on the topic, "A Defense of the Sacred Priesthood against Luther."

vestments, incense, and lovely music. Since then, I have sought to be a source of support for them as they have carved out different ways of survival for themselves—as some have "looked East," and some have decided to "stay and fight," and yet others have decided to "swim the Tiber."

At any rate, I am still indebted to Anglicanism for teaching me so much, and hardly a time goes by when I offer the Sacred Liturgy in English (I usually do so in Latin), that I don't make a special memento on behalf of those who showed me how to "do it right." I am happy to say that the Catholic Church in the United States today is nowhere near as confused as it was during my seminary days: Good seminaries are thriving (I hope you saw *The New York Times* article on this question on Easter Sunday), liturgical abuses are crawling to a halt (thanks to the influence of the junior clergy), and sound doctrine is being restored, especially through the new religious-education texts being published after consultation with our bishops' committee on the implementation of the *Catechism of the Catholic Church*. So, most of our seminarians today do not need to seek out their own "Smokey Mary's." Of course, sad to say, that venerable institution is itself mired in confusion these days, with priestesses functioning in a variety of ways—including concelebrating, even if not allowed to be the principal celebrant, oddly and (some would say) hypocritically enough.

SITUATING POST-CONCILIAR PRIESTHOOD IN THE TRADITION

When Canon Matheson invited me to share my thoughts with you on the theology of the priesthood in the Catholic Church since the Second Vatican Council, I did not hesitate for two reasons. First, I knew I would enjoy the company. Second, because I presumed the task would be "a piece of cake." My first intuition has certainly proven correct. The second is a somewhat different story.

Let me explain by sharing with you three quotations on the ministerial priesthood. The first goes like this: "By the sacrament of Order priests are configured to Christ the priest as servants of the Head.... Since every priest in his own way assumes the person of Christ, he is endowed with a special grace... [and hence] is better able to pursue the perfection of Christ, Whose place he takes." The second reads thus: Priests, "acting in the person of Christ and proclaiming His mystery, ... unite the votive offerings of the faithful to the sacrifice of Christ their Head, and in the sacrifice of the Mass they make present again and apply, until the coming of the Lord, the unique sacrifice of the New Testament. . . ." The last tells us the following: "The priests of the New Law are ministers of that true Mediator [Jesus Christ), administering in His name the sacraments of salvation." From where do they come? The first two are found in the documents of Vatican II, respectively from *Presbyterorum Ordinis* (no. 12) and *Lumen Gentium* (no. 28). The final one is from the *Summa Theologiae* of St. Thomas Aquinas.[2] In other words, the Catholic theology of the priesthood has not changed at all. In truth, one could not expect it to do so—although I will grant you that to hear some would-be theologians talk, one would suppose that a sea-change had occurred. In truth, Vatican II reclaimed the entire Tradition for the contemporary Church. As Father Aidan Nichols demonstrates:

> *Presbyterorum Ordinis* is a palimpsest, in which all these hands [the New Testament, Fathers, medievals, Trent] can be discerned at different points. So much is clear from the *references* appended to the document, which range from Scripture, the Fathers and St. Thomas to Trent and the modern popes, not forgetting the evidence of the liturgy and its formulations.[3]

In any event, lining up these texts and coming to the conclusion I did, I was then faced with the prospect of telling you that, on that account, my talk was over. But since I suspected that might leave too great a lacuna in the program, I pressed on.

So, what I would like to do this evening is to "tease out" some of the significance of particular trends in post-conciliar theology in three categories. First, I would like to ask you to consider that the fundamental notion underlying a theology of the priesthood arises from the New Testament doctrine of mediation. This will form the "meat and potatoes" of my reflections. Second, I intend to demonstrate how controversy has helped the Catholic Church articulate her positions more clearly and convincingly on two neuralgic issues: clerical celibacy and the ordination of women. Third, I hope to identify—ever so briefly—two areas that could benefit from further study: the meaning of the diaconate; how clergy and laity can and should interface within the one Body of Christ.

---

[2] *Summa Theologiae* IIIa, q. 26, a. 1.
[3] Aidan Nichols, OP, *Holy Order: Apostolic Priesthood from the New Testament to the Second Vatican Council* (Dublin: Veritas, 1990), p. 137.

1. MEDIATION

This past May marked the twenty-second anniversary of my ordination as a priest. And for these 22 years, I have celebrated Mass and administered the sacraments almost every single day and, often enough, more than once a day. By a conservative estimate, this means I have offered the Eucharistic Sacrifice at least seven thousand times. Some faint-hearted Christians might react with shock at what they would consider a blasphemous effort (or, actually, seven thousand such efforts) to "add to" the completed work of Christ on Calvary.

Let their fears be calmed. The definitive act of mediation between God and man took place in Christ's redemptive sacrifice, to be sure. However, this fact does not in any way render useless or obsolete (let alone sacrilegious or blasphemous) other, subordinate forms of mediation. St. Paul saw this so clearly that he offered it as a rhetorical question: "And how are they to believe in him of whom they have never heard? And how are they to hear without a preacher? And how can men preach unless they are sent?" (Rom 10:14f.). *Preaching* is an act of mediation. This is carried a step further in the dialogue between Philip and the Ethiopian eunuch, as the latter asks how he can understand Scripture "unless someone guides me" (Acts 8:31).[4] *Offering authoritative interpretations of Scripture* is an act of mediation. After the eunuch understood the message, he asked to be baptized, "and they both went down into the water, Philip and the eunuch, and he baptized him" (Acts 8:38). *Administration of the sacraments* is an act of mediation. Three small examples of human mediation attested to in the New Dispensation; dozens more could be brought forth, but our goal is not to engage in prooftexting. Rather, we are concerned to demonstrate: (a) that no experience of the divine is possible without human mediation (whether they be words, people, places, or signs); and, (b) that this is indeed the doctrine of the New Testament.

To accomplish this task, we need to look at the meaning of mediation, survey its place in the Old Testament, discover its role in the New Testament, and examine its function in the life of the Church.

A. *Mediation: A Definition*

The *New Webster's Dictionary of the English Language* defines the verb *mediate* thus: "To interpose between parties at variance with a view

[4] Cf. J. P. M. Walsh, "Dynamic or Formal Equivalence? A Response," *Theological Studies*, September 1990, 507.

to effecting agreement or reconciliation; to be in a middle or intermediate place." That will do quite well for our purposes. Thus, mediation is the action by which one is placed or places oneself between alienated parties, so as to bridge the gap; it is an act of unity. Webster's understanding is exactly the same as that of the biblical authors, to whom we now turn our attention.

B. *Mediation in the Old Testament*

Let us set the stage by a cursory glance at the concept of mediation in the Hebrew Bible.

The first full-blown act of mediation encountered is Abraham's intercessory activity on behalf of the citizens of Sodom (Gen 18:22ff.), and then two chapters later, for Abimelech (20:1–17). Moses served as a mediator between God and the Hebrews in many ways, not the least of which was receiving the Law in their name and then presenting it to them. Moses' intercession was so powerful that rabbinic thought expected never to see its like until the advent of the Messiah.

Mediation was not limited to individuals but was also found in the institutional pillars of Judaism: kingship, priesthood, and prophecy. The king represented the people before God even though he had no cultic role—until the days of the Messiah, when priesthood and kingship would be united: "The Lord sends forth from Zion your mighty scepter. Rule in the midst of your foes! . . . The Lord has sworn and will not change his mind, 'You are a priest for ever after the order of Melchizedek'" (Ps 110).

The Jewish priesthood was *the* organ of mediation, providing the Chosen People with the teaching and the rites which enabled them to enter into union with Almighty God. It was hereditary to ensure the on-going availability of this important work of reconciliation. Prophecy, on the other hand, was not handed down from father to son but was a charismatic gift, by which a personal divine intervention called a man and sent him on mission (see Is 6; Jer 1; Ez 1–3). The classical prophet united in his person two roles: that of intercession for individuals (1 Kings 17:20) or for the whole people (Amos 7:2; Dan 9:4–20), as well as that of imparting divine revelation (Jer 23:28). The prophet, then, stood between God and the people—to bring to the Lord their prayers and to repeat to the people what he had heard from the Lord. With these functions etched into the popular consciousness of a prophet's job description, no wonder that Moses would be seen as *the* prophet *par excellence*.

In the post-exilic period, God's Will was mediated to Israel by His Word, His Wisdom, His Spirit, His angels—all by way of preparation to hear about the Suffering Servant who would be the very embodiment of the "covenant to the people" (Is 42:6); should I be bold enough to say, its "incarnation"? Not too far-fetched, for the very last book of the Old Testament makes the identification clear: "Behold, I send my messenger to prepare the way before me, and the Lord whom you seek will suddenly come to his temple; the messenger of the covenant in whom you delight, behold, he is coming, says the Lord of hosts" (Mal 3:1).

C. *The Mediation of Jesus Christ in the New Testament*

It is interesting to note that the word "mediator" never appears in any of the Gospels, nor in the Acts of the Apostles. It does, however, surface, in four places in the epistles, three of which are in Hebrews (see 1 Tim 2:5; Heb 8:6; 9:15; 12:24). The Greek verb *mesiteuein* means "to prove a guarantee," "to give a security." The noun *mesites* refers to either a guarantor or an arbitrator. The rabbis of the day regarded this individual as the very agent of an agreement, the one personally responsible, not a mere representative of another.

The classical New Testament text, of course, is from First Timothy: "For there is one God, and there is one mediator between God and men, the man Christ Jesus, who gave himself as a ransom for all . . ." (2:5). The mediation here is in the "upward" direction (from men to God), and so there is a strong emphasis on Christ's humanity. His work of ransom or redemption is that of intercession or advocacy. While the New Testament makes mention of numerous mediatory instruments (e.g., angels, prophets, apostles), there is only one Mediator in the truest and fullest sense, namely, Jesus Christ. Why? Jesus is the ontological Mediator, that is, a Mediator at the core of His Being, for as true God and true man, He reconciles Godhood and manhood in His own Person. As both Priest and Victim, His Person is of greater worth than His work; in point of fact, one could say that His Person is His work, which pulls together the kingly, prophetic, and priestly offices of the Old Covenant.

In the God-Man, divinity and humanity are hypostatically united and thus provide for genuine mediatorship, which is not static but dynamic. Christ's redemptive work has a real dialogical character about it, for it truly opens up the lines of communication between God and man. It is worth observing that while the Father and the Son alike can rightly be called "Savior" (see 1 Tim 2:3), the title of mediator is proper to Jesus alone.

Jesus' unique mediation between God and man, however, does not exclude mediatorship within human society. In fact, these sacramental representations of Christ the sole Mediator are actually needed.

D. *Mediation in the Church*

That must seem like a bold assertion to some; in actuality, however, it would appear so only to those who fail to appreciate the meaning of the Incarnation and the mystery of the Church in relation to the Incarnation. Let us seemingly digress to analyze that relationship for a moment because it is foundational for understanding how Christ's mediation is made available today.

In the Incarnation we have the supreme proof of God's love for humanity (see Jn 3:16; 1 Jn 4:9f; Eph 2:4f.). St. Thomas Aquinas tells us that "Christ's humanity is a tool of His divinity: not a lifeless tool unable to move itself, but a tool with a rational life of its own able to involve itself in the doing of what is done through it."[5] And what was the task in which Jesus was "involved"? It was the work of mediation. Again, Aquinas helps us out:

> A mediator stands in the middle, separated from either extreme, uniting them by carrying things across from one to the other. Christ as man, set apart from God in nature and from the rest of men by the eminence of His grace and glory, communicates the commandments and gifts of God to men and makes amends and intercedes for men to God. So in the truest sense of the word He is, as man, a Mediator. The personal power to take away sin belongs to Christ as God, but making amends for mankind's sin belongs to Him as a man; and it is in this respect that He is called the Mediator between God and man.[6]

Mediation, of course, is but another name for priesthood. How was Jesus a priest? The Angelic Doctor places it all in marvelous perspective: "It is as man that Christ is a priest, not as God, though one and the same Person is both priest and God; but since His humanity worked as a tool of His Godhead, His sacrifice was the most effective sacrifice for wiping out sin."[7]

---

[5] *Summa Theologiae* IIIa, q. 7, a. 1.
[6] Ibid., q. 26, a. 2.
[7] Ibid., q. 22, a. 3.

The Incarnation, along with Christ's mediatory or priestly office, has an impact on the Church. The enfleshment of God continues in the Church, which is Christ's Body, albeit mystically. Nevertheless, the Body is united to the Head and the Head to the Body. "Because Christ received grace in Himself in such abundance, He was able to bestow it on others, and that is what His Headship means," says St. Thomas.[8] He likewise reminds us, with St. Paul, "that the whole Church is talked of as one mystical body by analogy with man's physical body, Christ being its Head, and its different members having different functions in the whole."[9]

Even Christ's grace of mediatorship has overflowed into the members of His Body, the Church. Aquinas spells this out in some detail:

> ... His headship He has shared with others. They too are heads, though not like Christ: for He is Head of the whole Church at all times in all places and at all stages, whereas others are local heads (such as bishops) or temporary (such as popes) or heads only over those at a certain stage (such as those still living their earthly life). Christ is Head in His own right and strength, others only stand in for Him.[10]

The contemporary theologian Otto Semmelroth explains it all this way: "And in comparison with Christ's mediatorship, it is derivative and analogous. But its reality is brought about by the operation of the redemptive grace of Christ which, of course, is not received merely passively by man but empowers him actively to share in Christ's redemptive action.[11] St. Augustine saw this clearly and put it powerfully: "God, Who created you without your cooperation, will not justify you without your cooperation."[12] Or as Father Raymond Brown has phrased it, "the message of the Incarnation is that there is no way to avoid the interplay of the divine and the human in approaching God."[13]

Now, one might ask: Is there any scriptural evidence for all this? I think so.

---

[8] Ibid., q. 8, a. 5.
[9] Ibid., q. 8, a. 1.
[10] Ibid., q. 8, a. 6.
[11] Otto Semmelroth, "Mediatorship," *Encyclopedia of Theology* (New York: Crossroad, 1981), p. 954.
[12] *Sermo* 169.
[13] Raymond E. Brown, "The Fundamentalist Challenge," *Catholic Update* (May 1990), p. 1.

The identification of Christ with His Church is pure Pauline theology, but many other texts develop the same theme in different ways. Second Peter tells us that we are to "become partakers of the divine nature" (1:4), which process began in the Incarnation and reached its fulfillment in the Lord's paschal mystery, thus bringing us into communion with the Father and the Son (see 1 Jn 1:3).

The mediation of Christ constitutes an appeal to humanity to become associated with Him in the work of salvation. Indeed, to be saved calls for nothing less. Jesus never hesitated to involve His disciples in His saving work. The One Who proclaimed Himself the Light of the world in John 9:5 assigned the self-same role to His chosen followers in Matthew 5:14. Similarly in John 9:4, Jesus describes His work as the effort of a "we." No, He was not loath to give voice to a strong participatory role for the apostolic band: "As the Father has sent me, even so I send you" (Jn 20:21). And so, we see them commissioned to preach the Word, to build up His Church, to baptize, to celebrate the Eucharist, and to forgive sins—all as signs and extensions of His divine power and all to be done under the authority of Him Who remains with His Church until the end of time.

Could Christ have acted differently? Certainly. Did He? No. Therefore, Christians must have the same healthy attitude toward the Church's participation in the work of salvation which the Church's Lord has. The Book of Revelation has several fascinating insights in this regard. The Church on earth is associated with the Lord in His royalty: "He who conquers, I will grant him to sit with me on my throne, as I myself conquered and sat down with my Father on his throne" (3:21). The Church in glory presents to God the prayers of the saints on earth: ". . . the four living creatures and the twenty-four elders fell down before the Lord, each holding a harp, and with golden bowls full of incense, which are the prayers of the saints; and they sang a new song, saying, 'Worthy art thou to take the scroll and to open its seals, for thou wast slain and by thy blood didst ransom men for God from every tribe and tongue and people and nation, and hast made them a kingdom and priests to our God, and they shall reign on the earth'" (5:8–10). The martyrs also beseech the Almighty to hasten the day of vindication (see 6:9ff.). The Kingdom begins in the Church on earth and reaches its fulfillment in Heaven.

The approach taken in this paper is the same as that used by Cardinal Newman. Henry Chadwick tells us that Newman sought to bring his evangelical listeners to "discern that they were learning much about the Church, about apostolic succession, about baptism and Holy Communion as *mediating the very presence of the Lord and His sacrifice* (emphasis added), but these themes are integrated into the grand theme of the necessity of reality and the quest for authentic holiness. The sacramental ecclesiology is there because of the means of grace and sanctification. The Lord gave sacraments because we need them, and we need them because they bring to us the grace and help necessary for the path to a sober, righteous and holy life." [14]

F. *Some Concluding Thoughts on Mediation*

St. Paul teaches that in the one Body of Christ the one Spirit distributes His gifts throughout the Body to provide for the Church's needs (see Eph 4:4). These gifts, alluded to at the outset as preaching, interpretation of Scripture, and celebration of the sacraments, are the concrete means by which Jesus the Mediator reaches all peoples of all times, until the day of glory when their necessity ceases. Far from detracting from the unique mediation of Jesus Christ, these charisms serve as the very ways by which the mediation done once and for all is presented to humanity today.

St. Thomas sums it up in this way:

> Christ, having reconciled man to God through His death, is the only perfect Mediator between God and man. Others can mediate between man and God in a secondary sense, cooperating by preparing the way or as ministers. The prophets and priests of the Old Law were such, announcing and prefiguring a true and perfect Mediator of God and men; and the priests of the New Law are ministers of that true Mediator, administering in His name the sacraments of salvation to men.[15]

Christian priests, then, are what St. Paul referred to as "stewards of the mysteries of God" (1 Cor 4:1).

Through the Lord's Incarnation and redeeming death, our relationship to Him and His Father is irrevocably altered: "No longer do I call you servants, for the servant does not know what his master is doing; but I have called you friends, for all that I have heard from my Father, I have made known to you. You did not choose me, but I chose you and appointed you that you should go and bear fruit and that your fruit should abide" (Jn 15:15f.).

---

[14] Henry Chadwick, "Newman's Significance for the Anglican Church," in David Brown's *Newman: A Man for Our Time* (Wilton, Conn.: Morehouse Publishing, 1990), p. 62.

[15] *Summa Theologiae* IIIa, q. 26, a. 1.

Yes, we are Jesus' friends, called to bear fruit that abides. As friends, we are collaborators in the work of salvation. Human mediation, then, is not abrogated by the New Covenant; on the contrary, it becomes more important than ever as the very means of living out our relationship with the One Who once deigned to assume a human body and, even more amazingly, willed to call us His friends.

Now, in order to test my hypothesis on the centrality of mediation, I did a cursory review of magisterial reflections on the sacred priesthood. A clear line moves from Hippolytus in the third century, through to Bérulle in the seventeenth century, to Newman and Manning in the nineteenth. Throughout the twentieth century, I found, time and time again, whether in the teachings of the Popes or of Vatican II or of various synods, the same, common thread: Human mediation as the key to interpreting and understanding the ministerial priesthood. We could start with Pope St. Pius X in his 1908 *Haerent Animo* (nos. 3f.) and continue on in 1935 with Pius XI's *Ad Catholici Sacerdotii* (nos. 8 and 33) and follow those up by various documents of Pius XII, like *Mystici Corporis* (1943), *Mediator Dei* (1947), and *Menti Nostrae* in 1950 (nos. 32, 35, 39, 52, 122). Then, on to Vatican II's *Lumen Gentium* (nos. 8 and 28; in fact, all of chapter 3) and *Presbyterorum Ordinis* (nos. 1–3, 5)—all of them make mediation their category of choice to explain the priestly office. Pope Paul VI went so far as to link up mediation and celibacy in his prophetic encyclical of 1967, *De Sacerdotali Caelibatu* (no. 21), something he may have found first in the work of Ephrem the Syrian centuries earlier. The 1971 Synod of Bishops directed its attention to a priesthood in crisis; it too relied on mediation as an apt notion to ground the priesthood in the Tradition of the Church (*De Sacerdotio Ministeriali*, nos. 10f.). Pope John Paul II has been thoroughly consistent in employing "mediation" as his personal hermeneutic, from his first discourse to the clergy of Rome in 1978 (no. 3), to his first Holy Thursday letter to priests in 1979 (nos. 3f.), to his landmark post-synodal exhortation on priestly formation, *Pastores Dabo Vobis* in 1992 (nos. 5, 12, 15), as well as in his Wednesday audience addresses on the priesthood during 1993. In point of fact, *Pastores Dabo Vobis* could not be any clearer: "Indeed, the priest, by virtue of the consecration which he receives in the Sacrament of Orders, is sent forth by the Father through the mediatorship of Jesus Christ, to Whom he is configured in a special way as Head and Shepherd . . ." (no. 12).

With "mediation" as our hermeneutical key, perhaps we can presently take a look at those "neuralgic" issues we identified at the outset. I am about to suggest that seeing the priest in a mediatorial or representative role leads logically to conclude that such an individual must be male and should also be celibate. Indeed, to mediate the benefits of the paschal mystery by celebrating the sacred mysteries, one ought to be conformed to the Mediator Himself as closely as possible.

II. DEVELOPMENT ON "NEURALGIC" ISSUES

A. *Clerical Celibacy*

I suppose the most important point to make here is a two-fold one: (a) The Church has had to fight to maintain the discipline of celibacy from the very beginning and at almost every point along the continuum since. So, that opposition should exist should not be surprising; were it not to exist, that would be cause for wonder. (b) Given the vociferousness of many of the twentieth-century opponents of clerical celibacy, it is not too remarkable that nearly every Pope of this century has spoken loudly and clearly on this matter, but especially (for obvious reasons) Paul VI and John Paul II. As I already mentioned, Paul VI devoted an entire encyclical to this topic in 1967. John Paul II wasted no time in his pontificate in letting wishful thinkers know that not only did he support the tradition but intended to give new force to it; hence, his first talk to the priests of Rome and his first Holy Thursday letter to the priests of the world underscored his firm conviction in this regard. Between Paul VI's document and John Paul's arrival on the scene, however, the 1971 Synod of Bishops made a major contribution by re-stating in the clearest of terms the determination of the worldwide episcopate to maintain mandatory celibacy: "The Synod does not wish to leave any doubts in the mind of anyone regarding the Church's firm will to maintain the law that demands perpetual and freely chosen celibacy for present and future candidates for priestly ordination in the Latin Rite."[16]

Well, that might all prove historically interesting or be the signs of the last dying gasps of the "institution" to hang onto an unpopular and indefensible practice. However, the determination of the Magisterium has served as an impetus for important theological and historical work to be done in this area. Let me offer some examples of what I mean.

---

[16] *Propositio* 11.

First, even the magisterial texts break new ground, or return to somewhat forgotten sources. I think it fair to say that much of Catholic thinking on priestly celibacy since the Reformation was rooted in a negative assessment of marriage, with that surely the case since the rise of Jansenism. Thus, celibacy was seen as a "higher" way of life because its alternative (marriage) was too connected to sexuality. Although that may not have been said explicitly, it tended to be a "coin of the realm" understanding among the Catholic people. The problem surfaced, though, when Vatican II (let alone John Paul II) fashioned a very positive and highly developed theology of Christian marriage. How to "justify" celibacy in those new circumstances? The most common and compelling image now used is that of the priest as an "eschatological sign," with celibacy as the hallmark of that aspect of his vocation. Truth be told, this was not a novelty; in fact, it simply required the Church to return to her storehouse to find our Lord Himself using that image as He counselled His disciples to be "angelic," that is, neither marrying nor being given in marriage (see Mt 22:30). A second and impressive approach used today is akin to the first, namely, that in a sex-saturated society like ours, celibacy is a powerful witness to the need for "pure" love (not in the sense that the sexual expression of love in marriage is tainted), but that modern man needs concrete, incarnate signs of selfless and undivided love. If priests can love like Christ, they fulfill a critical role in a world which has lost sight of disinterested, sacrificial love.

Second, historical studies on clerical celibacy have been extremely important. Since at least the eighteenth century, it was taken for granted that the West had mandatory celibacy in varying degrees from either the fourth or the eleventh century, depending on how you calculated it all and that the immemorial tradition of the East was that of optional celibacy, with the majority of clergy being married. Recent scholarship has made such theories untenable. Interestingly enough, the Vatican II Decree on Priestly Life and Ministry actually "buys" the idea that a married priesthood was normative in the East from the outset,[17] and even Pope Paul VI in his celibacy encyclical is notably timid in dealing with the Eastern practice.[18]

Several works have appeared in the post-conciliar period that are worth noting for their scholarship and the challenge they offer to the conventional wisdom of the past two centuries. Christian

---

[17] *Presbyterorum Ordinis*, no. 16.
[18] *De Sacerdotali Caelibatu*, no. 38.

Cochini[19] and Roman Cholij[20] provide a veritable *tour de force* of early conciliar and patristic texts to bolster their assertions. Cardinal Alfons Stickler[21] has popularized their work, while Stanley Jaki[22] has "piggy-backed" on their historical insights from the Early Church and made his own unique contribution in terms of more modern assessments of the charism of celibacy.

In summary form, the case of Cochini and Cholij runs along these lines. Clear evidence from the Early Church demonstrates that when married men were admitted to the priesthood, they and their wives gave up their marital rights and lived as brother and sister.[23] With the passage of time, the Church in the West took a slightly different tack by merely calling men who showed a capacity to live the charism of celibacy, not unlike the Lord's admonition found in Mt 19:12.

The first major departure from the expectation of priestly continence occurred with the Council of Trullo.[24] Its most problematic canon dealt with clerical marriages and effectively turned the entire Tradition on its head by not only permitting married men to be or-

---

[19] Cf. Christian Cochini, *Apostolic Origins of Priestly Celibacy* (San Francisco: Ignatius Press, 1990).

[20] See Roman Cholij, *Clerical Celibacy in East and West* (Herefordshire, Eng.: Flower Wright Books, 1989).

[21] See Alfons Maria Stickler, *The Case for Clerical Celibacy: Its Historical Development and Theological Foundations* (San Francisco: Ignatius Press, 1995).

[22] See Stanley Jaki, *Theology of Priestly Celibacy* (Front Royal, Va.: Christendom Press, 1997).

[23] Indeed, St. Paul speaks of various apostolic men who are accompanied not by a "wife" (as some mischievous English translations put it), but by a "sister" (see 1 Cor 9:5), that is, a Christian woman who tended to the needs of these men in much the same way as the women who accompanied Jesus (see Lk 8:1–3).

The movement away from married clerics who abstained from sexual intercourse when "on duty," to demanding "perfect continence," is already documented in the *acta* of the Council of Carthage in 390. Furthermore, the reason given for this discipline is the intercessory/mediatory nature of the priesthood *in se* (in itself) and not merely through isolated mediatory/liturgical acts. Another point to note regarding Carthage's dealing with the matter is that bishops, priests, and deacons alike fall "under the same obligation of chastity" because of their liturgical ministry, indeed, their liturgical way of life. Finally, it is worth observing that already in 390 we find a stress on the fact that the Fathers of Carthage are not inventing new legislation but simply enforcing what was "taught by the apostles and observed by antiquity [!] itself" (see Cochini, pp. 4f.).

[24] This council was an Eastern regional synod, convoked ten years after the Second and Third Councils of Constantinople and intended to enact disciplinary canons. This controversial synod had to wait nearly two centuries to find a Roman Pontiff to ratify its laws—and then only cautiously.

dained but by allowing for their continued use of marital rights. The legislation, however, was rather convoluted and demanded continence before one would celebrate the Eucharist. In many ways, unwittingly, Trullo set the stage for what would become the Protestant notion of priesthood by reducing priesthood to a liturgical role. The ontology of Holy Order (i.e., that a man is changed in his very being, which identity is a constant aspect of his existence) had been downgraded to functionalism (i.e., a man is a priest when he is "doing" something priestly). "Doing" had replaced "being"—the very dichotomy the eternal High Priest had reversed. A side-effect was the elimination of a daily Eucharist, due to the need for ritual purity. Not surprisingly, ten centuries later, the functional concept of priesthood among the Protestant Reformers would allow and even demand the departure of mandatory celibacy, as well as the loss of a daily Eucharist in the Reformation communities and even a regular Sunday Eucharist in most instances. In reality, the line of thought I have just offered is essentially the view of history which held sway for centuries in the Church of the West and was relegated to the sidelines, somewhat shamefacedly, in the Church of the East. Cholij concludes that Eastern churches that have returned to communion with the See of Rome and have subsequently restored mandatory celibacy have not engaged in a "westernization" of themselves; on the contrary, he says, they have led the way to a genuine "orientalization" since the earliest appreciation for clerical continence actually arose in the East.

Thus, responding to modern exigencies, both the Magisterium and the community of scholars have come up with new and deeper insights into a very ancient tradition.

B. *The Ordination of Women to the Priesthood*

I have often heard it remarked that the Catholic Church doesn't seem to take the Anglican Communion seriously. Certainly, that cannot be said of this century. Indeed, the Lambeth Conference decision of 1930 to allow for artificial contraception was immediately followed by Pope Pius XI's *Casti Connubii*, only four months later! And the famous (or infamous) attempt to ordain eleven women in Philadelphia in the summer of 1974 was responded to by a declaration of Pope Paul VI on November 30, 1975, which was then given much greater specificity in the declaration of the Congregation of the Doctrine of the Faith, *Inter Insigniores*, on October 15, 1976 (interestingly enough, the feast of St. Teresa of Ávila, one of the first female doctors of the Church!). Admittedly, I suppose this is not the kind of "seriousness" with which some Anglican divines would like to be taken by the Church of Rome, but Anglican decisions and actions are surely noticed.

The remote catalyst for Roman interventions from 1975 to 1995 on this matter was, of course, the contemporary woman's movement; the proximate catalyst was the decision on the part of Anglicans and other faith traditions to admit women to presbyteral and episcopal ordination—along with the subsequent drive by some groups within the Catholic Church to do the same. The magisterial statements all come down to a simple but profound fact of ecclesial life: The Church cannot ordain women—not *will* not ordain, or does not *want* to ordain—just *cannot* ordain. And the reason? Christ did not establish His Church and the ministry in such a way as to permit female priests. We find this expressed in three magisterial documents. In John Paul's apostolic letter, *Mulieris Dignitatem*, we read: "In calling only men as His Apostles, Christ acted in a completely free and sovereign manner" (no. 26). The Pope declares in *Christifideles Laici*: "In her participation in the life and mission of the Church, a woman cannot receive the sacrament of Orders, and therefore cannot fulfill the functions proper to the ministerial priesthood. This is a practice that the Church has always found in the expressed will of Christ totally free and sovereign, Who called only men to be His Apostles" (no. 51). Finally, the *Catechism of the Catholic Church* teaches that "the Lord Jesus chose men (*viri*) to form the college of the Twelve Apostles, and the Apostles did the same when they chose collaborators to succeed them in their ministry.... [T]he Church recognizes herself to be bound by this choice made by the Lord Himself. For this reason, the ordination of women is not possible" (no. 1577).

Now, these are hardly new insights, but even that realization is crucial to appreciate. The Church's ministry is not something that is ours to toy with; it is a given, a gift, to be handled with care. It would be rather amusing were the stakes not so high that some theologians who have such disdain for an infallible teaching office are seemingly prepared to accord more power to their own judgment or some other ecclesiastical body than even an infallible pope is prepared to do. What I mean is this: Both Paul VI and John Paul II have exhibited such a reverence for the Tradition (which is just another way of saying, the will of Christ) that they have indicated, in the strongest of terms, that they are not free to fly in the face of that Tradition. With no rancor, one could observe how true it is that "fools rush in where angels fear to tread."

While the Church has always known that she could not ordain women, explanations for this have varied from age to age. We might say that the conviction was absolute, while the rationale changed and evolved. It is likewise good to recall that the task of the Magisterium is to teach and/or define doctrine, not necessarily to explain it—a task more suited to theologians. Some of the arguments adduced in times past to refute proponents of female ordination would strike us as odd and, at times, downright demeaning to women. Others have withstood the test of time.

The theological underpinning for a correct view of priestly ministry is precisely that of mediation, which we have already explored together. It is that prism which sheds so much light on this controverted issue. As theologians loyal to the Magisterium have sought to expound the doctrine of the Church, repeatedly they have resorted to what is variously termed the "iconic," "representative," or "mimetic" concepts of how the ministerial priesthood relates to that of Jesus Christ. It is significant that, for all the historical and psychological differences between East and West, this "iconic" approach unites the response of East and West to this modern challenge.

How fundamental the mediatory dimension is can be gleaned from this comment of Samuel Terrien: "As long as a male priest claims that he re-enacts in a sacramental form the sacrifice of Jesus on the Cross and is thereby identified mystically with the living Christ—the Bridegroom of the Church—any discussion on the ordination of women will remain sterile."[25] And I would submit that Terrien is absolutely correct. In other words, basic realities—such as the identity of Christ, the meaning of His redemptive sacrifice, how the fruits of that sacrifice are mediated, the significance of a sacrament, the nature of the relationship between Christ and His Church—such realities are all touched upon by the supposedly simple decision to ordain or not to ordain women. In point of fact, I think one can say that the vast majority of those favorably disposed toward female ordination have already eschewed the traditional concerns I have raised.

One of the great benefits accruing to the Church with this debate is a deeper sense of all these allied issues. Hence, theologians such as Louis Bouyer, Hans Urs von Balthasar, Max Thurian, Joseph Cardinal Ratzinger, Albert Vanhoye, Aidan Nichols, Peter Kreeft, Alice von Hildebrand, and many more have come forth to take on various aspects of the question; I should not overlook the

---

[25] Samuel Terrien, *Till the Heart Sings: A Biblical Theology of Manhood and Womanhood* (Philadelphia: Fortress Press, 1985).

masterful contribution of the Anglican E. L. Mascall, either. At any rate, the Church's overall theology has been enriched as we have been led to see how this is related to and now causes us to reflect more deeply on a host of topics, such as authority in the Church, the force of Scripture and Tradition, sexual symbolism, Mariology, the mystery of femininity, personal rights and the common good, the identity of the priest, and the meaning of vocation. In other words, the drive to ordain women is bringing about in our time the same type of theological enrichment as occurred at the time of the great Christological controversies. But the teaching authority of the Church has intervened, in the words of *Ordinatio Sacerdotalis*, "that all doubt may be removed regarding a matter of great importance" (no. 4). The hope is that, "with all doubt removed," we shall no longer waste our energy in fruitless endeavors but will turn our attention to more profitable concerns, many of them allied to and impinging on the original controversy. Or, as Newman saw so well: "Error may flourish for a time, but truth will prevail in the end. The only effect of error is ultimately to promote truth." [26]

III. AREAS TO BE DEVELOPED

Vatican II set in motion certain developments within the ministry of the Church. As might be expected, a realignment in one area may call for one in another.

The first has to do with the re-discovery of the diaconate as a permanent and stable ministry in the West. It seems to me that the permanent diaconate is a ministry in search of an identity and theology. To be frank, I find myself in league with a beleaguered school of thought which questions the very sacramentality of the diaconate, that is, whether or not it participates in the Sacrament of Order. I admit at the outset that, although Trent shied away from declaring it to be a part of Order, subsequent development has proceeded in that direction, with a cautious move in its favor at Vatican II in *Lumen Gentium* (no. 29) and even stronger support from Pope John Paul II and the *Catechism of the Catholic Church*, with Ludwig Ott assigning it the theological note of *sententia certa*. That having been said and respectfully noted, I call as my witness no less a liturgical and patristic scholar than Louis Bouyer.[27] My logic runs thus: There is nothing that a deacon can do after ordination that any lay person

---

[26] "Christianity and Scientific Investigation," in *The Idea of a University* (New York: Longmans, Green, 1923), p. 478.

[27] See *Woman in the Church* (San Francisco: Ignatius Press, 1979).

cannot do without ordination but with appropriate delegation. If that is so, then what "power" or "character" could have been conferred by the Sacrament of Order? The liturgy of ordination also assists us as we consider that at the consecration of a bishop, all bishops present impose hands on the ordinand; at a presbyteral ordination, all priests present impose hands. At a diaconal ordination, what do deacons do? Nothing. Is this but a living out of the principle of *nemo dat quod non habet*?

The question is more than merely academic. For if we do not really know who a deacon is, we have even less idea of what he should be doing. If his "ordination" does give him some unique responsibility or power, we should know that—and we should ensure that others in the Church do not usurp his specific ministry. On the other hand, if the diaconate is not actually a part of Holy Order, but a "sacramental" like the old subdiaconate or minor orders, then there is nothing to prevent the admission of women.

The second post-conciliar concern revolves around the proper limits for lay activity within the Church, especially as that is connected to priestly ministry. In the euphoria of the immediate aftermath of the Council, many theologians and pastors alike accorded to the laity a host of responsibilities of an "intra-ecclesial" nature— even though the Council's vision for the laity was much more "*ad extra.*" Some of the practices tended to get considerably out of hand, obfuscating the uniqueness of the ministerial priesthood and causing confusion in the minds of the faithful. The 1971 Synod of Bishops treated this topic with some anxiety (no. 4). In 1987, Pope John Paul promulgated *Christifideles Laici* and warned against the "clericalization of the laity" (no. 23) and the concomitant "laicization of the clergy." Ten years later, in unprecedented fashion, eight dicasteries of the Holy See felt compelled to warn against a variety of abuses.[28] Lay preaching at the Eucharistic Sacrifice (art. 3.1), regular distribution of Holy Communion by the non-ordained (art. 8), lay anointings (art. 9), etc., were all tagged as problematic practices which needed to be eliminated, as well as an indiscriminate use of the word "ministry" for the activity of the non-ordained (art. 1).

In this situation, we see how conciliar reception works negatively as well as positively within the Church, that is, how the Church can evaluate whether or not certain eventualities are genuine developments of conciliar teaching. Given the "cottage industry" which has

---

[28] See *Instruction on Certain Questions Regarding the Collaboration of the Non-ordained Faithful in the Sacred Ministry of Priests* (Washington, D.C.: United States Catholic Conference, 1998).

grown up around so-called "lay ministries" of every kind, it will not be surprising to find this theme revisited frequently by Church authority into the foreseeable future.

CONCLUSION

As we conclude our meanderings through post-conciliar notions of priesthood, two thoughts come to mind. The first is that the great Fathers of the Church were not only superb theologians, they were also pastors, shepherds. The second is akin to the first: Those Fathers were also renowned for their holiness of life. How many of the "greats" of contemporary theology would we put forth as either pastors or saints? While a certain "scientific" precision is in evidence in some cases (but certainly not in all or even the majority), what is so conspicuous by its absence is a love for the Church when a cold, calculating, and clinical approach masquerades as sophistication and "professionalism."

Not desiring to fall into the same trap myself, I would like to end by placing all our considerations within a faith dimension. For all but eighteen months of my 22 years of priestly life and ministry, I have had the person of Christ "mediated" to me by a priest who knows not only the theology of the priesthood but has lived it to an extraordinary degree. His priestly service to me has helped make me be a better, more effective priest. That priest, of course, is Pope John Paul II. During the golden jubilee year of his ordination, he took the occasion to pen some reflections on the meaning of the priesthood, to which he loves to refer as "gift and mystery."

Looking at the priesthood since Vatican II, as we have been doing, automatically implies taking a historical view. The Holy Father does that very well, and I would like to allow him to have the last word on our topic:

> Fifty years as a priest is a long time. How much has happened in this half-century of history! New problems, new lifestyles, and new challenges have appeared. And so it is natural to ask: What does it mean to be a priest *today*, in this time of constant change, as we approach the Third Millennium?
>
> Certainly the priest, together with the whole Church, is part of the times in which he lives; he needs to be attentive and sympathetic, but also critical and watchful, with regard to historical developments. The Council has pointed to the possibility and need for authentic renewal, in complete fidelity to the Word of God and Tradition. But I am convinced that a priest,

committed as he is to this necessary pastoral renewal, should at the same time have no fear of being "behind the times," because the human "today" of every priest is included in the "today" of Christ the Redeemer. For every priest, in every age, the greatest task is each day to discover his own priestly "today" in the "today" of Christ to which the Letter of the Hebrews refers. This "today" of Christ is immersed in the whole of history—in the past and future of the world, of every human being and of every priest. "Jesus Christ is the same yesterday and today and forever" (Heb 13:8). If we immerse our human and priestly "today" in the "today" of Jesus Christ, there is no danger that we will become out-of-date, belonging to "yesterday." Christ is the measure of every age. In His divine, human and priestly "today," the conflict between "traditionalism" and "progressivism"—once so hotly debated—finds its ultimate resolution.[29]

---

[29] Pope John Paul II, *Gift and Mystery* (New York: Doubleday, 1996), pp. 83f.

Gentlemen and Scholars: Priests for the Third Millennium

An address delivered to the students of St. John Vianney Seminary
Denver, Colorado, October 24, 1999

Thirty-one years ago I began the journey on which you have embarked—six weeks after *Humanae Vitae*—a very rocky road to the altar personally, but also a tempestuous period in the Church-at-large; I think it fair to say that my years of priestly formation were perhaps eight of the worst years in modern Church history. Now, going on 23 years as a priest, I must say, "It was all worth it, and yes, I would do it all over again."

I thought it might be good for you to hear such sentiments since often the years of formation seem interminable and, not infrequently, the process is less than appealing. In those moments, remember Pope Pius XII's remarks to the seminarians of Rome: One's vocation is not to the seminary, but to the priesthood. That, of course, is the goal you must keep not only in view but in focus. And know that many elder brothers stand on the other side of the finish line cheering you on, waiting to welcome you formally to the greatest fraternity in the world.

Locally, you are fortunate to have a superb priest as your Rector, and need I say how blessed you should reckon yourselves to have Archbishop Chaput as your father in God—a man whom I have been graced to count as a friend for over a decade.

While awaiting your full admission to the brotherhood of the ordained, however, there's much work to be done, and I am delighted to have been asked to make some small contribution toward that effort.

Our thoughts this evening are directed toward consideration of the need for priests of the third millennium to be, first of all, gentlemen and scholars. Our attention will be concentrated on the human or natural qualities needed, in contradistinction to but not opposed to the supernatural. I believe there is good justification in our tradition for this approach: St. Thomas Aquinas reminds us that grace builds on nature; Pope John Paul II uses this very paradigm in *Pastores Dabo Vobis*, where we find the following: "The whole work of priestly formation would be deprived of its necessary foundation if it lacked a suitable human formation" (no. 43). And the recent circular letter from the Congregation for the Clergy exhibits the same perspective, as we read: "There are many other acts [of priestly work] in which the human qualities of the minister acquire notable importance."[1]

Your goal, my friends, should be to become churchmen. A churchman is not a hireling or a hanger-on or an ecclesiastical bureaucrat. There is a significant difference here, just as there is between a politician and statesman. The emphasis here is on the art or craft, as well as on the idea of love and devotion to a calling, rather than a job or a position of political expediency or an avenue of upward mobility and self-aggrandizement.

A good working definition of a gentleman comes to us from the pen of none other than the great Cardinal Newman. He said: "It is almost the definition of a gentleman to say that he is one who never inflicts pain." Interestingly enough, we find that line in his *The Idea of a University*;[2] in other words, Newman saw an intimate connection between gentlemanliness and scholarship. Indeed, he was himself the very embodiment of the terms, and I can think of no better model for a young ecclesiastic to emulate than this consummate gentleman and scholar.

My list of qualities would run like this: courage of convictions; confidence; enthusiasm; joy; scholarship; prudence; class. The list is not exhaustive, but it does provide us with a good start.

1. *Courage of Convictions*

First, we must look at "convictions"; then, "courage."

One great weakness of "the old days," in my estimation, was that so many people did all the right things for no reason or for the wrong reason; all too often, what was exhibited was mindless, blind obedience. Think about women religious as a case in point: Tell me, if you can, how someone can go from nine yards of black serge, swathing nearly every part of the body, to a JC Penney pantsuit within 48 hours! Or priests, who went from rigid and unthinking mouthing of the "party line" to public or private dissent. The problem, of course, was that we had too many ecclesiastical meteorologists, that is, individuals simply content with discovering which way the wind was blowing.

---

[1] *The Priest: Teacher of the Word, Minister of the Sacraments, Leader of the Community*, II, 1.
[2] In "Knowledge and Religious Duty."

One should not take positions lightly but, once taken, they should be stuck to, because they are grounded in the truth and, thus, unshakable. Intimately connected to this is the belief—an indefatigable belief—in the existence of objective truth. And compromise is the enemy of truth. In some seminaries the new men are told in very blunt terms: "Keep your mouth shut until the stole hangs straight." If that happens, a pattern is set in place: If I can't be myself or reveal my true convictions until ordination, then why not until I am guaranteed a good first assignment? And if then, why not until my first pastorate? If then, why not until I get a really good parish? And if then, why not until some purple buttons decorate my cassock? Eventually, a man wakes up on the morning of his fiftieth anniversary and discovers he has never taken a stand on behalf of anything. What a tragedy! Now, I'm not talking about looking for trouble or being intractable on matters which admit of a variety of solutions, but there does come a point when silence does give consent. The line must be drawn in the sand at some time in one's priestly life.

In *Salt of the Earth*, Cardinal Ratzinger has some very harsh words for bishops (and by extension, other clerics) who simply avoid conflicts, under the guise of being "prudent." He says: "The words of the Bible and of the Church Fathers rang in my ears, those sharp condemnations of shepherds who are like mute dogs; in order to avoid conflicts, they let the poison spread. Peace is not the first civic duty, and a bishop whose only concern is not to have any problems and to gloss over as many conflicts as possible is an image I find repulsive."[3]

2. *Confidence*

This topic is tied to our first point: Know who you are and what you have to offer—then run with the ball. Nothing is so disconcerting as a man who ends declarative sentences with question marks. Granted, all sentences needn't conclude with exclamation points, but periods are good.

As you should know by now, self-confidence breeds confidence in others; just look at the reaction of people to John Paul II. Note, however, that self-confidence is not arrogance.

When a spiritual dimension is added to our picture, we have even more reason for confidence, for we are ambassadors of the Son of God and His Church, with a two-thousand-year glorious and proud

[3] *Salt of the Earth* (San Francisco: Ignatius Press, 1997), p. 82.

Tradition, a philosophical and cultural system which fashioned Western civilization, responsible for any greatness it ever knew. Furthermore, it is important to realize that the very best forms of psychology, sociology, and philosophy completely reinforce our theology—which is why we are getting so many converts from those fields today. Therefore, there is no need to be skittish or apologetic.

3. *Enthusiasm*

Because we are confident, we should be enthusiastic. The word *enthusiasm* comes from the Greek, meaning "God in me." Enthusiasm, not surprisingly, is contagious. Allow me to offer an example of what I mean.

When I was a sophomore in high school, we had as our English teacher Sr. Stella Grace—a *grande dame* close to 80 years of age, a brilliant woman, a great educator, and an exemplary religious. Our new high school was already building an extension and our English class was held in the cafeteria, with five other courses being taught simultaneously. And there was Sister with forty boys for American Literature, most of whom had not an iota of interest in the subject. But because she loved it, she made us love it. A footnote on the story: Sr. Stella Grace died during our senior year, and, by a unanimous vote of the class, our yearbook was dedicated to her. This outpouring of love and devotion for a nun by high school kids is all the more remarkable when one recalls that clergy and religious were generally viewed with suspicion and even hostility by the rebellious youth of the sixties.

Part of enthusiasm involves not being afraid to give personal testimony to undergird one's preaching and teaching. Pope Paul VI, in *Evangelii Nuntiandi*, made an excellent point: "Modern man listens more willingly to witnesses than to teachers, and if he does listen to teachers, it is because they are witnesses" (no. 41). For instance, in exhorting teens or the engaged to premarital chastity, use yourself as an example of one who lives celibate chastity and who likewise leads a happy, fulfilled life.

Some years ago, a man spoke to me about his new parish priest. "He's a nice man, Father; in fact, I think he may even be a holy man, but he's just got no fire in his belly!" "Fire in the belly." That's a down-home way of talking about enthusiasm. Stalin once remarked that if he had seven men like Francis of Assisi he felt confident that he could conquer the world for Marxism in one year. Cardinal Newman, surveying the English landscape of his time and—remember—always the consummate model of temperance—observed, "it would be a gain to the country were it vastly more superstitious, more bigoted, more gloomy, more fierce in its religion than at present it shows itself to be."[4] The mediocrity bothered him immensely. Of all things, let's allow Jean-Jacques Rousseau to have the last word on this matter. He wrote: "Leave those vain moralists, my friend, and return to the depth of your soul: That is where you will always rediscover the source of the sacred fire which so often inflamed us with love of the sublime virtues; that is where you will see the eternal image of true beauty, the contemplation of which inspires us with a holy enthusiasm."[5] Sacred fire and holy enthusiasm: That says it all.

4. *Joy*

What is joy? It is possession of a calm assurance amid the vicissitudes of life. It is not a Pollyanna-ish, unrealistic view, so that if the roof caves in, you say, "Praise you, Jesus. Now I can see the sky." That's not joy; that's nuttiness.

No, joy allows one to see reality for what it is and to put everything into perspective. For a man of faith, that entails viewing all things *sub specie aeternitatis*. That is, operating from the conviction that Christ has conquered; that the war has been fought and won; that all which remain are the skirmishes He has given over to us.

Being joyful is more profound than being happy. People can be happy in mental institutions. Joy is more abiding, more deep, and less ephemeral—a permanent condition, which is why Jesus can promise "and no one will take your joy from you" (Jn 16:22).

Joy enables us to bear our crosses without becoming weary, depressed, or negative. Like enthusiasm, joy is also contagious. Which is why Nietzsche was correct in saying that if Christians wanted him to consider their God, they would have to look more redeemed and more joyful. All too many pious souls have made an entire spirituality out of looking glum and, hence, what bad salesmen they are for the Gospel which is, above all else, "good news." St. Teresa of Ávila, St. Philip Neri, and many other saints had a tremendous sense of humor and similarly a strong aversion to people who had equated a sour puss with sanctity. As "marked men," don't forget how important it is to look joyful in secular society; what a countersign it is

---

[4] *Apologia pro Vita Sua*, 46.
[5] *La Nouvelle Héloïse* (1761; ed. M. Launay, 1967), pt. 2, letter 11.

to see priests and nuns on city streets looking as though they had just emerged from a three-hour root canal.

On an autobiographical note, permit me to share an anecdote with you. Over my years in the priesthood, I have sent about fourteen young men to the seminary—either former students or directees. For quite some time, I used to bring them all together once a year for a few days of "R and R." On one such occasion, as I was putting the finishing touches on dinner and they were all on the porch having a drink, with my "teacher's ears," I heard them regaling each other with stories about me, as each one tried to top the previous one with a particularly bizarre tale. At which point, I emerged from the kitchen and said, "Well, boys, say what you want but all of you would agree on one thing: As loony as I might be, I was the human instrument or catalyst for your being where you are right now." Then I went on, "Tell me something, however. Just what was it about me that pushed you over the line into priestly formation?" Mike stood up (I had been a teacher and administrator for him as a high school student) and said, without batting an eyelash: "You always looked like you enjoyed being a priest!" I replied, "Even the day I suspended you from school in your junior year?" He retorted, "Especially that day!"

The story is cute and funny, but the point is key: We must be imbued with joy interiorly, if we are to project it externally. And if we don't appear joyful, we'll never attract anyone to the Church, let alone to the priesthood.

5. *Scholarship*

If one thing characterized priesthood fifty years ago (especially in Europe, even if less so here), it was the priest as a man of learning, that is, possessing a broad grasp of knowledge, a true Renaissance man—an in-depth knowledge of a few areas and a gentleman's acquaintance with many, many more, so that he could have an intelligent conversation with just about anyone.

Priests were trained in seminary to be perpetual students and to set aside time for study as much as for prayer, which simply followed the Jewish approach to things. Orthodox Jewish observance of the Sabbath to this day is quite restrictive, but two things can and ought to be done with gusto: Prayer and study. Interestingly, under the rubric of study, one finds included any discipline or science whatsoever, because all truth is one and should lead a person back to the Creator God.

As a professor of education and former high school teacher and administrator, I find it particularly sad to see a decline of education in general, but it's even worse for priests and seminarians. Beyond that, we now encounter in all too many clerical quarters an almost full-blown anti-intellectualism. How often have you heard classmates complain about academic demands, ending their tirade with, "What do they want me to be—a saint or a scholar?" As though they were mutually exclusive! But recall St. Teresa of Ávila, who said that, if confronted with the mutually exclusive choice for spiritual director of a saintly priest or a theologian, she would always opt for the theologian.

Over ninety years ago, the co-founder of New York's Dunwoodie Seminary theological journal, Father Francis P. Duffy, penned these lines: "Lack of faith is not our difficulty, unless it be that worst form of infidelity which fears to look at the truth. Our main drawback is a certain intellectual sloth which masquerades as faith." [6]

What would he say today? For not too many decades ago, the priest was the best educated man in any parish; today, all too often, especially in suburbia, he is the least educated. This explains the hesitancy, the poor self-image, the lack of confidence, the resort to gimmickry. What is the solution? Embark on an intellectual self-improvement plan by becoming friends with the secular classics and the Catholic classics. During my last year of full-time high school work, I offered an elective to the ten best and brightest seniors we had: "The Catholic Intellectual Tradition," which introduced them to two thousand years of great Catholic thinkers. They couldn't get enough.

Seminarians can afford no less than high school seniors. Gain an exposure to and appreciation for literature, art, music; be able to use these in the pulpit, the classroom, and the confessional, not to impress but to teach effectively and memorably. If the best you can do is cite the latest films or rock tunes, you're selling everyone short: your audience (young and old alike), yourself, the Gospel, the Church.

Learn languages. First, classical languages, which give you entrée to the minds of the greatest men in history and access to a worldview and mode of thinking logically and precisely which will put you in good stead for your whole life. Latin and Greek also serve as your personal introduction to the Tradition of the Church; I'm sure you recall the Holy Father's comments to the university students in Wadowice this past spring when he chided them for not learning

---

[6] Thomas Shelley, "What the Hell Is an Encyclical?" *U.S. Catholic Historian* (Spring 1997), p. 93.

the classics and embarrassed them all by quoting from memory several lines of *Antigone* in the original Greek! Without these languages, you will be lifelong hostages to either ignorance or other people's translations of these treasures. Liturgically, you will be at the mercy of ICEL.

Second, modern languages: You cannot imagine how pleased people are when you speak or even attempt to speak their language. Finding myself in New York City cabs more often than I prefer, I look at the driver and his name-plate, surmise his ethnicity, and then try to speak at least a few lines in his native tongue. Invariably, his face lights up. My effort tells him the Church cares about him; in a rather hostile, threatening, and uncomprehending world, immigrants need to know that their priests are concerned about them. Beyond that, languages introduce a person to different and enriching thought patterns and cultures—an important experience for any would-be minister of the Gospel.

Professional, academic preparation was also underscored in that circular letter of the Congregation for the Clergy, to which I alluded a few minutes ago. It reminds us:

> We live in an information era characterized by rapid communication. We frequently hear experts and specialists on the television and radio. In a certain sense, the priest (who is also a social communicator) has to compete with these when he preaches to the faithful. Hence, his message must be presented in an attractive manner. His apostolic spirit should move him to acquire competence in the use of the "new pulpits" provided by modern communications and ensure that his preaching is always of a standard congruent with the preached word.

It goes on to encourage us "to acquire a noble and dignified self-presentation and poise." It spells this out in great detail when it asserts that "the human 'key' to effective preaching of the Word is to be found in the professionalism of the preacher who knows what he wants to say and who is always backed up by serious remote and proximate preparation. This is far removed from the improvisation of the dilettante. . . . Care should therefore be taken with the meaning of words, style, and diction."[7]

I could offer another dozen suggestions in this category, but I think you get the idea. Let me leave this topic by offering you an image about priests and pursuits of the mind: You know the intellectual level of the priesthood has declined when you go to a man's

---

[7] II, 2.

room and find his shelves are filled, not with books but with stuffed animals!

6. *Prudence*

Let's start by saying what prudence is *not*: It's not doing nothing; it's doing the right thing under the right circumstances. Sometimes that means silence and patient waiting, yes; but also, speaking and doing as discernment dictates.

Those of us to be priests in the third millennium will be faced with massive mop-up operations bequeathed to us by a generation of neglect by bishops and priests, finding expression in ignorance of the basics of the Catholic Faith; a lost sense of the sacred; misguided notions of freedom, conscience, and autonomy. To us has been confided the task of the Catholic Restoration. A revolution is easy to pull off; a restoration requires vision and insight—the wisdom of Solomon, which is the practical ability to do and say the right thing at the right time, being neither a bull in a china shop nor a Mr. Milquetoast. It demands the ability to determine negotiables from non-negotiables and then the willingness to stand by those decisions, whether popular or not. Josef Pieper put it well: "Prudence means purity, straightforwardness, candor, and simplicity of character; it means standing superior to the utilitarian complexities of mere tactics."

An ancient Roman proverb advises: *Quidquid agis, prudenter agas, et respice finem*. Since I'm sure you're all classical scholars, undoubtedly no translation will be necessary, but just in case someone didn't catch the nuance of the Latin, it comes out this way in English: "Whatever you do, do prudently and look to the end." The *Catechism* reminds us that prudence should not be "confused with timidity or fear" (no. 1806); rather, St. Thomas had it right when he called it "right reason in action."[8] Indeed, the Wisdom Literature equates prudence with wisdom, as we hear Solomon pray in Hebraic parallelism: "Therefore I prayed, and prudence was given me; I pleaded, and the spirit of Wisdom came to me" (Wis 7:7 NAB).

7. *Class*

Last but by no means least, class. (After all, seven is the number of perfection.)

---

[8] *Summa Theologiae* II-II, q. 47, a. 2.

At the outset, let me make sure you do not misunderstand what I mean by "class." I'm not calling for a "preppie priest," but I am looking for one who realizes he bears a dignity beyond his own. Therefore, the way we dress, eat, walk, and talk are all critically important, for people will judge the message by the messenger—whether we like it or not. Simply put, "God is in the details."

At your age, we were given a course in clerical etiquette—yes, a three-credit course, complete with textbook! Some of us laughed about it, but I must say that I have never been embarrassed by following its guidelines, nor have I ever embarrassed the Church.

Let me offer several examples of what I have in mind here.

1. All too many rectory dining rooms or seminary refectories are little more than cattle troughs, and that atmosphere is transferred by these clerics to all their other environments, as well.

2. So many of the brethren have no sense of how to dress, indicative of a most unprofessional attitude, let alone being in violation of Church law. For an ecclesiastic not to dress properly is actually quite clericalistic, because it is a refusal to live up to the faithful's expectations and seeks privilege by being different or odd, calling attention to the self. To be perfectly honest, aside from the gym and the beach, I cannot conceive of a priest in lay clothes; I am supported in that position by paragraph 66 of the *Directory for the Life and Ministry of Priests* from the Congregation of the Clergy. Archbishop Sepe, in the press conference releasing the document, was asked if the Church envisioned a priest going out to dinner in a clerical collar. He answered: "He's no less a priest in the restaurant than at the altar."

Beyond that, it is important for people to see us doing *normal* things: dinner, movie, play, concert, shopping. In truth, I have made a kind of apostolate out of engaging people in those situations with a friendly smile or an apt comment, and I'm happy to say my priests and seminarians have seemed to pick up the practice, too. This concept is reinforced by the same circular letter we have encountered earlier this evening, as it declares that we must "understand the significance and pastoral role of the discipline concerning clerical garb, to which the priest should always conform since it is a public proclamation of his limitless dedication to the brethren and to the faithful in his service to Jesus Christ." Don't miss the adverb "always." And then comes the salutary reminder: "The more society is marked by secularization, the greater the need for signs."[9]

---

[9] Ibid., IV, q. 3.

That having been said, I'm not talking about wearing just a sloppy or dirty old clerical shirt. We must be attired clerically, but appropriately so. Our clerical etiquette professor also gave us some handy rules of thumb which I pass on to you: On Sundays, cassock and cuffs; for activities when a layman would be expected to wear a suit, a rabat and suit for us; when a blazer would work for the layman, the same for us; and then, Fr. Hinrichsen's famous category of "clerical casual," a black shirt and sweater for games, parties, and the like. We're not aiming to produce a fastidious Anglican cleric who's all dressed up with nowhere to go, but we are hoping for a cultured gentleman.

Why am I spending so much time on the clothing question? Not just because it is so neuralgic in so many quarters today but also because it is intimately connected to bigger questions of priestly identity. First, because constant clothes-changing is unhealthy and effete. Second, we all unfortunately know of young priests who subscribe to the "dual wardrobe" theory, that is, Gammarelli cassocks and Brooks Brothers lay attire. That approach is both foppish and unevangelical. Third and most important of all, one's priestly identity must be integrated into one's total identity and should not be able to be compartmentalized. We exhibit self-assurance when we are comfortable with our role and person—that's a thumb-nail definition of class. When we hear talk about being able to "relax" only apart from one's priestly identity, we are looking at a spiritual problem and probably a psychological one, too.

3. Although we could treat the following item in a discussion on celibacy, let's do it here because it flows naturally from what has been said. Be certain that all your relationships not only *are* good but also *look* good. Don't give parish gossips something to work with; they'll find enough without your help. Along similar lines, be manly. That doesn't mean that every priest or seminarian must be able to point to a Varsity letter in high school football, nor that every ecclesiastic need look and act like John Wayne. It does mean, however, if I may be frank, that he can't look or act like Lola Falana!

4. A special word about courtesy in all its forms. Let me highlight three of them, however: using titles for people, especially elders; writing thank-you notes; responding to telephone calls. Use of titles like "Mister" and "Missus" should not be consigned to the dustbins of history. Europeans, for instance, are horrified at how easily we Americans address total strangers by their first names. For clergy, particularly young men, using a title to address one's senior is a sign of humility and an acknowledgement of the other person's

dignity. If that person graciously suggests using his first name, that's a different story. With regard to older priests, be especially attentive. While many of our elder brothers in the priesthood are very fond of the junior clergy, particularly due to their doctrinal orthodoxy, they often express amazement at their perceived flippancy about titles. For a 25-year-old priest to address a 70-year-old priest as "Joe" is a grievous lapse in common civility. Ironically, these are just as frequently the fellows who are upset when some nuns or laity fail to call them "Father." Senior priests, most of whom could have baptized you, have borne the heat of the day, and they deserve our respect in any and every way we can show it. I have a simple rule of thumb for myself: (a) In introducing myself to a brother-priest, I never use a title for myself. (b) In addressing any priest older than myself, I always call him "Father"—unless explicitly directed otherwise. (c) I never, even if told otherwise, call men who were my teachers or pastors when I was a boy or a seminarian anything but "Father."

On the latter two concerns of thank-you notes and phone messages, the best way to ensure that you fulfill these duties of charity and even justice is to handle them immediately, so that other events do not squeeze them out or make them forgotten. In my experience, I think it fair to say the average layperson would be willing to forgive a priest almost anything other than these two offenses—and they happen to be the most common lapses of priestly courtesy, I think.

5. Other areas demanding attention include, but are not limited to: care in grammar and language; off-color jokes; drinking to excess (folks may say that "Father let his hair down," but all too many really want us to let our guard down, to drag us down to their level and thereby reduce our capacity to "preach" to them); gluttony; smoking (there's nothing so offensive as putting one's nicotine-stained fingers into someone's mouth or blowing one's smoky breath through a confessional screen); being well-groomed (hair need not be a crew-cut but shouldn't be either the "shaggy dog" look or the "fresh-from-the-salon" image; if you have facial hair, don't make yourself a contender for Rasputin's successor; make sure finger nails are clean and cut). And, of course, no boorish, loutish, or boisterous behavior.

Some may think this has all been a bit too much, but don't forget our Lord's approach, which may be summed up as, "faithful in small matters, faithful in greater affairs" (see Mt 25:21). Class, you see, is demonstrated by attention to small matters which, in turn, reveals respect for self, one's people and the God we are privileged to represent.

Concluding Thoughts

Well, that's the end of my laundry list. So permit me just this final reflection. When I was a boy, the greatest compliment which could be paid to anyone was that he was "a gentleman and a scholar." I still subscribe to that theory. Our people still have that desire, often unarticulated. We find Micah in the Old Testament saying to the young Levite, "Be to me a father and a priest" (Judg 17:10). That request follows on the heels of an interesting remark by the sacred author, namely, that "in those days there was no king in Israel; every man did what was right in his own eyes" (17:6). Centuries later, St. John Vianney—your special patron—noted that if you left people without a priest for twenty years, you'd come back and find them worshipping beasts! My experience tells me that the saint wasn't exaggerating.

The renewal of the Church in the United States, my dear young Levites, depends—in my judgment—on a priesthood filled with gentlemen and scholars. May their tribe increase, and may you always be in their number.

Celibacy and the Meaning of the Priesthood

From Priestly Celibacy: Its Scriptural, Historical, Spiritual, and Psychological Roots (Mount Pocono, Pa.: Newman House Press, 2001)

More than twenty-five years ago, as a young seminarian, I brought my group of inner-city altar boys to a high school seminary for the day, where they were introduced to priestly formation and the various options that existed within a priestly vocation, including the difference between religious order priests and diocesan or secular clergy. The staff and students were extremely gracious and even allowed the boys the use of the outdoor pool. At the end of the day, the rector informed me that it had been decided the poor kids needed a good meal: thick steaks, french fries, homemade cherry pie, and ice cream. My charges were ecstatic, but one reaction I will never forget. When beholding the culinary delights, fourth-grade Cubit blurted out: "Wooo-ee, if this be poverty, bring on chastity!" Many people, including many practicing Catholics, have no deeper an understanding of clerical celibacy than my little ten-year-old server.

I would beg the reader's indulgence to be just a bit autobiographical. I was an only child, went to Catholic schools my whole life, perceived a call to priesthood on the first day of kindergarten (and never wavered from that goal), never met a Protestant until I was in seventh grade, and entered the seminary at the age of seventeen. Now, some will express amazement at such a description of a young life, but, believe it or not, my story could be replicated by thousands of American priests, especially growing up in the Northeast in the nineteen-fifties and -sixties. Given such a Catholic ethos, certain things were taken for granted—in a good sense. One of them was that a call to priesthood did indeed usually come in one's youth and that it should be acted on as soon as possible, in line with the Lord's remarks about putting one's hand to the plough and not looking back (Lk 9:62). Within that first set of presumptions was another: That if one were to be a priest, he would spend his entire life in the unmarried state. No one ever thought it bizarre or the least bit worthy of discussion—just as normal and natural as the expectation that one's parents would never be divorced.

Then came the late nineteen-sixties, with the collapse of societal norms, with the questioning of every tradition imaginable, with the misbegotten euphoria of the post-Vatican II era; and attitudes toward priesthood in general and celibacy in particular began to change dramatically. It was in those years that I found myself in the seminary, which is intended by the Church to be an eight-year preparation for priestly life and ministry in every detail. In other words, no newly ordained priest ought ever be able to say truthfully that he was surprised by some essential aspect of his existence for which he was not given adequate grounding. By 1968, however, thousands of priests had begun a massive exodus from the priesthood; indeed, a departure greater than what the Church experienced at the time of the Protestant Reformation. Sad to report, by the end of the pontificate of Pope Paul VI in 1978, more than a hundred thousand men had petitioned for what is technically known as a "rescript of laicization"[1] and had received one.

Within that climate, I was supposedly being prepared for ordination. Many of my professors had close friends and classmates who had either left the priesthood or were planning to do so; many of my professors ended up leaving, too. Will anyone be shocked to learn, then, that never once in eight years did I ever (a) have a course in celibacy; (b) have a retreat or day of recollection devoted to the topic; or (c) hear a spiritual conference or homily on that theme? And yet, that is the truth with one notable exception. The few times that the topic of celibacy did come up for discussion, we were told that, by the time we were ordained, celibacy would be optional! More than twenty years into the priesthood, I smile when I think

---

[1] A rescript of laicization is a document, signed by the Pope, acceding to a man's request to leave the active ministry and to return to the lay state. Under Pope Paul, such a document also usually granted the petitioner a dispensation from celibacy and from the recitation of the Divine Office—two obligations assumed at that time at subdiaconate and now taken on at diaconate. A "laicized" priest remains a priest forever but cannot function as such and, in fact, cannot perform any liturgical role whatsoever, cannot teach theology, and cannot administer any Catholic educational institution.

Not infrequently, we hear people say that we never would have lost all these men if it hadn't been for the law of celibacy. No objective research bears out that assertion. My own personal observation and experience suggest something very different. I knew more than thirty men who had "left the priesthood," only one of whom left precisely to get married. Most left because of disillusionment with the Church or the priesthood in general. Of course, having left and having been dispensed from the promise of celibacy, it would not be odd that they would consider marriage. One final codicil on this aspect of Church history: Statistics show that more than three-fourths of these clerical marriages have ended in divorce, and the Holy See reports that tens of thousands of "laicized" priests have asked to return to active ministry.

how wishful thinking and ideological conditioning can be so off-base. Engaged couples attending a three-session pre-Cana conference have a better chance of hearing the essentials of married life than my generation of seminarian did in regard to the priesthood. Thanks to the leadership of Pope John Paul II and many good, young bishops, that situation has changed for the better.

Having had many wonderful priest-friends throughout childhood and adolescence, and having lived celibacy for twenty-five years before ordination, I think I did understand both the expectations of the Church and the practical pitfalls. Very early in my priestly life, I became involved in ecumenical work. The one, consistent theme I heard from non-Catholic clergy was how wise the Catholic Church was to mandate celibacy for her clergy. Why? These ministers told me three things: (1) Optional celibacy means mandatory marriage; that is, any man who would freely choose celibacy would be thought to have a questionable sexual orientation, in the minds of most congregations. (2) Marriage and ministry do not go together, so little so that most of their wives were miserable and most of their children had an unabated resentment toward organized religion because of their perception of having been cheated out of a father by "the Church." (3) Having a married minister does not eliminate sexual scandals; truth be told, Protestant clergy have an even higher share of such, with adultery, pedophilia, and homosexual liaisons occurring with depressing regularity.[2] I took seriously the counsel of these brothers in Christ and have never forgotten it.

A Theology of Celibacy

While all of the above information may be interesting, it still does not explain why the Catholic Church requires celibacy of her priests

[2] John Henry Cardinal Newman saw this very clearly when he wrote—over a century ago—from his stance as a former Anglican clergyman: ". . . I state my deliberate conviction that there are, to say the least, as many offenses against the marriage vow among Protestant ministers, as there are against the vow of celibacy among Catholic priests. . . . But if Matrimony does not prevent cases of immorality among Protestant ministers, it is not celibacy which causes them among Catholic priests. It is not what the Catholic Church imposes, but what human nature prompts, which leads any portion of her ecclesiastics into sin. Human nature will break out, like some wild and raging element, under any system; it bursts out under the Protestant system; it bursts out under the Catholic; passion will carry away the married clergyman as well as the unmarried priest. . . . Till, then, you can prove that celibacy causes what Matrimony certainly does not prevent, you do nothing at all" (*Lectures on the Present Position of Catholics in England*).

who belong to the Latin Rite.[3] Of course, and in truth, the connection between priesthood and celibacy is not unique to Catholicism. We find such linkage in various pagan cults of Greece and Rome and, even more radically, in Stoicism's overall rejection of sexual pleasure. While these historical precedents may offer interesting angles of insight or a "natural" intuition in this regard, Christian faith sees something much deeper here.

Catholics believe that through the Sacrament of Holy Order a man is "configured" to Christ the High Priest. In other words, no Catholic priest "has" a priesthood of his own; rather, he shares in the priesthood of the one and only Priest of the New Covenant, Jesus Christ. Our participation in that priesthood needs to be as full and visible as possible; "maleness" is one such sign, and celibacy is another. The first is an absolute, while the second is not—although the appropriateness of the sign of celibacy touches very closely on the nature of the priesthood.

Jesus was a priest at the core of His being, which is to say that He did not simply function as a priest on certain occasions (e.g., in offering Himself to the Father on Good Friday); rather, His entire life was an oblation given to the Father, thus uniting within Himself the roles of Victim and Priest. The priests of the Old Covenant functioned at the Temple according to a schedule; while "on duty," they lived at the Temple to ensure ritual purity. Among other things, that meant abstaining from marital intercourse. The tenth chapter of the Epistle to the Hebrews teaches us that our great High Priest fulfilled all those holy sacrifices by His one eternal offering; in that moment, He also abolished priestly functionalism. That is, priesthood is not what one *does* but who one *is*. Since the Lord's entire life was a priestly offering, His observance of continence was not an on-again, off-again phenomenon. And it was the self-same approach to which He called His disciples when He urged them to leave house, wife, brothers, parents, and children "for the sake of the kingdom of God" (Lk 18:29).

Therefore, we see that the Twelve, although probably many of them were married, were obedient to the Master's command; they

[3] It should be noted that the Catholic Church consists of many "rites," which differ in some accidentals (such as liturgical forms and discipline), all the while professing one faith, in communion with the Bishop of Rome. The Latin or Roman Rite is the largest by far of them all and is actually larger than all the others put together; this rite and a few other so-called "Eastern" or "Oriental" rites mandate celibacy, while the others permit a married man to be ordained, albeit he cannot remarry should his wife die, and bishops are chosen solely from the ranks of the celibate clergy.

left all to follow Him in a radical response to prepare the way for that time and place in which "men neither marry nor are given in marriage" (Mt 22:30). Was this expected? Hardly. Judaism had a keen sense of the meaning and beauty of marriage and family.[4] Jesus' approach went against the goad here, but that was not the only instance of such a departure from the expected pattern of teaching or behavior on His part. Can we forget that for centuries Jewish law had permitted divorce and remarriage? Our Lord's reversal of that norm was so unexpected that it caused the disciples to suggest that perhaps it might be better not to marry at all (Mt 19:10)! The Savior was not simply pleased to be counter-cultural (although He was certainly that); He was quite intent on presenting Himself—and any who wanted to be a part of Him—as eschatological signs, that is, as living pointers to the age to come, wherein every human good (even married love) is subsumed into the *Summum Bonum* (the Highest Good), allowing God to be "all in all" (1 Cor 15:28).

Clear evidence from the Early Church, discussed elsewhere in this volume,[5] demonstrates that when married men were admitted to the priesthood, they and their wives gave up their marital rights and lived as brother and sister.[6] With the passage of time, the

[4] Yet, even within Judaism, one finds certain of the prophets living celibately, and convincing evidence from Qumran suggests that at least some members of that community lived in celibacy. Interestingly enough, rabbinic literature also recounts a tradition that Moses—after beholding God on Mount Sinai—never again had sexual relations with his wife, the obvious implication being that once one had seen God, all other relationships and loves paled into insignificance. See, in this regard, Anthony Opisso's "The Perpetual Virginity of Mary in the Light of Jewish Law and Tradition," in *The Catholic Answer* (July–August 1996).

[5] Roman Cholij, *Clerical Celibacy in East and West* (Herefordshire, England: Flower Wright Books, 1989); also Christian Cochini, *Apostolic Origins of Priestly Celibacy* (San Francisco: Ignatius Press, 1990).

[6] Indeed, St. Paul speaks of various apostolic men who are accompanied, not by a "wife" (as some mischievous English translations put it), but by a "sister" (1 Cor 9:5), that is, a Christian woman who tended to the needs of these men in much the same way as the women who accompanied Jesus (Lk 8:1–3).

The movement away from married clerics who abstained from sexual intercourse when "on duty" toward demanding "perfect continence" is already documented in the *acta* of the Council of Carthage in 390. Furthermore, the reason given for this discipline is the intercessory and mediatory nature of the priesthood *in se* (in itself) and not merely through isolated mediatory or liturgical acts. Another point to note regarding Carthage's dealing with the matter is that bishops, priests, and deacons alike fall "under the same obligation of chastity" because of their liturgical ministry, indeed, their liturgical way of life. Finally, it is worth observing that already in 390 we find an emphasis on the fact that the Fathers of

Church in the West took a slightly different tack by calling only men who showed a capacity to live the charism of celibacy, not unlike the Lord's admonition found in Mt 19:12.

The first major departure from the expectation of priestly continence occurred with the Council of Trullo.[7] Its most problematic canon dealt with clerical marriages and effectively turned the entire Tradition on its head by not only permitting married men to be ordained but by allowing for their continued use of marital rights. The legislation, however, was rather convoluted and demanded continence before a priest could celebrate the Eucharist. In many ways, unwittingly, Trullo set the stage for what later became the Protestant notion of priesthood, reducing priesthood to a liturgical role. The ontology of Holy Order (viz., that a man is changed in his very being, which identity is a constant aspect of his existence) had been downgraded to functionalism (viz., a man is a priest when he is "doing" something priestly). *Doing* had replaced *being*—the very dichotomy the eternal High Priest had reversed. Not surprisingly, ten centuries later, the functional concept of priesthood among the Protestant Reformers came to allow, and even demand, the departure of mandatory celibacy.

Besides the ontological nature of the priesthood, celibacy is particularly appropriate because Catholic theology assigns a sacramental meaning to Matrimony as well as to priesthood. It was undoubtedly this very notion which brought Paul to conclude that the married state and full-time discipleship were in conflict (see 1 Cor 7:32–33). Now, while some observers have argued that Paul simply had a negative assessment of marriage, an objective reading of the passage will not bear out such a reading. It would seem that Paul is saying, however, that given the radical nature of Christian discipleship and the pressing (and good) demands of marriage, the two states are incompatible within one person. Seen in this light, what the Apostle was holding out for and what the Latin Church has opted for is an understanding of Matrimony and Holy Order as both deserving of a full commitment, with no divided existence. Far from being a negative judgment on marriage, then, the Church's position exalts

---

Carthage are not inventing new legislation but simply enforcing what was "taught by the apostles and observed *by antiquity itself*" (Cochini, pp. 4–5; emphasis added).

[7] This council was an Eastern regional synod, convoked ten years after the Second and Third Councils of Constantinople and intended to enact disciplinary canons. This controversial synod had to wait nearly two centuries to find a Roman Pontiff to ratify its laws—and then only cautiously.

Christian marriage and urges taking that vocation and sacrament seriously—as seriously as priestly ordination.

Clerical celibacy also bears an eschatological meaning, that is, it points man here below to a life to come. As we saw earlier, our Lord Himself spoke about this dimension when He reminded His audience that in the age to come human beings take on an angelic aspect as they exchange their physical desires for contemplation (see Mt 22:30). Celibacy, then, is not simply a lifestyle, it is a message—a prophetic message—that helps the human race in general and Christians in particular to remember that there is more to life than the sensual and encourages them not to get lost in the ephemeral. In our contemporary, sex-saturated world, this word needs to be spoken as often and as loudly and clearly as possible. In fact, the silent presence of Catholic clergy and religious on the streets of the secular city constitutes a most eloquent testimony to the existence of the transcendent and stands as an on-going invitation to the world to move beyond that which is passing; this witness is not unlike that of Ezekiel, who is told by the Lord that his very life should stand as a sign for the people (see Ezek 24:24). The priest, as an *alter Christus*, experiences in his person a foretaste of the life of Heaven by being focused solely on God; and, on the basis of his personal experience, he likewise appeals to his fellow men to follow him as he has followed Christ. The Eucharistic Sacrifice, the eschatological sign *par excellence*, is similarly celebrated most fittingly by one who is himself an eschatological sign. In 1988, then-Archbishop J. Francis Stafford summed up this aspect of clerical celibacy thus:

> Since Christ was unmarried, we may find it strange at first that the [Second Vatican] Council speaks of fatherhood in Christ. Yet the hymn *Summi Parentis Filio* speaks of Christ as "Father of the world to come." If we bear in mind what St. Paul teaches us about the spousal love of Christ for His Church, we will see that this "world to come" is nothing less than the child of that union, the fruit of that love.... It is not for nothing that the priest is addressed as "Father" by his people.
>
> As with the fatherhood in Christ, that of the priest points to the world to come: His solitude and earthly barrenness, a prefiguring of death; his prayer, pastoral charity and spiritual fruitfulness, a sign of God's power which is at work now to sanctify and so to yield eternal life.[8]

---

[8] J. Francis Stafford, "The Mystery of the Priestly Vocation," *Origins* 18.22 (Nov. 10, 1988).

Celibacy in Practice

While the Church has always taught that the celibate form of life, chosen for the Kingdom, is higher than other forms of life, she has also taught that the celibate person is not thereby automatically granted access to holiness of life. States of life are conceptual and objective; persons are actual and subjective. Therefore, it is important to note that, objectively speaking, a consecrated celibate *ought* to be holier than anyone else in the Church, but we also know that that does not necessarily happen in all cases. The theology of celibacy—like the theology of marriage—can be diminished or even perverted when lived by weak, sinful human beings. And so, it might be well to round out our reflections by looking at what the charism of celibacy can and should do for both the individual and the Church, as well as offering some practical observations about its living.

Several "negatives" might be grouped together to advantage:

(a) Celibacy is not merely a "rule" or "external norm." Or, as Pope John Paul II warned in a post-synod apostolic exhortation on priestly formation: "For an adequate priestly spiritual life, celibacy ought not to be considered and lived as an isolated or purely negative element, but as one aspect of a positive, specific and characteristic approach to being a priest" (*Pastores Dabo Vobis*, no. 29). When viewed from a juridical or legal perspective, this style of life can appear almost inhuman and is certainly robbed of its inner meaning and beauty, just as marriage would be if deemed little more than a "remedy for concupiscence." Rather, celibacy is a charism freely bestowed by the Lord upon certain members of His Church, for the salvation of those individuals and for the good of the whole Church and the salvation of the entire world. Just as it is freely bestowed, so too must it be freely received, never simply grudgingly endured but always joyfully and lovingly embraced. When celibacy is seen as a burden, neuroses surface, as does aberrant behavior, made manifest in repression or unhealthy forms of compensation. Which leads to the next point.

(b) Celibacy is not bachelorhood. When regarded as merely being unmarried, celibacy devolves into a lifestyle in which material comforts, the drive for power, or ambition replaces sexual pleasure. Not a few priests have been heard to say, "My Cadillac is my wife!"—a theologically and spiritually precarious, as well as a psychologically devastating, attitude.

(c) Celibacy is not contrary to human nature. Interestingly, *The*

New Celibacy, by Gabrielle Brown, a non-believer, offers some of the strongest support for this way of life. Her research is professional and dispassionate, and therefore well worth reading.[9] Father Stanley Jaki's study also contains fascinating endorsements of celibacy (or at least back-handed compliments) from such unlikely sources as Ignaz Döllinger, George Sand, Friederich Nietzsche, Rolf Hochhuth, George Bernard Shaw, and Ernest Renan.[10]

(d) Choosing celibacy is not a matter of opting for what is good (celibacy) over what is bad (marriage), but of considering two "goods" and selecting one that is objectively better. As was noted earlier, pitting one style of life against another is counterproductive and unbiblical. Celibacy is not a statement against anything; it is a statement in favor of something—the Kingdom of God and eternal life. Pastoral experience demonstrates that when married life is highly valued, celibate vocations flower in the Church; similarly, priestly celibacy gives powerful support to married couples. Consecrated celibacy and Christian marriage are not in competition or rivalry with each other; they complement each other, as marriage is a sign of Christ's present love for His Church and celibacy points to the future consummation of that love in Heaven.

One of the consistent objections leveled against clerical celibacy is that the temptations of modern society are "too great" to sustain such a burden. Let's examine that statement a bit. Following such logic, one would have to conclude that, given the promiscuous nature of most sexual activity today, commitment to a spouse in a stable, permanent, and exclusive union is equally untenable. We

---

[9] In that volume, we find statements like the following:

"Celibacy is a style of life known only to humans."

"There are many priests, nuns and monks who have confronted and accepted their sexual natures so completely that they are happily and comfortably celibate."

"Freud was surprisingly open to the positive results of celibacy. He observed that people can achieve happiness by transcending sexuality for a higher experience of love and took examples from religious life."

"Celibacy can both strengthen a man and soften him."

"In ancient Rome, despite its dissolute reputation, the effort of continence was greatly admired and thought to represent a superior nature and a character verging on the divine."

"Love is less likely to be restricted in its nonsexual expression than in a love relationship focused on that one overriding concern—which often occurs when sexuality dominates the relationship."

"Those [celibates] who have achieved a permanent state of pleasure or fulfillment are said to radiate a kind of energy of love which is constant, unbounded, brilliant, and truly universal."

[10] Stanley Jaki, *Theology of Priestly Celibacy* (San Francisco: Ignatius Press, 1998).

know, however, that the Latin proverb has it right in asserting, *Abusus non tollit usum* (Abuse doesn't take away use). In other words, the mere existence of the possibility of a problem does not automatically rule out the correct use of a particular faculty or institution. Rather, the solution is to return to the sources for a kind of refresher-course at both the intellectual and affective levels. Temptations against marital fidelity are not inventions of the twenty-first century; they are as old as the institution of marriage. Love, commitment, prayer, and hard work are the keys needed to ensure fidelity. The same keys are needed to maintain a celibate commitment. If a priest took seriously the centrality of Holy Mass and the Divine Office in his daily life and worked hard in his pastoral endeavors, he would generally be well insulated from the most egregious assaults on his consecrated celibacy. Furthermore, when priestly identity is strong and one's priestly life is fulfilling, celibacy is rarely if ever a difficulty—not unlike observing marital chastity for the happily married.

Of course, one cannot gainsay the importance of personal discipline in all this. Fifteen centuries ago, St. Augustine (who had ample personal experience with sexual licentiousness) asked this telling question: "Why do you follow your own flesh? Turn round, and let your flesh follow you" (*Confessions*, book 4.11). In other words, emotions must be ruled by the intellect—whether those emotions are grounded in ordinary physical or biological urges or in a desire for companionship and human love. It is extremely important for future priests to be taught how to be alone without being lonely. Many married people can testify—sadly—that although they have shared a house with a spouse for decades, they lead lonely and disconnected lives. Priestly solitude should be a most welcome aspect of a life that seeks to develop the mind and a contemplative mode of existence. Developing interesting and healthy hobbies is also critical for appreciating one's own company, while keeping loneliness at bay. Good priestly fraternity is the best way to guarantee that one is not overpowered by lonesomeness. Employing these safeguards to clerical celibacy is no more than what the Second Vatican Council referred to as "mak[ing] use of all the supernatural and natural helps which are now available to all" (*Presbyterorum Ordinis*, no. 16). As Pope John Paul II has said, "it is prayer, together with the Church's Sacraments and ascetical practice, which will provide hope in difficulties, forgiveness in failings, and confidence and courage in resuming the journey" (*Pastores Dabo Vobis*, no. 29).

Sometimes we hear it said that married priests would be better counselors and role models to their flocks, in that 95 percent of the lay faithful are married. Once more, the assertion does not hold up under scrutiny. Must an oncologist have cancer in order to deal effectively with cancer? Must a teacher revert to childhood to "relate" herself to first-graders? Nor can one point to an iota of evidence that married Protestant clergy and rabbis have any greater effectiveness in pastoral situations with the married than do celibate priests. In fact, the only serious research on the topic, conducted by the priest-sociologist Andrew Greeley, showed clearly that young married women actually prefer celibate priests as their spiritual "confidants" for a variety of reasons, not the least of which is that such relationships seem to enhance their relationships with their husbands.[11]

Not infrequently yet another challenge to celibacy is raised with the claim that, while celibacy may have "worked" in another time and place, it can't do so today in a host of locations from North America to Africa to Latin America. The argument usually continues on to say that this is no more than giving due consideration to inculturation and acknowledging the "coming of age" of regional Christian communities. But if—as we have attempted to show—celibacy *is* related to the ontological nature of the priesthood and *is* intimately tied to the eschatological dimension of Christian life and *was* clearly an integral part of Christ's invitation to apostleship, how can we treat it as an expendable commodity? Father Aidan Nichols handles this challenge to celibacy most deftly when he writes: "To say that local churches, in given parts of the globe, cannot be expected to produce celibate ministers of the Gospel is to say that they cannot be expected to reproduce an intrinsic element in the experience of the apostles. And this seems a strange way in which to recognize the Christian maturity of such churches!"[12]

In other words, this approach is—in reality—a slap against a particular culture, essentially holding that the evangelical commitment or sexual self-control of its time or place is so minimal that potential priests in its environment are incapable of doing what priests have done for centuries. To debate the topic incessantly is actually to do a great disservice to potential candidates, especially when one reads of the determination on a 1990 synod in this regard: "The Synod does

---

[11] Aidan Nichols, "Celibacy as Witness," *The Tablet* (Aug. 26, 1989), pp. 968–970. This same article also mentions *en passant* that "the burden of being a married priest is pretty heavy, too, *especially for the priest's wife*" (emphasis added).

[12] Aidan Nichols, *Holy Order: Apostolic Priesthood from the New Testament to the Second Vatican Council* (Birmingham, Eng.: Veritas, 1990), p. 164.

not wish to leave any doubts in the mind of anyone regarding the Church's firm will to maintain the law that demands perpetual and freely chosen celibacy for present and future candidates for priestly ordination in the Latin Rite."[13]

The contention is occasionally made that insistence on a celibate clergy is ecumenically counter-productive. No less a priest-scholar and ecumenist than Father Raymond Brown takes on this objection forthrightly: "Precisely because the witness of celibacy is conspicuously lacking in many other Christian churches, the Roman Catholic Church has an ecumenical *duty* to the Gospel to continue to bear an effective witness on this score" (emphasis added). He goes on:

> Perhaps this would be possible without a law, but one must admit that it is the law of priestly celibacy that makes it clear that those who accept it are doing so for the sake of Christ and not simply because they prefer to be bachelors. Some of the forms of optional celibacy being proposed would soon lead to obscuring the vocational character of celibacy and would reduce it to a personal idiosyncrasy.[14]

We often tend to forget that ecumenism is a two-way street. While Catholics surely have many things to learn from their separated brethren, our non-Catholic brothers and sisters also have a few things to learn from Catholics—and the value of a celibate clergy is one of those things, in my estimation.

The most obvious benefit of celibacy is pastoral, as it "is lived in an atmosphere of constant readiness to allow oneself to be taken up, as it were 'consumed,' by the needs and demands of the flock" (*Pastores Dabo Vobis*, no. 28). In saying this, Pope John Paul II was merely echoing the Fathers of the Second Vatican Council, who declared that "this perfect continence for love of the Kingdom of Heaven has always been held in high esteem by the Church as a sign and stimulus of love, and as a singular source of spiritual fertility in the world" (*Lumen Gentium*, no. 42). Who can fail to be impressed by the missionary labors of millions of priests in history or the witness of thousands more in the gulags and concentration camps of this century? Can one doubt that their celibacy allowed them—even challenged them—to be such constant and faithful signs of Christ's saving message of truth and love? Humanly speak-

---

[13] Cited in *Pastores Dabo Vobis*, no. 29.
[14] Raymond E. Brown, *Priest and Bishop: Biblical Reflections* (London: Chapman, 1970), p. 26.

ing, could we have expected such dramatic testimony from one rightly concerned for the welfare of a wife and children? Much less dramatic—but no less impressive—is the pastoral service of hundreds of thousands of celibate priests whose day begins before sunrise and ends as the clock's hands move into a new day. Like a candle, the celibate priest fulfills his mission by "burning himself out" for Christ, His Gospel, and His Church.

Apart from these more "pragmatic" considerations on celibacy,[15] a quick re-reading of what I have written here shows that I have often relied on comparisons between priesthood and marriage. And I think that, although accidental in part, this tendency has been fortuitous. Both vocations are highly demanding, requiring tremendous amounts of self-sacrifice. In fact, I am reminded of an exhortation that once formed part of the Sacrament of Matrimony. The bride and groom were instructed that for a marriage to succeed, self-sacrifice had to become a fixture in the relationship. But the text went on to note, both realistically and hopefully: "Sacrifice is usually difficult and irksome; love can make it easy; perfect love can make it a joy." It is the Church's conviction—after centuries of experience—that perfect love can make celibacy a joy for the priest himself and for the whole Church he serves.

Some Concluding Reflections

Pulling together theology and spirituality, we bring to mind that as all was being consummated on Calvary, we encounter three virgins—Jesus, Mary, and John—forming the *ecclesiola*, the "little Church" about to be born from the wounded side of the Lord. That Church embodied the seeds of a virginity destined to bear fruit, both in time and unto eternity. It is the Church's hope and desire that her celibate clergy (and her consecrated religious too) would show forth to the world, in a unique manner, the Church's identity as both the virginal mother and the fruitful spouse of Christ.

Proposition number 11 of the 1990 synod on priestly formation embodied this hope:

> The Synod would like to see celibacy presented and explained in the fullness of its biblical, theological and spiritual richness, as a precious gift given by God to His Church and as a sign of

---

[15] Two other "practical" works on the subject are: Peter M. J. Stravinskas, *Essential Elements of Religious Life Today* (Libertyville, Ill.: Marytown Press, 1987), and Federico Suarez, *About Being a Priest* (Princeton, N.J.: Scepter Publishers, 1996; repr. 2009).

the Kingdom which is not of this world, a sign of God's love for this world and of the undivided love of the priest for God and for God's People, with the result that celibacy is seen as a positive enrichment of the priesthood.[16]

This book is itself a small effort toward the realization of that desire of the Synod Fathers.

---

[16] Cited in *Pastores Dabo Vobis*, no. 29.

An Open Letter to My Brother Priests

(Originally published by New Hope Publications, 2005)

Dear Fathers,
In Pope John Paul II's address to the American cardinals in Rome two years ago, he issued a call for "a holier priesthood." Thirty-five years ago this past September, I entered the college seminary at Seton Hall University. These two facts, along with a long career as professor and journalist, combine to make me conclude that I might become a holier priest myself by helping others priests become holier, for I have often found that reflecting on a topic can have the salutary effect of bringing about not only a deeper appreciation of the matter but also a deeper experience of the reality for myself and others, as well. With that in mind, may we make it our goal that this mutual reflection on the Sacred Priesthood would bring our vocation into clearer focus and thus cause it to be more fervently lived?

Let me assure you from the outset that there will be nothing new in this letter, for two reasons really. First, as a person, I am not much given to coming up with new ideas or clever angles; more importantly, though, as a priest, my job is not to create novelty but to "hand on to you what I myself have received," as St. Paul put it. Furthermore, there will be no particular effort to prioritize the listing of concerns, because they are all interrelated. These observations come from my own 26 years as a priest and from observing the priestly lives of others—with positives and negatives alike. My hope is that these thoughts might serve as "food for thought" for each of you personally and likewise as "talking points" for various gatherings of priests, formally and informally.

Prayer

Our fundamental task as priests is to put others into contact with the Triune God, which presumes that we have a relationship with that same God. That relationship began with our Baptism and has been fostered by each and every sacramental encounter since then. It is moved along in a particular way by personal prayer. The adage is as true today as it was when first uttered centuries ago: *Nemo dat quod non habet.* As priests, we are the official "pray-ers" or intercessors within the community of the Church. While liturgical prayer is the heart of the matter, it can be rather lifeless if it is not supported and sustained by private, personal prayer. If a married couple does not attempt to communicate with each other, except for engaging in that activity which is the peak of their relationship, their intercourse will be less than the full experience God intends it to be. Indeed, all the little acts of kindness, love, and intimacy on a day-to-day and hour-by-hour basis lead up to—culminate in—the peak moment. I think the application should be apparent for us: If the only time we pray is as ministers of the sacraments, we are cheating ourselves out of the depth of meaning the Lord intends for us and, by extension, we are thereby cheating our people, too.

Therefore, please make personal prayer and *lectio divina* the building blocks of your spirituality. At the same time, one must situate the Liturgy of the Hours or Divine Office at the very heart of our spirituality. I am more convinced of the truth of that today than I was twenty years ago. The Liturgy of the Hours flows from the Holy Eucharist and leads back to it.

Which leads to my last item in the prayer category: Holy Mass. Offering the Eucharistic Sacrifice is the most priestly thing we can ever do; indeed, it was the act for which we were ordained. As our Holy Father never tires of reminding the whole Church: the priesthood exists for the Eucharist, and the Eucharist is actualized through the priesthood. The Church is never more the Church than when she celebrates the Lord's self-offering to His heavenly Father—and the priest is never more a priest than in that privileged action.

Hence, I want to encourage you to make the centrality of the Eucharist a reality in your life. Among other things, that means never missing a day of celebrating the Eucharist, unless prevented by sickness or some other serious cause. A day off or lack of congregation should never impede one from making this vital contact with Christ the High Priest. While a priest may not want to be locked into a set time for celebrating Mass on a day off, it should nonetheless be viewed as an essential element of his walk with the Lord on that day as on any other. Similarly, if the lay faithful are not given to regular participation in daily Mass, Pope John Paul suggests that if you make them aware of your performance of that sacred action, it can actually become a catalyst for them to see the value in this supreme act of worship.

On the other hand, many of you feel the clergy "crunch" most acutely by having to binate or trinate on a regular basis, in order to meet the pastoral demands of your people. You are to be thanked for this heroic effort. At the same time, allow me to issue a caution.

We all know that "familiarity breeds contempt," which is the very reason the Church is skittish about having her priests celebrate the Eucharist more than once a day. Do not permit yourselves to fall prey to the demon of routine, which spawns haste, irreverence, inattention, and lack of devotion. Some of the ways to avoid these pitfalls is by using all the legitimate options the Church gives us in bringing about variety in our celebrations: having recourse to all four eucharistic prayers; employing votive Masses or the formularies for various special intentions, instead of relying on the Sunday orations all week long; calling upon the principle of "progressive solemnity," so that the degree of solemnity (amount of singing, use of incense and number of candles, quality of vestments and vessels) is a true reflection of the event being celebrated. I am sure many of you saw the results of a recent *Adoremus* survey which indicates that the most frequently voiced complaint of the Catholic people in regard to the Sacred Liturgy is the irreverence and casualness of the celebrant. We should not be stiff or stilted in our leading of liturgical worship, but we certainly should never be irreverent or casual. On the day of our ordination, we promised to "celebrate the mysteries of Christ faithfully and religiously as the Church has handed them down for the glory of God and the sanctification of God's people." Or, as the plaque that hangs in many sacristies urges: "Priest of God, say this Mass as though it were your first Mass, as though it were your last Mass, as though it were your only Mass."

This leads naturally to a final exhortation: that the Sacred Liturgy be offered according to the mind and norms of the Church. As *dispensatores mysteriorum Dei*, we are the servants of the liturgy, and not its masters. Our personal preferences must be subjected to the wisdom and law of the Church, which we solemnly promised to obey at our ordination. *Sacrosantum Concilium* teaches forcefully that "no other person, not even a priest, may add, remove, or change anything in the liturgy on his own authority" (no. 22). Disregard for the Church's rubrics is a sin of disobedience but also an act of clericalism, whereby we arrogate to ourselves the right to make our vision of worship that of the whole Church and foist that on our people. "Erector set" approaches to liturgical presidency is ultimately unfair to the people we serve because it denies them their baptismal right to worship according to the approved rites of the Church; it is equally unfair to our brother-priests because it puts them in the awkward position of having to justify their own fidelity to the rubrics or of having to explain another priest's infidelity to the same. Please do not presume that you know better than the Church.

By all means, make the Sacred Liturgy come alive for your flock, but do it properly. Richard Burton became acknowledged as a great Shakespearean actor, not because he changed the Bard's texts, but because he so put himself into them that audiences were brought to experience them in a completely new and vibrant way. That is our challenge as leaders of liturgical prayer.

Work

If the first verb in the Benedictines' motto is *"ora,"* we know the second is *"labora."* Human beings, by the divine plan, find meaning and fulfillment in work and, I daresay, in hard work. Labor is one of the most concrete ways that we share in the creative activity of Almighty God. The Book of Genesis tells us that one of the curses leveled at Man after the Fall was not work but work "by the sweat of the brow." In other words, work that would be perceived as arduous, tedious, and perhaps often enough meaningless. God forbid that our work as priests should ever be considered in any of those ways. If any human being's work makes that person a co-creator with *the* Creator, how much more should we esteem *our* work, which is nothing less than a participation in Jesus Christ's re-creation of the world as He prepares to present it to His heavenly Father at the end of time.

Thus, while I would not want any priest to drive himself to an early grave because of an imprudent and slavish work ethic, I do hope that every man goes to bed each night tired due to a full day spent in the service of the Kingdom. And that produces a good and restful sleep. On numerous occasions in the Gospels, we hear Jesus counsel His disciples to commit themselves to long hours in the task of preaching, teaching, and healing in His Name. In point of fact, He Himself gives not only the charge but the example for a selfless pouring out of one's time and energy in this effort. This sense of urgency comes across loud and clear in a unique way in St. Mark's Gospel, leading us to conclude that no opportunity should be missed, no stone left unturned, no person unapproached with immediacy to share the Gospel message. That should serve as our model of evangelical ministry.

If we intend to follow Christ's example of hard work—and we should—we likewise need to imitate His example in other ways. We discover that even the Son of God had to "re-charge" through communion with the Father and through "get-aways" with His disciples or even on His own. We have already considered the first.

Time off is important, and each person requires different modes and amounts of such time. For some, a standard, weekly day off is almost necessary; for others, accumulating time can work better. The fundamental issue, however, is that we all need recreation which, not accidentally, has the etymology which suggests that this leads us the better to create or work once we have been re-created. Days off and vacations with priest-friends—co-disciples—are always good and healthy, and they should be encouraged. Time by oneself can also be valuable, but I would warn against developing a solitary character, which can become a breeding ground for loneliness and isolation.

While working even long hours can be positive experiences, guard against "busyness." So often priests tell me that they find themselves bogged down in an almost endless round of meetings, leaving them feeling more like bureaucrats than priests and also causing them to ask at the end of the day if anything worthwhile has been accomplished. Be judicious in your use of time and personal energy; make sure that those precious resources are not wasted. Thus, it is a worthwhile project, every so often, to chart out how you spend your days and to determine if better organization and more careful delegation could spare you for more direct pastoral and sacramental work.

Every trade has it pet failings. In my experience, I suspect one of ours is self-pity. All too often, priests seem to succumb to the "woe is me" syndrome, which harbors the notion that our lives are so much harder and less satisfying than everybody else's. If you are tempted to become a victim of this disease, I think it might be good to consider that most of the fathers in your parishes work far longer and much harder than most of us. How many of them put in forty-hour weeks and then work a part-time job, as well, in order to keep their children in Catholic schools? For how many is a Saturday or Sunday little more than another day of work, albeit in a different venue, so that a house can be painted or kids chauffeured? How many of them get a month's vacation and a week's retreat? And even if they did, where could they afford to go? No, even from a very clinical, objective stance, we priests have been given many special gifts by the Lord because of our vocations, special considerations which the lay faithful do not begrudge us. However, we need to appreciate those facts, lest we wallow in self-pity, which can cause us personal and ministerial difficulties. On the contrary, joy in the service of God's People ought to be our hallmark, because we count ourselves blessed to have been chosen to labor in the Lord's vineyard.

Study

When I was a youngster, it was commonly thought that every priest was a scholar; one doesn't hear that said too much any more. Of course, in those days it was not unusual for the priest to be the only educated man in a parish. Thank goodness, the level of education has been raised for everyone since then. However, I sometimes wonder if the educational achievement of our priests has kept pace with the overall educational accomplishments of our people. Regardless of what kind of education a priest received in high school, college, and theology, it is important for him to have a strong appreciation for the value of study and to perceive it as a lifelong process and goal. Indeed, it is essential for a healthy, wholesome, human, Christian, and priestly existence.

I find it fascinating that as strictly as Orthodox Jews observe the Sabbath, study—of any subject, not just the Torah—is permitted and even encouraged. The rationale is simple and clear: Study of any aspect of knowledge leads one ultimately to the Source of all knowledge, Who is God Himself. We priests need to adopt that mindset. It should apply, in the first place, to on-going theological education, for which there are so many wholesome opportunities. I am sure you would agree that few of us would feel comfortable entrusting our medical needs to a physician whom we knew to have done nothing to update himself since leaving medical school. The application to our lives should be apparent.

Beyond formal programs of study, we can chart a personal course of theological development by reading. I am thinking, for instance, of committing oneself to undertaking a book-of-the-month club approach to theological investigation—done on one's own or with others. Of course, a priest should always read carefully and immediately documents from the Holy See, especially the writings of the Holy Father. Every priest ought to subscribe to at least one solid and serious theological journal, in addition to one of a more pastoral bent. All this keeps us up-to-date and thinking with the Church— and thus more secure in our service to the People of God.

Lifelong education is not theological alone; it extends to the totality of human concerns, as the pagan Roman Terence knew when he declared, "*Nihil humanum mihi alienum est.*" Therefore, cultural and historical pursuits are likewise important in making us well-rounded men, who can use these avenues as ways of growing in our understanding of humanity and helping our people to do the same. I suppose what I'm hoping for is the re-emergence of a Renaissance gentleman, who can foster that unity of faith and culture so dear to the heart of Pope John Paul.

Witness

Christians witness to their faith in Christ in many ways, and priests do, too. What I want to highlight under this heading is a very specific form of witness, unique to us priests—the wearing of clerical garb. We do not wear distinctive garb simply because the law of the Church requires it. Rather, the Church requires it because it is important for us (it reminds us who we are) and for the world (it reminds society of a transcendental dimension to modern life). And so, embrace opportunities to be visible public witnesses to Christ, His gospel, and His priesthood. Seek them out; create them.

It seems to me that it is more necessary than ever for our people and society-at-large to see us doing very normal, natural things—shopping at a mall; filling up the tank at a gas station; going to a movie; enjoying a dinner at a restaurant. If they see us doing things beyond the strictly "cultic" or ministerial (what we might call "job-related" activities), our credibility will be enhanced, which will have very positive effects in crucial areas like evangelization and vocation recruitment. Be proud to be Christ's special representatives, and use your public persona to reflect the kindness and joy of the Lord in the secular city, which so needs "ardent but gentle" witnesses to something beyond what it has to offer.

Celibacy

This is not the forum for a full-blown discussion of priestly celibacy, but I do want to highlight some key notions. From time immemorial, this apostolic way of life has shaped the Catholic priesthood in the ways of close configuration to Christ the Priest and in service to the Church and the world. That is why every Pope of our time, as well as the Fathers of the Second Vatican Council and the various synods of bishops of the post-conciliar era have all stressed the Church's total commitment to this charism and its critical connection to the Sacred Priesthood.

Celibacy is, first of all, God's gift to you and then your gift back to Him. Because it is a gift, a grace (*gratia*), it needs to be cherished and safeguarded. It is safe to say that many of our brethren who have strayed from a proper living of this charism did so through carelessness at first and even recklessness in some instances. A married man does not and cannot maintain fidelity to his wife in a casual sort of way; marital fidelity demands constant vigilance. So does fidelity to evangelical continence. No one wants priests to be cold, aloof, and rigid, as means of protecting their celibate commitment, but some commonsensical practices are certainly in order.

How often we heard the Sisters in grade school admonish us that "an idle mind is the Devil's workshop." This was not a scare tactic to keep children in line; it is a fundamental truth of human existence. That is why it is crucial for us to keep occupied with worthwhile activities and to ensure that we are living happy, fulfilled, priestly lives; that's the positive approach. The *via negativa* is just as important: Avoid the near occasions of sin, whether they come from television, videos, the internet, magazines, or other people. Foster good, healthy relationships with men and women alike. How can you be sure these relationships are healthy? I have always found a good rule of thumb to be this: If I would be afraid or uncomfortable to be with that person publicly, it is probably a sign of trouble.

At a more spiritual or theological level, it is necessary to return repeatedly to the uniqueness of the priestly vocation; celibacy seen in that context makes sense—and apart from that, not at all. Accept the sacrifice entailed, but recall that Christian marriage involves many sacrifices, albeit of a different kind. Celibacy lived according to the mind and heart of our great High Priest can and will make us both more loving and more lovable. That's what we committed to as either deacons or sub-deacons, and that's what we must keep in constant focus.

Gratitude

Gratitude has been called the most fundamental of all virtues by thinkers as diverse as Aristotle, Cicero, and Aquinas. I suspect that this is because gratitude always implies another and, for believers, *the* Other, thus placing us in a relationship which helps us recognize that, in the words of the great Rabbi Abraham Heschel, "all that we own, we owe." It is important for all people to appreciate what they have and who they are, but that is especially critical for us priests. God has been so immeasurably good to us, first of all, in giving us the gifts of life and faith, and then, even more graciously, calling us to share in His work of the sanctification of His People. What a blessing and what a grace! But do we take it all for granted all too often? Have we ceased to be amazed at the dignity that is ours? And if so, is it any surprise that we also fail to be grateful?

Over and above the Lord's generosity to us, I am constantly struck by our people's generosity to the Church—to our many works, to our institutions, and to us priests personally. Do we offer prayers of thanksgiving for them, bringing them to mind during the Eucharistic Sacrifice and the Liturgy of the Hours? Do we express our gratitude to them personally, both verbally and in writing, especially after particularly gracious acts performed for the Church or on our own behalf?

It was no accident that the Lord Jesus desired that we perpetuate His memory and presence among us by offering the Eucharist, that is, by making a thank-offering. To be truly eucharistic people is to be grateful people. As the one who presides at the eucharistic action, the priest must likewise preside over and foster an attitude of gratitude in the Christian community.

Generosity

The Triune God is the absolute model of generosity. In the work of creation, the Father exhibited lavish abandon by fashioning a universe of nearly incredible diversity, beauty, and vastness. Therefore, not one star or two, but billions of them. Not a single rose, but millions. Not a couple of different types of animals, but thousands of species. In the work of redemption, the Son did not spend an hour or two showing us how to be truly human, but a lifetime. Nor, in the consummation, did He shed but one drop of His Precious Blood (although that would have "done the job"), but every single ounce, pouring out His life like a veritable libation. In the work of sanctification, the Holy Spirit poured forth His entire life-giving breath upon the Church, providing her not with the bare minimum needed for salvation, but granting her the fullness of the means of salvation, so that she might experience Heaven even while still on earth. Yes, my brothers, the Holy Trinity has shown us how to be generous, and we need to be models of that for those entrusted to our pastoral care.

The most precious commodity anyone has at his disposal is time. Therefore, be as available to others as God has been to you. Ours is not a nine-to-five job. The "do not disturb" button on the telephone or the answering machine in a perpetual "on" position are signs of unavailability. When away from the phone, make a point of responding to all messages with due speed to indicate your interest and commitment, as well as your respect.

Second, realize that Almighty God has given you certain talents

He has given to no one else. They are not your personal possession, to be hoarded or even hidden. Remember how harshly our Lord portrays the master in demanding a reckoning of the talents. What we have received is intended to be used for the glory of God and the good of His Church.

Third, share your financial resources with those in need. No priest I know is on public assistance or food stamps (nor should he be), and probably none is a millionaire, but all should be examples of sacrificial giving to their people. Surely, we must be prudent in our giving, for we are responsible for our own retirement, among other things, but that should not preclude our contributing to the various works of charity toward which we would encourage our people to give. Priesthood does not remove the obligation of charity; on the contrary, it impels toward an even greater sense of responsibility for the welfare of others.

One way we can have enough to give to others is by living a spirit of evangelical poverty. We secular clergy do not profess a vow or promise of poverty, but we are certainly called to live it by being detached from material possessions (whether they be cars, stereo systems, or clothes) and by being prudent, just, and charitable in our use of money. Our faith informs us that the all-generous and ever-generous God is never outdone in generosity; He always responds not only in kind, but beyond our wildest dreams, expectations, and hopes.

Fraternity

We know from secular and Christian literature alike that the hallmark of the Early Church was their oneness of mind and heart. "See how they love one another," was the reaction of the general populace, and their very visible and tangible love became a means of evangelization. When I was a boy, the boast of the priesthood was that it was a worldwide fraternity, such that simply seeing another man in a Roman collar identified him as a brother. Sad to say, ideological conflict has marred the unity of the priesthood in recent decades in many ways as priests have sometimes grown suspicious of each other or, in more extreme cases, even enemies of one another. This is a counter-sign, like disunity within the Christian community in general, causing scandal to the lay faithful and even to those outside the Church. If the men who share in Christ's Priesthood are not united by a common profession of faith and by the bonds of charity binding brothers, how can we expect our ministrations to be fruitful? How can we expect our people to believe, let alone the unbelieving world?

Hospitality toward other priests and acts of kindness toward them should be standard operational procedures among us. When a priest needs a shoulder to cry on; when a priest needs someone with whom to rejoice; when a priest needs a sounding-board, he should be able to rely on the fraternity of the priesthood. When he can't, we should not be amazed to discover that he seeks that kind of support and affirmation from those outside the priesthood, with all too predictable results in many instances.

Perhaps the fundamental problem is that we have lost sight of the meaning of friendship and need to re-capture the classical appreciation for its true meaning. Is it not significant that Jesus chose to relate to His chosen ones as friends? Is there not at least a hint in that choice that He expects us to regard His friends as our own, friends with whom we share the deepest aspects of our lives and for whom, like Christ, we are even willing to lay down our lives? That is Gospel preaching at its most convincing. Being friends of the Lord and of one another then gives us a credible platform from which to preach the need for all Christians to be friends. If that concept were in place, I daresay that we would not find our youth engaging in pre-marital intercourse, or married couples involved in adulterous affairs, or anyone else exhibiting dysfunctional forms of behavior. Why? Because friendship never manipulates, uses, or degrades; it always challenges, inspires, and elevates, just as Jesus did for His friends.

Holiness

As Pilate asked, "What is truth?" so too do some ask, "What is holiness?" And like Pilate, they frequently do not really want an answer. Priests, however, are in the holiness "business." Our life's work is to sanctify ourselves and those committed to our care. Hence, it should not be either a rhetorical question or a futile one.

It has been a truism of pastoral theology for centuries that a parish is as holy as its priest. Priestly holiness, then, ought to be our prime concern. Let's begin by stating what it is not. It is not sanctimoniousness, nor being what we used to call a "pious fraud." It is a manly quality of equilibrium—being comfortable in the presence of God; being able to face God; being able to be totally honest with His people. And that is contagious: One who is holy makes others want to become holy. Holy priests, you see, make their people holy who, in turn, make the world holy, which is the whole purpose for the existence of the Church—to bring as much of the human race to God and His Heaven.

We priests are holy when we live lives of fidelity, integrity, and discipleship. In fact, it is essential that one be a true disciple before attempting to be a minister of the Church. Otherwise, we would be endeavoring to teach others to be something that we have never been ourselves, which is clearly a "mission impossible."

On our road to holiness, which is a lifelong pilgrimage, we need landmarks and cartographers. The landmarks are found in the Church's patrimony of doctrine, morality, and spirituality; the cartographers are our confessors and spiritual directors. Which leads me to our next consideration.

Sacrament of Penance

The very best means of personal growth is through devotion to the Sacrament of Penance and Reconciliation. Permit me to urge you to make a commitment to use regularly—at least once a month—this extraordinary stimulus to holiness, along with a sincere daily examination of conscience. It seems to me that a priest cannot be an honest promoter of this Sacrament if he is not an enthusiastic recipient of it first, as the Holy Father has reminded us on numerous occasions. Its greatest value for priests is that it provides us with a check on ourselves, fosters sensitivity to even minor offenses against God, and offers grace for the struggle of the life of Christian discipleship, keeping us honest and making us holy.

Wholesome Appreciation of Self

The New-Agers didn't invent the value of self-knowledge and self-appreciation. The ancient Greeks urged one another to "know thyself." But who am I? In the sixties, it was fashionable for grown men to assert that they didn't know who they were; not a few of them were priests. How sad.

In this effort at gaining self-knowledge and, then, self-appreciation, the example of St. John the Baptist can offer us much. Do you remember how he identifies himself? First, he says who he is *not*; then he says who he *is*. In addition to seeing himself as that famous "voice crying in the wilderness," he likewise considered himself to be "the friend of the Bridegroom." That is, the best man at the wedding, the one responsible for seeing that everything would go well at the wedding feast. Isn't that an apt "job description" for a priest? The one responsible for ensuring that Christ's Bride, His Church, is suitably prepared to meet her Lord and Spouse.

To get to that lofty calling, however, requires some very basic information about oneself, which includes knowing one's assets and liabilities as a person and as a Christian. In this process of personal discovery—and it too is generally a lifelong process—one must be neither an optimist nor a pessimist. Realism is what is required. The realist sees what God sees. He is not depressed by weaknesses, for the Christian realist knows, with St. Paul, that "it is when I am weak that I am strong" and that "I can do all things in Him Who strengthens me." Nor is he overly impressed by strengths, for he also knows that if he should boast (and sometimes one should), he "should boast in the Lord," the source of every strength of character and personality we possess.

And so, the sign in the executive's office makes eminently good sense: "Be patient with me. God isn't finished with me yet." We are all "works in progress," who must always be open to personal growth and development, especially in the natural and supernatural virtues.

Zeal

When we know ourselves, we are then in a position to do great things for the Lord. The Evangelist John applies the words of the Psalmist to Jesus: "Zeal for your house consumes me." Zeal is gusto in service to the Kingdom. For all too long we have had massive doses of institutional maintenance, but that never converts anyone. Rarely does it even keep anyone within the bonds of communion. We priests must be zealous without falling into zealotry, which can drive people away just as surely as clerical indifference. What should we be aiming for?

Some time ago, a man I met on a plane spoke to me about his new pastor. When I asked him what he thought of him, he replied: "He's a nice man, Father. He's a good man. He might even be a holy man, but—he's got no fire in the belly!" Fire in the belly, that's what we all need. Wasn't that the quality that enabled St. Peter to bring three thousand to Christ on the first Pentecost? Wasn't that what motivated men like St. Paul and St. Francis Xavier to go to the far ends of the known world to preach the Gospel? And wasn't that also what moved the circuit-riding priests of another century to lay the foundations for the Faith and the Church, on which we continue to build? These were "driven" men, driven by the Holy Spirit to accomplish great things for Christ. We must duplicate in our own time and place their drive to preach, to teach, and to witness to the Gospel of Jesus Christ. The work is exciting and exhilarating; its motive force comes from zeal.

Our Lady

With every passing day, I become more certain that devotion to the Mother of God is not optional or an "add-on" for any Christian, let alone a priest. Devotion to the Blessed Virgin can never be soupy or sentimental but filial—*filii ad Matrem*. Litanies in her honor, meditation on her role in salvation history, imitation of her virtues, especially those of evangelization and charity demonstrated in her visitation of Elizabeth, are all most profitable for a priest. Most profitable of all is the Rosary, which, as Pope John Paul has recently noted so persuasively and eloquently, is that "school of Mary" in which we can "contemplate the beauty of Christ."

The sixteenth chapter of St. John's Gospel speaks about a mother's sorrow being turned into joy. The nineteenth chapter of that work portrays Mary at the foot of the cross at the moment of the most intense sorrow, but it goes on to show her receiving the Beloved Disciple (i.e., each one of us) into her care as she becomes the Mother of many sons, but most especially the Mother of her Son's brothers in His Priesthood. John, the virginal priest, represents us in a unique way.

Just as our Lady stood by the altar of the Cross, so too does she stand at the foot of every altar since then, inviting us to join her as she joins herself to her Son's sacrifice, and ours to His, as well.

O Mary, Mother of Christ, Mother of the Church, Mother of Priests, make us all holier priests—and thus make us worthy of the promises of Christ.

Made in the USA
Middletown, DE
05 February 2024

48578732R00179